I Lay
This Body
Down

POLITICS AND CULTURE IN THE
TWENTIETH-CENTURY SOUTH

SERIES EDITORS

Bryant Simon, *Temple University*
Jane Dailey, *University of Chicago*

ADVISORY BOARD

Lisa Dorr, *University of Alabama*
Grace Elizabeth Hale, *University of Virginia*
Randal Jelks, *University of Kansas*
Kevin Kruse, *Princeton University*
Robert Norrell, *University of Tennessee*
Bruce Schulman, *Boston University*
Marjorie Spruill, *University of South Carolina*
J. Mills Thornton, *University of Michigan*
Allen Tullos, *Emory University*
Brian Ward, *University of Manchester*

I Lay This Body Down

THE TRANSATLANTIC LIFE OF ROSEY E. POOL

Lonneke Geerlings

The University of Georgia Press
ATHENS

Paperback edition, 2026
© 2022 by the University of Georgia Press
Athens, Georgia 30602
www.ugapress.org
All rights reserved
Set in 9.5/13.5 Miller Text Roman by Kaelin Chappell Broaddus

Use of any part of this book in training for any
artificial intelligence (AI), large language model (LLM),
machine learning technologies, or similar generative language
system without license is expressly prohibited.

Printed digitally

EU Authorized Representative
Easy Access System Europe—Mustamäe tee 50, 10621 Tallinn,
Estonia, gpsr.requests@easproject.com

The Library of Congress has cataloged the
hardcover edition of this book as follows:

Names: Geerlings, Lonneke, author.
Title: I lay this body down : the transatlantic life of Rosey E. Pool / Lonneke Geerlings.
Other titles: Transatlantic life of Rosey E. Pool
Description: Athens : The University of Georgia Press, [2022] | Series: Politics and culture in the twentieth-century South | Includes bibliographical references and index.
Identifiers: LCCN 2021056445 | ISBN 9780820362076 (hardback) | ISBN 9780820362069 (ebook)
Subjects: LCSH: Pool, Rosey E., 1905–1971. | Netherlands—Biography. | Women political activists—England—London—Biography. | Holocaust survivors—England—London—Biography. | Translators—Netherlands—Biography. | Civil rights—United States—History—20th century. | African Americans—Civil rights—Southern States. | Civil rights workers—Southern States—Biography.
Classification: LCC DJ219.P66 G44 2022 | DDC 949.207/092 [B]—dc23/eng/20211217
LC record available at https://lccn.loc.gov/2021056445

Paperback ISBN 978-0-8203-7805-3

"That piece of yellow cotton became my black skin."
—ROSEY E. POOL, ca. 1968

CONTENTS

Acknowledgments xi

Introduction 1

CHAPTER 1 Amsterdam, 1905–1927 9

CHAPTER 2 Berlin, 1927–1939 27

CHAPTER 3 Westerbork, 1939–1945 43

CHAPTER 4 Amsterdam, 1945–1949 65

CHAPTER 5 London, 1949–1971 79

CHAPTER 6 Hilversum, 1958 95

CHAPTER 7 Up North / Down South, 1959–1960 113

CHAPTER 8 Mississippi, 1960–1963 127

CHAPTER 9 Alabama, 1965–1966 143

CHAPTER 10 Befriending Langston Hughes, 1945–1967 155

EPILOGUE Pursuing Ghosts 169

Sources and Methodology 173

Notes 179

Bibliography 213

Index 229

ACKNOWLEDGMENTS

Preparations for this book began in late 2013, when I began to explore options for completing a PhD, after I had worked in several archives for some years. It was Anneke Ribberink who linked me to Susan Legêne, who together with Diederik Oostdijk, would become the supervisors of my PhD project. I can honestly say that these years were to that point the best of my life, and I have them to thank for it. Doing the PhD enabled me to travel the world, encouraged me to look beyond my boundaries and preconceptions, and even gave me the space to make mistakes and failures—a highly undervalued element of research and personal growth. I matured during the PhD, and I owe it largely to Susan and Diederik. I could not have wished for better supervisors.

There are so many people I want to thank, but first is Peter Paardekooper, my partner who stood by me and functioned as a sounding board and a 24/7 commenter. I could not have done this book without him: I discussed all my discoveries and conclusions with him, and we together visited many of the places to which Rosey Pool traveled. Moreover, I want to thank my family, my parents, and my sister and brother, who encouraged me endlessly. All my friends, the members of *Helleveeg*, other bands—you know who you are. A special thanks to a relative of Rosey Pool, whom I could always talk to: Rudi Wesselius and his wife, Maja.

I also want to thank the people at the University of Georgia Press, including especially Nathaniel Francis Holly, who was a great fan of Rosey Pool from the start and kickstarted this project as soon as I e-mailed in my book proposal to him. I honestly could not have wished for a better editor. MJ Devaney did a great job copyediting the manuscript and provided great suggestions. And other people from the Press who were indispensable included Jon Davies, Christina Cotter, and Candice Lawrence.

Three people in particular influenced my thinking and writing: Anneke Ribberink, on women's history and biographies; Dienke Hondius, on the intersection of racism and anti-Semitism; and of course Babs Boter, with her meticulous knowledge of literary theory, gender, and history. You are the best.

I found great support in the "intervisie" group that was formed by a set of PhD students and my colleagues, including Jos van Beurden, Marieke Oprel, Michel van Duijnen, Caro Verbeek, Miel Groten, Berend Mul, Fieke Smitskamp, Tjalling Bouma, Marja van Heese, Heleen Blommers, and Maaike van den Berg. During my internship at NWO there were people who similarly supported each other, including Eva Mulder, Job Vossen, Jolien Cremers, Kim van Gent, and Niké Wentholt. Some other colleagues at the VU were helpful, each in their own way, including (in no particular order) Karin Lurvink, Hans de Waardt, Frans Huijzendveld, Pepijn Brandon, Martha Visscher-Houweling, Chiel van den Akker, Bettine Siertsema, Bart Wallet, George Harinck, Christoph van den Belt, Widya Fitria Ningsih, Wouter de Vries, Jos de Weerd, Alexander Geelen, Ab Flipse, Martina Amoksi, Inger Leemans, Erika Kuijpers, Riedwaan Moosage, Wybren Verstegen, Serge ter Braake, Antske Fokkens, Kristine Steenbergh, Gea Dreschler, Nelleke Moser, Dirk Visser, Janet van der Meulen, and, of course, Liesbeth Geudeke. I might have forgotten some, my apologies. All of you were indispensable, always ready to discuss research, academia, and the quality of coffee at the VU.

Other valuable colleagues at the VU included Amrita Das, with her knowledge on literature and her humor; Marijke Huisman, who gave commentaries on early versions of chapters; Nancy Jouwe and Wim Manuhutu, who were endlessly supportive; and Dineke Stam, who gave me advice for diaries on Otto Frank. I was able to discuss my research during guest lectures at the VU as well in courses taught by Ronald Kroeze, Norah Karrouche, Tijl Vanneste, and Dienke Hondius. Eric Akkerman and Onno Huber largely made the digital part of this research possible.

A special shout-out to archivists worldwide: you are the real heroes. I especially want to thank Annette Mevis (formerly of Atria) for her great tips, Jo Baines (formerly of Sussex) for her advice; Gertjan Broek and Erika Prins of the Anne Frank House; Guido Abuys of the Westerbork memorial center; Barbara Schieb of the *Gedenkstätte Deutscher Widerstand*; Frans van Domburg of the Stichting 1940–1945; Jasper Snoeren of the Institute for Sound and Vision in Hilversum; Beverly Cook of the Chicago

Public Library (this woman deserves a statue); and Carlijn Keijzer of the NIOD, who discovered letters written by Pool in Westerbork. To all the archivists I forgot to mention: THANK YOU.

I greatly benefited from exchanges with international scholars at some summer schools I went to: on European Jewish history (Brighton, UK), Cold War history (Vienna, Austria), transnational history (OPG), and people I met at specialized courses on Digital Humanities, databases, and networks analysis, as well as on intersectionality, oral history, food history, and many, many more.

There was great institutional support from the Huizinga Institute for Cultural History (Paul Koopman and Afke Berger) and the expert group Unhinging the National Framework that was initiated by Babs Boter. Also helpful were some people I randomly e-mailed and who surprisingly e-mailed back. Some I'd like to thank in person include Brooks Marmon, for his work on AMSAC and South Africa; Hugh Wilford, for his knowledge on AMSAC; Bart de Cort; James Davis (NYU), for his insights on Rosey Pool; Marlen Eckl (Frankfurt area) and David Jünger (Sussex), for our collaboration in Münster; Ben Braber, for his research on the Van Dien resistance group; M. J. O'Brien, for sharing his knowledge on Tougaloo College; Myriam Everard, for her tip on an IISH archive; Dawn Skorczewski, for her suggestions on my chapters; Volkert Visser, for his help with Nodegoat and everything digital; Andrina Tran, who did research for me at Yale University; and of course Ellen de Vries, for great talks and collaboration on Nola Hatterman; Nanka de Vries at the RIAS.

I also want to thank the entire board of the Association for Gender History (VVG) and all the—current and former—editors at Historica, the journal for gender history. I truly enjoyed doing interviews together with Kirsten Zimmerman, Greetje Bijl, and Laura Nys.

I want to mention some other helpers along the way: Shima Jalal Kamali, for her tips on Langston Hughes; Clive Webb (Sussex); and Shaul Kelner, Ellie Flier, and Jeana Pointdexter, who enabled me to speak at Vanderbilt University in 2017. A special thanks goes to Diarmuid Hester (formerly Sussex, now Cambridge), who also saw how special Rosey Pool was and who organized an entire festival around this amazing woman, in 2018. Finally, I want to thank Sandra Rottenberg for her zest to promote Rosey Pool after my dissertation was completed.

This project has financially been supported by a PhD grant from the Netherlands Organisation for Scientific Research (NWO) that included a generous travel grant as well. I was able to do two international fellowships: one at the British Library in London, financed by the Eccles Centre;

and another one at the Bundesarchiv in Berlin, made possible by the European Holocaust Research Infrastructure (EHRI). Other financial support came from the German Historical Institute (GHI) in Washington, D.C., to attend a conference; the EAAS, for research in the United States; and the Catharina Halkes Fonds, for research in Chicago. Additional funding came from VU's CLUE+ to invite international scholars. And finally, thanks to the Institute for Sound and Vision, where I researched my chapter on *Advocaat pro deo* in even more detail as a guest researcher. All of these institutions helped creating this work. Thank you.

I Lay
This Body
Down

INTRODUCTION

Tuesday, 7 September 1943, a sunny September day in Camp Westerbork, a Nazi transit camp in a distant corner of Holland, was one of the darkest in Rosey Pool's life. It was the day she set foot on a train to Auschwitz.

During her fifteen weeks in the camp, she had seen several trains arrive and quickly depart. Now she heard her name when the deportation list was read aloud. Together with almost a thousand others she packed her suitcase with some of her hastily thrown together belongings and stepped into the train. The cattle car was dark, cramped, and terrifying. Through the open door she caught a last glimpse of the camp—and of her home country. Then an SS officer appeared, ready to lock and seal that door. Without thinking, Pool stepped out of the cattle car. The German guard, clearly annoyed, nodded toward the door, implying that she ought to get in again. But she told him in fluent German that she was "on transport duty" as well. Slightly confused, the guard looked at her upper arm where there should have been an armband to prove her rank. "Oh," she responded as lightly as she could. "I must have lost it in the bustle." The guard muttered, "Don't let it happen again." As if walking in slow motion, Pool returned to her barrack. She did not dare look back. The train with 987 people left Camp Westerbork minutes later and set off for Auschwitz. Only eight of them would survive. Or nine, if we include Rosey Pool.

Pool carried the guilt about that day for the rest of her life. Depression, frustration, and anger took root in her mind, where they became a darkness that never went away. She swore to herself never to think about

Figure 1. Pool with a small child in Huntsville, Alabama, where she taught in the mid-1960s.
SOURCE: F010635, Jewish Historical Museum, Amsterdam.

that moment again, let alone talk about it. Until she arrived in the United States two decades later, she maintained her vow.

In 1964, the then fifty-eight-year-old Pool was invited by English professor Sterling Brown to speak at Howard University in Washington, D.C. Since her escape twenty years earlier, Pool had become a specialist in African American literature, which she had become interested in perhaps as early as the 1920s, when as a student she claimed to have stumbled on the work of Countee Cullen. Through her involvement with the socialist movement, her interest in the literature of African Americans developed into a political stance as well, as she learned more about injustices against this oppressed minority. She started collecting the African American poetry that occasionally appeared in Dutch newspapers and journals. While editors usually chose poems by Langston Hughes, Claude McKay, or Jessie Fauset, they also published Dutch translations of some poems by Sterling Brown.[1] Pool soaked these works up like a sponge. Still, Black literature and culture remained a hobby, nothing more.

During World War II, however, Pool's interest in Black culture became "something so different and something so personal," something "very deep and very real." In Camp Westerbork she learned the "true meaning" of Black works of art, she believed. In late July 1943, after she had been in the camp for several weeks, the news arrived that the Italian dictator Mussolini had stepped down. This hopeful message spread like wildfire throughout the camp, arousing smiles, laughter, and joy. The first fascist leader was out, and it probably would not be long before Hitler would step down as well, they told themselves. Their joy did not go unnoticed by the camp guards. That evening the inmates were called together and told that they were forbidden to visibly or audibly laugh or show other signs of merriment. Disobeying this rule would lead to severe punishment. This mandate reminded Pool of a Sterling Brown poem, which she recited later that same evening to her fellow inmates. The poem is about a fictional character named Slim Greer who faces an uncannily similar situation: a law in Atlanta, Georgia, that prohibited African Americans from laughing outdoors. The poem "Slim in Atlanta" "held us up" in the camp, Pool told Brown almost twenty years later, when she finally met him at Howard University, the prestigious black college where he taught. She felt a "very deep debt of gratitude towards the [Black] race" for the writing that had helped pull her through a parallel situation.

During Pool's visit to Howard University, Brown set up an intimate poetry reading with, among others, the poet Samuel Allen and Howard librarian Dorothy Porter. Brown himself started off Pool's visit by reading some of his old Slim Greer poems. Pool then went on to relate, for the first time in her life, what had happened to her in Camp Westerbork and during World War II and how Black American literature had been a beacon of hope during that time. Pool recalled one night in 1943 in her barrack, where she, along with about six hundred women and children, passed the long, dreadful days. That night, a child next to her said, "If there were only [something] that we could concentrate on . . . and get our thoughts away from the misery." "There were tears in Sterling Brown's eyes when . . . I told him how, on that night of July 26th 1943, I had acquainted my 'block' with Slim Greer's adventure in Atlanta, Georgia," Pool later recalled.[2] The group then tried to say some prayers, but that "just didn't work," Pool said, "because the majority were Jews, and there were Protestants, there were Catholics, there were communists." But then someone said to Pool, "You know so many of those American Negro songs and poems," adding that perhaps she could think of something from among them that would help. One song immediately came to mind. And she sang, until the entire barrack softly sang with her:

> I walk in the starlight,
> I walk in the moonlight,
> I lay this body down.
>
> I'll lie in the grave,
> And I stretch out my arms,
> I lay this body down.
>
> I go to the judgment,
> In the evening of the day,
> I lay this body down.

Singing "I Know Moonrise" became a ritual, night after night, Pool recalled. It became their "nightly prayer," even "twice a week when the death trains were standing outside." The burial song "united us and gave us a moment of serenity."[3]

A long, emotional silence followed after she finished speaking, strikingly audible on tape. Sterling Brown cracked the silence by asking, "Would you teach at Howard?"[4] This encounter exemplified the sort of uncompromising acceptance Pool encountered in America, a sense of belonging she had longed for. No mistrust or suspicion, no criticism. Just a shoulder to cry on. In Black America, she finally felt "home" again.

As a Holocaust survivor and activist fighting against segregation in the Deep South, Pool connects histories that are often studied and relayed in isolation. The story of her life allows us to explore intersections between

European and American history, showing us where the experiences of Jewish Europe and Black America converge. Pool's story also allows us to see how she dealt with tragedy, trauma, and loss. At its core, this book is about resilience and hope. Indeed, Pool's life story demonstrates the power of reinvention for dealing with both challenging personal circumstances and the traumas of global history.

Anne Frank's Teacher, Langston Hughes's Friend

Rosey E. Pool (1905–71) hardly lived an ordinary life. She was a translator, an educator, and an editor, but also much more than that. Her life was amazingly rich, eventful, and transnational. She witnessed the rise of the Nazis in Berlin firsthand; she taught many pupils, including Anne Frank; she participated in a Jewish resistance group; she escaped from a Nazi transit camp; she witnessed independence movements in Nigeria and Senegal; and she was involved in the American civil rights movement. Pool was part of many of the critical moments of the twentieth century. We cannot understand who she was without looking at the contexts she was situated in, which often informed her actions. By pausing to examine where she was and when, this book illuminates Pool's various identities, passions, and political causes.

Defining Pool surely has not been an easy task. During my five years of research it became clear to me just how fluid and malleable her identity was. Each context she found herself in called for different behavior, different choices, and, occasionally, radically different personalities. It is easiest to define her by noting what she opposed: she was antimilitarist, antifascist, antiracist, antisegregationist, and anticolonialist. Defining her by what she was also helps draw attention to the different types of work she did. She was a recitist, a poetess, an activist, a translator, an educator, a resistance fighter, an anthologist of African American poetry, a biographer, a writer, a literary agent, and an actor. All of these roles testify to her ability to reinvent herself time and time again. Yet there were stable elements in her personality. From her teenage years until her sixties, she remained a mercurial and creative, charismatic, big mouthed, witty, and opinionated person. Her constant reinvention was her particular way of dealing with the traumas of the twentieth century.

Pool also drew on individual lives and stories—that she often recounted with microscopic precision—to exemplify the larger arguments that gave her life and work meaning. She frequently told the story of Anne

Frank, whom she taught during the 1940s, to American audiences, to highlight the similarities between Nazism and Jim Crow. She promoted the career of actor Gordon Heath in the Netherlands to fight racial prejudice and anti-Black racism. And when she was in Mississippi in the early sixties, her own life story illuminated another sort of racial oppression in the Western world. Often Pool was absolute in the connections she made, prone to sweeping, sentimental statements. Individuals and their stories were crucial to the way Pool made sense of her world.

Pool's public talks offer powerful examples of the importance she assigned to the stories she told. Though she was often stubborn in the opinions she held, she typically fought for the right sorts of causes. Indeed, she had her greatest cultural impact with her talks in the South, which she delivered at a time when the civil rights movement was a risky enterprise that was not certain to succeed. In the midst of that revolution many people found her talks utterly inspiring. One African American student who heard her speak at Fisk University recalled, "At this point, just before the beginnings of the nation-wide civil rights movement, it was very exciting and validating of Black culture to hear a European who was so passionately dedicated to [Black poetry]." Students fell in each other's arms after hearing her speak, overwhelmed by emotions, she remembered.[5] Pool's talks helped galvanize activists as they began participating in the growing civil rights movement.

Forgotten, yet Not Lost

It seems curious, then, that this woman has almost been forgotten. Despite her extraordinary life and significant achievements, she is largely absent from existing historiography and from most archives—except her own. To compile a narrative, I had to dig Pool's story up from her largely unexplored archives scattered across different continents and research multiple separate histories from the labor movement to the negritude movement. Because she lived and worked in various countries, she does not fit into nationalist narratives, which has made it difficult for archivists and scholars to pin her down. Judaism, the socialist movement, negritude, the Bahá'í faith, and even the Girl Scout movement all had transnational organizational structures and were based on internationalist ideals. Most of these movements, of course, also faced fierce opposition. Another reason she is absent from historiography and popular memory is that she had no family to keep her legacy alive after her death. She had no children, and almost all of her family was killed in the Holocaust.

Remarkably, Pool is also often missing from scholarship on the movements she played a part in. A notable exception, however, is the work of Anneke Buys, whose 1986 thorough and detailed unpublished manuscript on Pool's life has been tremendously important to my own research.[6] The interviews that Buys conducted with friends, colleagues, and collaborators of Pool's during the 1980s proved crucial to my understanding of the first forty years of Rosey Pool's life.

Pool's eventful life also led me to delve into more unfamiliar territory: lesbian subcultures in Nazi Germany, histories of obesity, and African American tourism in the Soviet Union. Repeatedly I was led to "other" voices in history: those of protesters, the oppressed, and people on the fringes of society. From her antifascist affiliations to her anticolonial work and her antisegregationist activism in the American South, her life was very much a countercultural story that focused on the "other"—or shadow history—of her time. Her life brings to light underexamined aspects of the twentieth century while simultaneously offering a different perspective on familiar events.

What perhaps stands out the most is Pool's resilience throughout her life. She had an almost limitless capacity for self-invention, a seemingly endless energy, and a courageous willingness to throw herself into challenging circumstances time and again. Partially it was her trauma that kept her going. But her activism led her to a deeper understanding of her own experience as well as that of others. Pool's life story shows that if anything good can come out of tragedy, it is the determination to prevent it from ever happening again. After each terrible event she recommitted to righting the wrongs of the world. And she encountered the wrongs of the world long before she faced the horrors of the second World War. To fully understand Rosey Pool's life, her zest, and the choices she made, we need to go to Amsterdam, where it all started.

CHAPTER 1

Amsterdam, 1905–1927

Her last name, Pool, was a silent reminder of her family history. Her Jewish ancestors had fled Eastern Europe in the seventeenth century, and as was common, their place of origin became their last name. Yet Rosey Pool often did not quite feel Jewish, nor did she show a particular interest in Judaism. She only entered a synagogue once, after a teacher had come into her loud classroom and shrieked in dismay: "What is this here, a classroom or a Jewish church?!"[1] The teacher was assuming that unlike Christian churches, synagogues were lively and bustling. This suggestion stirred Rosey's interest, and at her request her mother took her to the Portuguese synagogue, one block away. However, her teacher's assumption proved wrong, and Rosey thought the "time-worn decorum" was disappointingly boring. She was thereby immediately cured of her religious curiosity.

Rosey (or "Roosje," as she still went by) grew up in a "mixed" Jewish family: her father was of East European Ashkenazi descent, while her mother was of Portuguese Sephardic descent. Such a "blended" marriage would have been unthinkable before the late nineteenth century. Before that there were two separate Jewish communities in the Netherlands, each with their own customs, their own organizations, and their own distinct accents. Until the Batavian revolution, Jews were formally a separate community with self-government, operating independently from the state. But after 1795, Jews were also recognized as citizens, allowing them to move around freely and take on professions they were previously shut out from. It was the start of Jewish emancipation and integration in Dutch society. Throughout the nineteenth century, modernization and also secularization drastically changed formerly tight-knit Jewish communities. More and more Jews began abandoning Jewish religious

Figure 2. Pool, around three years old, with her mother, Jacoba Pool-Jessurun, Amsterdam, circa 1908.
SOURCE: F010617, Jewish Historical Museum, Amsterdam.

customs, traditions, and language and integrating themselves into Dutch Gentile society. Jews were well represented in Amsterdam, the nation's capital. About 12 percent of the population was Jewish, and owing to its countless Jewish shops, the famous Jewish market, and the Jewish Quarter, Amsterdam was lovingly called Mokum Aleph (literally "City A," the best or first city) and occasionally the "Jerusalem of the West."[2]

When Rosey's father, Louis Pool (1876–1943), arrived in the city in the early 1880s, Dutch society was divided among different pillars—Protestant, Catholic, liberal, and socialist. Each group had its own newspapers, schools, shops, and hospitals. Jews that had integrated into Dutch society fell into two categories. While upper- and middle-class Jews often joined the liberal group, the lower classes were often intrigued by the promises of socialism. Although Louis Pool came from a family of Jewish cattle traders and was thus part of the upper middle class, it appears that his family became impoverished after his father passed away in 1882. Together with his mother and three siblings he left Rotterdam and via Woerden they arrived in Amsterdam in 1887 and settled in the heart of the Jewish Quarter. It was only a matter of time before Louis Pool left his Jewish religious background behind. When he was in his early twenties he immersed himself in socialism. A multitude of "red" organizations had sprung up, including workers' choirs, leftist libraries and cinemas, socialist sports clubs, and the Social Democratic Workers' Party, all of which became an indispensable part of the socialist movement in Amsterdam. By the 1900s, socialism had become a lifestyle.

In those circles he probably also met Jacoba Jessurun (1880–1943), a commissioner's daughter. She was a real Amsterdamer, born into a family of diamond workers and traveling salesmen. They married in 1901—not in a synagogue but in the Handwerkersvriendenkring, an association for Jewish laborers and craftsmen. Afterward, they moved in above the cigar shop that Louis Pool had taken over in 1898 at Nieuwe Hoogstraat 18. Pool became a busy volunteer, and later he even joined the board of a local Social Democratic Workers' Party chapter. Soon he was in touch with famous political "dissidents," including the legendary party founder Frank van der Goes, who produced the first Dutch translation of Marx's *Capital*.[3] Rosey's father was a teetotaler and active in the Dutch Association for the Abolition of Alcoholic Beverages (also known as the "Blue Knot"). In his advertisements he ironically advised his clientele that his tobacco was "the best cure against alcohol abuse."[4] From his shop, Louis Pool also collected money for poor children and provided free tobacco and discounts on coffee to unemployed laborers.[5] Socialism was clearly his way of life. On the first floor was a "tiny living room" according to one eyewitness, which was used as a meeting place for Social Democratic Workers' Party meetings and preparations for activism.[6] However, the birth of Rosa ("Roosje" or "Ro") in 1905 and of her brother Jozef ("Jopie" or "Jo") in 1915 put the political work of her parents on hold.

The first years of her life Pool was called "Roosje," literally little rose. She only changed it to the more sophisticated "Rosey" when she was a teenager, inspired by her grandmother's Anglophilia. Both her parents and her grandparents had big hopes for the young girl, seeing in her a path for the family's upward mobility. Her mother went to great lengths to keep her away from her extended family, who lived in the deepest corners of the Jewish Quarter. Young Roosje herself did discriminate between social classes, she recalled. When she showed an interest in "the busy, shiny-eyed, Spanish or Papiamento-speaking women" of her mother's Portuguese-Jewish family her mother put a stop to it. Her mother did not want her little girl to get near the livestock market above the Portuguese Religion School in the Weesperstraat. Her mother was especially horrified by the live chickens, with their feet tied together and their heads dangling down, waiting to be sold. "My parents were very open-minded people," Pool noted. "But well . . . 'there are boundaries.'"[7]

Most Dutch Jews lived hybrid lives, being both Dutch and Jewish at the same time.[8] Rosey's parents also combined a socialist lifestyle with a handful of Jewish traditions. "They were Jewish at Rosey's home, but not religious," one acquaintance remembered. "They probably had a white tablecloth on the Sabbath, that's it," the acquaintance added, referring to the traditional Jewish festive day.[9] The Pool family's everyday Dutch was in a natural way peppered with Yiddish words and expressions. Pool occasionally spoke of her "vague Jewish ancestry," and she recalled that her family contrasted their own world (that of the "yids") with that of the others (the "gojim," Gentiles): "When we were having a particularly delicious meal," Pool remembered, "someone might say: 'I wouldn't care to give that to a goy.' And when someone told a lousy joke, the listener would respond: 'Where did you get that goish story?'"[10] Much later she somewhat reluctantly admitted that at home they referred to non-Jews as "stupid, annoying, and inferior." And yet those comments were not meant to be hurtful but merely to mock, and, furthermore, "they remained within the inner circle of yids."[11] The Jewish/Gentile divide was partly a social construct and partly self-imposed, as there were few formal restrictions on Jews at the time. Rosey's street was clearly mixed:

> Next to us was a non-Jewish milkman, on the other side of the road a craft and fancy soap store run by two unmarried sisters. Eikelenboom that store was called. I do not know if that was the name of the shop or of the sisters. Next door, non-Jews had a shoe shop. Just around the corner, in the Zanddwarsstraat, there was Hennetje, a non-Jewish licorice and children's candy shop and the non-Jewish barber shop with its wooden outdoor sidewalk. . . . [O]n the first and second floors [lived] a Jewish diamond worker family and a non-Jewish woman who worked outdoors.[12]

Pool anachronistically compared her old neighborhood to American inner cities of the 1960s: "Just like Negroes and white people in the United States live in the same street, but do not live together," so did Jews and Gentiles in Amsterdam.[13] But although Pool later occasionally spoke to American audiences about "the old Amsterdam Jewish 'ghetto'" from before the war, segregation was not strictly practiced, and there were differences between the ways Jews were treated and the way African Americans were treated.[14] Most notably, Pool had no recollection of being othered based on her race. "I cannot remember that people *smoused* [*kiked*] openly in our neighborhood," Pool said. Then again, there were certainly similarities in the way each group was treated. "Mild antisemitism" was common and even broadly socially acceptable.[15] More seriously, Jews were also barred from a wide range of high professional and political positions.[16] In Rosey's elementary school, the reputable Anna Visscherschool, which was conveniently located opposite their house, "a vast majority" of the students were Jews but no teachers were, to her knowledge. "I cannot remember ever having known a Jewish teacher. Maybe there weren't any in those days."[17] Jews could integrate in Dutch Gentile society, but there remained invisible walls in the Jewish ghetto that were impossible to climb.

From Girls Scouts to the Socialist Youth

Rosey was one of the few in her class to go to the First Girls *hogere burgerschool*, Dutch secondary school.[18] Some classmates remembered her as "outgoing" and "very cheerful and fond of laughing," but that she also liked to study.[19] This made her a bit of a mix of both of her parents. While her father was a sophisticated "gentleman" who loved literature and business, her mother was the more outgoing one, with a captivating personality.[20] Rosey inherited her ability to socialize and easily make friends, although she did not get along with everybody. For reasons unknown she could not stand one particular classmate named Ine den Hollander, whose brother ironically became a specialist in African American history.[21]

Being bullied had by far the biggest impact on the young Roosje. The reason she was bullied, she thought, was because she was an "exceptionally fat child"; the other children called her names like "fatty" or "roly-poly." One nickname especially got to her: *bulletje bloedworst*, "fatty bloodpudding." The term always reminded her of the time she witnessed the slaughtering of a pig at her father's family farm in Woerden. "It was a nightmare," she recalled, when the hot blood gushed from the pig moaning its last breath. Whenever she heard "fatty bloodpudding" her own heart was "ripped" open in the same way "the butcher's knife had ripped open that poor leg-bound pig's."[22] Later Pool reflected that being bullied as a child made her more receptive and sensitive concerning race and especially regarding issues facing nonwhite people. Pool's obesity became a stigma that separated her from her peers. And as "a fat minority of one," as she put it, it was not difficult for her to understand discrimination in any form.[23]

Considering her personality, it is unlikely she was a passive or submissive victim. She was probably more of a "provocative victim," who reacts aggressively to being bullied.[24] Rosey was striking in appearance, and she was never afraid of upsetting others. Some eyewitnesses recalled that even in her parents' cigar shop, she would challenge the professors who came there to buy cigarettes. Yet Rosey was also a sensitive child, and for a while she retreated into herself. "When the other children were making trouble, she kept aloof and continued to focus on her work," one anonymous source revealed. "Friends that visited her were kept busy by her mother; she hardly paid them any attention."[25] Around this time, she also displayed a cheeky rebellious side. One classmate remembered that once "Roos had drawn something on a school desk." She could not remember what it was she drew, but when the teacher confronted her about it, Rosey lied and outright denied having drawn it.[26] We might conclude she was troubled by something at this point in time. However, lying at such an early age can also be a sign of intelligence: it is an indication that a child understands that different people may have different knowledge of the situation and that there is a difference between what the child knows and what people around him or her know.[27]

Pool thus was an intelligent and curious child, and she also showed a remarkable interest in the divine. Although her cautious curiosity about Judaism dissipated after a visit to the synagogue, when she was a young teenager she re-embarked on a spiritual quest. Rosey joined the Girl

Scouts, through which she met one of her best friends, Mies Beugeling. "I always had Jewish friends," Beugeling said, recalling that Rosey often dropped by on Sundays with her mandolin. "One time she confided in me that she did not feel much for her own faith."[28] Rosey seemed to be searching for something to fill a spiritual gap in life, and so, this friend took her to a meeting of Dienaren van de Ster in het Oosten (Servants of the Star in the East), the youth club of the local Theosophical Association.

By the time she was sixteen, she seems to have come to fully embrace the socialist lifestyle of her parents. Perhaps her thinking at this time was influenced by the emergence of the antimilitarist movement in the early 1920s, largely a result of World War I (during which the Netherlands had remained neutral). Around 1921 she joined the Workers Youth Center, the Social Democratic Workers' Party youth organization that was a sort of socialist scouts.

The Workers Youth Center was where Rosey explored and developed her talents. "I've always wanted to write, teach and perform, and I am doing exactly that," she noted.[29] She first performed when she was eighteen in a play put on by a local theater group called Intimate Original Art.[30] At the center she recited poetry and sang and was recognized by her peers, who found her interpretations extremely captivating. Several eyewitnesses recalled she was "wonderful at storytelling" and praised her talent for public speaking as well.[31] The loneliness of her former school days was now left behind: people enjoyed this quirky girl eager to sing on the stage. Her membership in the center clearly showed her desire to be part of a group; however, the urge to become an autonomous individual was also very strong.

Her performances were also politically motivated. People were wildly idealistic in the 1920s; they dreamed of a new world based on social justice, of uplifting of the masses, and of class solidarity. Prominent socialists tried to foster individual self-improvement through cultural education, encouraging people to become *Kulturmenschen*, "civilized human beings." Pool was deeply involved in the Institute for Laborers Development, an organization that sought to bring high culture to "ordinary" Social Democrats and to attract new followers with entertaining talks.[32] This was related to a central idea in the socialist movement of this day, namely, that not only society but also people themselves could be transformed and uplifted and could become the best version of themselves within a lifetime.[33] Pool's talks on Flemish folk stories fit in that tradition of educating workers and letting them grow into better people. Pool received a rave review when she gave her audiences a full-on experience by using a Flemish dialect in these talks.³⁴ Her passion and enthusiasm for the subject always made a great impression on her audiences, and soon she became a socialist personality who needed few words of introduction. "Rosey Pool will be there with her books and her storytelling," one organization announced, "and that says enough."³⁵

"Rosey" was becoming a recognizable brand, and her main interest was Dutch literature that focused on labor issues. She frequently read poetry by Frits Tingen, a blind socialist poet, Leonhard Frank, a German writer, and Dutch Social Democratic Workers' Party icon Henriette Roland Holst. But her favorite poet was Margot Vos, also a member of the Dutch Social Democratic Workers' Party, who often wrote about the exploitation of laborers and feminist issues. Rosey willingly stepped into the spotlight but always with a goal that was more or less the same: to fight for the underprivileged—a commitment that would become stronger throughout her life.

When Pool relayed her life story in the years after World War II, she never mentioned her participation in the socialist movement. She had concluded that there was only one noteworthy thing from that period, which was when, in 1925, she claimed to have discovered the poetry of the African American poet Countee Cullen. This discovery was, according to her, "the beginning of a lifelong interest in the poetic self-expression of America's darker ten percent."³⁶

If it is true she had come across the work of Cullen in 1925 (and there is not enough evidence to suggest it is), this would have been extraordinary, since Black literature was a small niche among Dutch readers. Occasionally, as happened during the interwar period, Black literature drew the attention of a wider, mainstream audience, most often in Amsterdam. Although "Negrophilia" never became quite the rage it did in Paris around that same time, there were occasional upsurges or "hypes" around indigenous African art, jazz music, and the Charleston dance. In the mid-1930s, a short-lived jazz craze struck Amsterdam. The Negro Kit Kat Club became a haven of jazz, largely thanks to the handful of Surinamese people who lived in Amsterdam at the time.

However, Pool did not participate in the jazz fad. By this time she had moved to Berlin, and although she regularly visited her old hometown, when she was in Amsterdam she spent most of her time with socialist and communist groups. These two worlds were not entirely separate, though. African American literature and poetry was a popular topic of leftist journals, which from time to time published special issues on "Negro" themes, as did *Groene Amsterdammer* in 1930 and *Links richten* in 1933. Leftist groups saw the situation of African Americans, whom they called the "Negro proletariat," as the ultimate proof of the hypocrisy and vile nature of American capitalism.

In the postwar context of the Cold War, Pool censored her entire "red" phase, claiming that Black poetry had been her sole interest during this period: "Perhaps [there are some] that remember how I sung spirituals when I was a young student and recited Langston Hughes on Workers Youth Center evenings," Pool said in a radio interview in the late 1960s.[37] But although eyewitnesses indeed recall that Pool was already interested in the Black cause, the available sources deny that this was her only or even main interest.[38] She in fact showed an enthusiasm for a wide variety of subjects, and the "Black cause" was perhaps one of them, although there is no evidence she ever talked about this in public. It is likely that the ensuing Cold War encouraged her to rewrite this episode from her life.

A highlight was the yearly Pentecost meeting in the countryside (the first day of Pentecost is a collective day off in the Netherlands). Workers Youth Center members took care of entertainment by playing music, singing, reciting poetry and literature, dancing, and performing plays. At the Pentecost meeting of 1930—that attracted around twenty-one hundred visitors—Pool sang a song called "Burn, Rise, Burn," which was perhaps the song she was singing in one of the few photographs that has survived from this period (see figure 3). The (now lost) lyrics were printed out on a handout so that everybody could sing along.[39] Not only did she have a "beautiful voice," one friend remembered, but she "spoke without a Jewish accent."[40]

This comment is revealing, because the Workers Youth Center offered opportunities to explore Jewish culture. Jeanne Mug-de Gooijer, for example, was well known for her performances of Hebrew and Yiddish songs at center meetings.[41] So many Jewish young people like Pool participated in cultural activities that the center was described as having a "Jewish atmosphere," which one eyewitness interpreted as "a desire to live in a more outgoing way."[42] During this period Rosey did not appear to be particularly interested in Jewish culture or religion, nor did she look Jewish. Only once, in March 1927, did Pool show interest in writers who wrote about Jewish topics, when she read the poetry of Hyman Overst (1883–1927), a Jewish socialist "people's poet" who was not only known for his revolutionary poetry but also his stories about the Jewish ghetto. She did occasionally speak at labor organizations like the Jewish Diamond Club Concordia and the Handwerkersvriendenkring that most often attracted workers of Jewish descent even though they were general meeting places for members of the socialist movement.[43]

Figure 3. Pool, around twenty-four years old in a reform dress, accompanied on lute by Wim Gaffel with Jeanne Mug sitting between them, circa 1930.
SOURCE: BG B10/979, International Institute of Social History, Amsterdam.

And yet "Jew" and "Jewish" were labels that Pool rarely used and only ambivalently identified with. As a secular socialist, she did not practice the Jewish religion or follow Jewish traditions, nor did she speak Yiddish or Hebrew. In other words, there was little distinctly Jewish about Pool. Moreover, it would not be enough to simply describe her as Jewish, since there were many differences and divisions among Dutch Jews at the time; there were Zionist and assimilationist, orthodox and liberal, Ashkenazi and Sephardic, left-wing and right-wing Jews.

Nevertheless, Pool no doubt had reasons for her ambivalence about her Jewish background. Although there is no such thing as race biologically or genetically speaking, race is certainly a social construct that comes with traditions, customs, and social realities. Secular Jews' standing in prewar Dutch society was unsettled. They still faced discrimination, both disguised and overt. The friend's comment about how Pool did not have a Jewish accent exemplifies benign antisemitism: he regarded Pool's ability to mask her Jewishness as a positive thing.

Rosey in her youth can be summed up as a woman who embraced the modern age. Beginning in the late nineteenth century, Dutch women were finally admitted to universities and increasingly worked outside the home, and in 1919, they achieved the right to vote. The twentieth century seemed to offer endless possibilities to them in terms of education, work, and fashion as well. The reform dress that Rosey wears in the photograph, a dress without a corset, was an outspoken symbol of freedom and the possibilities for women that modernity brought. Pool liked to explore the many paths that were available to her, and she refused to be pinned down by her background.

Among the "In Crowd" of Future Socialist Leaders

In July 1923, two months after her eighteenth birthday, Rosey Pool obtained her *hogere burgerschool* diploma. As was common for women in her day and age, she chose to enroll in a one-year course to train for secondary school teaching in Dutch.[44] People who knew her claim that she wanted to go straight on to college but that her father expected her to earn a "useful" degree first.[45] Reportedly, Rosey was furious and eloped with her boyfriend to protest. Eventually when the thrill of her elopement had worn off, her mother had to come to get her. "The boyfriend was a vegetarian," Pool confided years later to an American friend whose daughter also had run away, "and when my mother turned up somewhere in Belgium to find out if I wanted to link up with my family, gosh, was I happy to run home with her. I remember I ate a huge steak that night at a hotel in Liège. Never tasted any steak better."[46] Apparently Rosey had adopted her boyfriend's vegetarian lifestyle—which was quite bon ton among socialist intellectuals—yet she never made it her own. The herbivore boyfriend was carelessly left behind.

She did not tell that same American friend that her escape was part of a scandalous affair. During her flight Pool found out she had become pregnant. For a moment her life was about to go in a completely different direction. She had a miscarriage, however, and it seemed that afterward everyone, including Rosey herself, tried to forget that the flight and pregnancy ever happened. Almost miraculously and despite this turbulent period, Rosey did obtain her teacher's degree.[47] She probably went on to the university and took courses in Germanic languages.

Her student days were formative: during this time, her political beliefs cemented, and she improved her organizational skills. She started out ambitiously, taking courses while also volunteering on several boards. Perhaps she was driven by the expectations she thought her family had of her. Her younger brother, Jopie, was not intelligent. According to eyewitnesses, he was "not the brightest bulb in the box."[48] He may have had a mental disability, but he was in any event unable to pursue an education. Apparently wanting to realize her parent's dreams of social mobility, she now took decisive steps to kick start her career in the socialist world.

Almost instantly she enrolled in the Social Democratic Student Club and became treasurer of its Amsterdam chapter. The club members often met at the Handwerkersvriendenkring, the same place her parents had gotten married two decades before. It was both a student association and political discussion group, and its members talked about the aims and future of socialism, often operating on the basis of "strong principles," one eyewitness recalled.[49] As this was the only leftist student club in town, it was the place to be for ambitious socialist intellectuals. Pool was surrounded by future doctors, professors, politicians, and ambassadors who would become the leaders of the leftist and socialist Netherlands, including Hilda Verwey-Jonker, who later became a prominent politician. She called the motley crew pictured in figure 4 the "in crowd" of the socialist movement.[50] Verwey-Jonker also recalled that the club was utterly different from the "flirty" associations in Leiden and the "bourgeois" ones in Amsterdam. The club offered a place for "good intellectual contact."[51]

Surrounded by "good" socialists, Pool clearly blossomed. In figure 4, one of the few remaining photographs from this period (figure 4) she is wearing a flower dress that does not convey the impression of an ambitious young woman. Her weight also contributed to that. One eyewitness even tenderly remembered her as "a very cozy, fat mummy," hardly a compliment for a twenty-two-year-old woman.[52] Yet against the odds, Pool had a string of admirers. One fellow club member recalled one specific admirer, named Jan Oudegeest Jr., who was "madly in love" with Rosey, who stood out with her eloquence and wit. He courted her for quite some time, but Rosey ignored him.[53]

Perhaps she was struggling with her sexual orientation, but she could also simply have been too busy, caught up in what insiders called the "school of revolution"—with countless talks, lectures, film screenings, and poetry readings. This next generation of the elite was trained in socialism and took on Marxism, humanism, anticolonialism, antinationalism, antimilitarism, and other classic left-wing topics. Although there is only evidence of a few events Rosey attended, she likely attended many more. At the age of eighteen she went to a massive antifleet law demonstration, protesting against the use of colonial naval forces in the Dutch East Indies.[54] And in 1926, when she was twenty-one years old, she was deeply impressed by a "wonderful lecture" that Social Democratic Workers' Party leader Wil-

Figure 4. Pool (on the left) at a meeting of the Social Democratic Student Club, near the Handwerkersvriendenkring (an association for laborers and craftsmen) in Roeterstraat, Amsterdam, 1927. She stands next to Hilda Verwey-Jonker.
SOURCE: F010621, Jewish Historical Museum, Amsterdam.

lem Albarda delivered. She seemingly wholeheartedly supported his Marxist thesis of how the economic situation and big business conglomerations contributed to the "proletarianization" of the people. "The world is on its way to Socialism," Rosey noted hopefully after his talk.[55] A new world seemed to be around the corner, and perhaps she envisioned becoming a revolutionary herself as well.

International Comradery

Because she came from a socialist family, Rosey was very familiar with the idea of internationalist solidarity and the worldwide struggle of the proletariat. Those ideals came to the fore in January 1926, when she went to a conference in Leiden of the Dutch Student Association, which focused on the Middle Dutch, or Diets, language. Over 160 students from the Netherlands, Flanders, and South Africa met there for a conference to discuss their "common language". In the Social Democratic Student Club's journal, *Kentering* (a word that means "turning point"), Rosey wrote in advance of the conference that she truly looked forward to young people "who spoke the same 'Diets' language with only a difference in dialect" finally getting to know each other's "national character," and she hoped that everybody would conclude that they were actually one. However, she was extremely disappointed when the Leiden delegation opened the conference by stating that "the highest honor of a people is expressed in nationalism."[56] That sentiment went fully against the socialist idea that nationalism was an artificial construct meant to keep people (and laborers) apart. Her loathing clearly shows how much of her thought was influenced by the internationalist socialist movement, which predicted a proletarian revolution that would make nationalism redundant.

In *Kentering* she also published her own writing for the first time. The first poem she ever published, when she was twenty-one years old, was inspired by a Workers Youth Center Pentecost meeting she had recently attended:

> PARTY
>
> Music which sings happy days—sing through my entire heart,
> The sound of those happy days surge—pierce my happy heart.
> There were people—young!
> And all were mates—happy!
> The flag song was sung,
> A May sun is blossoming like never before.
>
> Oh, the flapping of the flags in the air,
> To feel the rising of those bright colors,
> Above the world. In a happy sound,
> The world full of young scents of spring.
>
> The Communal voice then convened across the earth:
> "Young Comrades—come!!"
> The earth-beauty then bedecked itself,
> And every flower shone.
> Many young hands reached for each other,
> Around every head a beam of light then shone,
> Future dreamlands then lay bare,
> And life became a lovely round dance.[57]

Replete with socialist references—flags, May, and comrades—this poem does not show much of Pool's personality. Yet some elements stick out. Although the narrator seems to be part of the "round dance" of young and idealistic youngsters, the tone is also rather observational. The poem combines a distant, descriptive tone ("There were people") with an insider's view ("life became a lovely round dance"). The poem reflects Pool's personal and lifelong struggle between her wish for a radical autonomy and her longing to be part of a group. The phrase "all were mates" depicts an ideal world in which people are one and at peace with each other that was sadly often out of reach for Pool, as she was herself a bit of an outsider. In other words, it is likely that the poem speaks to how Pool wanted the world and her own life to be. Ironically, the poem signals that Pool wanted her voice to be heard, and yet she did not use her own voice: it is the communal voice that is represented.

In her public appearances she always recited the works of others, never those she had written. Pool gained notoriety with her poetry readings, which were generally not stand-alone events but were tacked onto lectures by notable figures, usually men. She read poems on such topics as the future of the class struggle, alcohol and civilization, and—in a sign that her spiritual quest was still not quite over—socialism and theosophy."[58] Her captivating readings made her famous in what insiders lovingly called "the movement." According to one friend, she was able to "narrate wonderfully" and to easily keep listeners interested.[59] By the end of 1927, her fame had grown so much that the twenty-two-year-old Pool was being introduced as "Miss Rosey Pool, the famous young Amsterdam recitist," and photographs of her were prominently featured in socialist newspapers in order to attract listeners.[60]

Most of her recitals were held in or near Amsterdam, but it was only a matter of time before Pool was also asked to come speak on the new socialist radio station (VARA, founded in 1925). The significance of this radio station cannot be overestimated. It grew substantially in the years after 1925, largely because it was one of the few that not only broadcast party propaganda but also classical music, lectures, and poetry readings, the goal being to reach and uplift the "masses."[61] Members of the socialist "establishment," including the prominent leader Henri Polak, did not approve of this approach, as they feared that radio would only distract workers and would prove to be a hindrance to "enjoying good literature [and] serious study" and to "practicing music and visiting performances."[62] This reactionary statement was a faint sign the Social Democratic Workers' Party was out of touch with the changing times, and in the following years the size of VARA radio's audience grew so rapidly it even outnumbered that of the party itself.[63]

Pool found herself in the middle of this exciting, progressive new medium. She now reached a national audience, and her fame grew within the socialist movement and beyond. Pool recited poetry after notable politicians like Carry Pothuis-Smit and Goswijn Sannes delivered radio lectures and also made several appearances with pianist Nora ("Noor") Kinsbergen, who was probably a relative on her mother's side.[64] The two young women also collaborated as members of the Socialist Artists Circle. Pool was one of the founders of this club, along with Kinsbergen and Jef Last and socialist greats including Fré Cohen, Henriette Roland Holst, and Peter Alma. With lectures on the inevitability of socialism's triumph and the proletarian view on life this club seemed to align with other socialist organizations. Although their goal, which was to bring socialist intellectuals and laborers together in a peaceful fraternization, sounded innocent, this group was part of the radical left wing of the Social Democratic Workers' Party.[65] It was a political stance that Pool was increasingly drawn to.

In mid-1927, as her reputation and her career were taking off, she made a drastic change: she got engaged to a German lawyer and moved to Berlin. She abruptly left her old life behind and along with it the reputation that she had so carefully built up over the preceding few years. Her sudden disappearance was odd. She had suddenly popped up in the Workers Youth Center, one eyewitness remembered, and "then disappeared just as quickly for inexplicable reasons."[66] Some thought she had had a falling out, perhaps with Max Haringman, one center leader with whom she was close friends. One eyewitness retrospectively compared her to a 1980s Dutch politician who was forced to resign after it was revealed that he did not have a university education. What he seemed to suggest was that something similar was the case with Pool: "She presented herself as better than she actually was," the friend said.[67]

It does appear that Pool misrepresented herself. Although the archives of the Germanic Studies Department at the University of Amsterdam are lost, this department was very small. Because the department had only a few professors and just a handful of students, it was a tradition that each graduate was announced in national newspapers. Pool's name indeed pops up in newspapers of August 1927, around the time she was supposed to graduate as well, but not for an academic degree: it was announced that she obtained a primary school teaching certificate for German, a much lower degree.[68] Although it remains possible that she took university courses in the German Studies Department, it is highly unlikely she ever graduated. On future resumés Pool often left it ambiguous whether she graduated or not: "I was trained to be a teacher in elementary schools before entering Amsterdam University to read Germanic languages with drama as a sideline and a focus on poetry. (Folk literature and music entered into that too, and has stayed with me.)"[69]

Her rush to leave the Netherlands in 1927 as well as her subsequent efforts to deliberately cover up this period of her life looks like an admittance of guilt. She clearly felt shame. Perhaps she was uneasy about her behavior, given that she was living a lie that was bound to come out. She was a creative woman, so it is curious she did not use her imagination to tell the story in a different way. A solution might have been what her friend Jef Last did: he also dropped out of college and started working as a sailor, a trajectory he afterward fabricated into a heroic story of a socialist intellectual who immersed himself in the lives of true laborers rather than stuffy academics. Pool could easily have used the same narrative, but she chose to remain silent. Perhaps such an adventurous story was not an option for women. Still another factor is that these socialist youth organizations were supposed to be places where you could make friends for life, but for many of Pool's friends, life was to be much too short. Recollections of this period may have been emotionally taxing as she got to think about those that did not survive the war, especially as so many Jews and radical socialists were killed by the Nazis. Her creativity was perhaps blocked whenever she thought about this period, making her silence not so much a choice as a necessity: this joyful period brought back too many painful memories.

Solidarity of a Loner

Acting collectively and being part of a group was such a defining aspect of early twentieth-century political movements that it would be anachronistic to emphasize Pool's individuality too much in this period. But while she always wanted to be part of something larger than herself, she never embraced communal thinking. She clearly stood out—her irresistible charisma and playfulness set her apart—and she also loved being in the spotlight.

During her experiments, she eagerly tried out different identities. Remarkably, she did not experiment with a Jewish identity at the time, although she did have a clear religious interest then, which was perhaps stirred by fierce antireligious sentiments in the socialist movement. One historian has remarked that those sentiments were "painful" for Jewish socialists, "even when they did not go to the synagogue any more every Saturday."[70] Jews saw being antireligious as rejecting a part of themselves; this adamant secularism paradoxically also fostered a spiritual interest in Pool. It was an interest she never quite lost, and she would spend the rest of her life searching for religious fulfillment, first in theosophy, then Catholicism, and later in life in the Bahá'í faith.

The socialist movement as well as modern life required Pool to leave behind many things: the Papiamento-speaking family she found so captivating, the "Jewish church" she so curiously explored, and the impoverished part of her family that was still slaughtering pigs. As she started to make a living out of teaching, literature, and poetry, she and they were put worlds apart. Her former self thus became a casualty in the social mobility that she and her parents aspired to. As a teenager and in her twenties Pool was trying to become not just a better person but a different person.

This compulsion to become a different person was no doubt what led her to tell the lies she told throughout her life. Although it is dangerous to project too much of her later identity on the young "Roosje," the creative narrating of her life story and goals is consistent in a certain way. Whether it was lying about not having carved things in her school desk or prevaricating about attending university or striving to improve herself, Pool was always trying to be somebody other than who she was. They were signs of what Pool wanted to become. Pool certainly embraced that desired self-image and not only wanted to transform herself into a better person but also improve society in general. Yet if these were growing pains, she only fully matured in Berlin, where her new life was about to begin.

CHAPTER 2
Berlin, 1927–1939

In 1927 the twenty-two-year-old Pool made an interesting decision: to go away as far as possible and leave the Netherlands behind. At an international student conference in 1926 she met a German law student named Gerhard F. Kramer (1904–73).[1] An ambitious student, he worked his way through college while serving as president of a Berlin Social Democrat student union.[2] Eyewitnesses described him as a "decent man" and said that he was "very handsome ... when he was young."[3] Pool fell in love and was ready to settle down, as was expected of young women her age. Barely a year after she met Kramer, she moved with him to Berlin.

Although the Weimar Republic had struggled with profound political and financial problems in the late teens and early twenties—war reparations had to be paid, hyperinflation drove people to desperation, and war veterans flocked the streets begging for money—an unexpected economic boom in the last half of the 1920s, generally known as the "goldene Zwanziger Jahre," turned the country around, creating great prosperity, especially for a happy few.

Cultural life blossomed: modernist Bauhaus architecture, expressionist movies, and unconventional art experiments by Dada artists made Berlin the center of modernity. But what Berlin was most notorious for was its hedonist and extravagant nightlife. In the 1920s and early 1930s male prostitutes worked between the Kurfürstendamm and the Nollendorfplatz, looking for international sex tourists. Those streets were also infamous for the number of cocaine addicts living on the edge. In addition, countless eyewitnesses remembered crossdressing on the streets, by men and women alike. Underground gay and lesbian clubs became

Figure 5. Pool dressed in black, possibly at the funeral of her grandmother Roosje Pool-van Blankenstein (1849–1935), which was held in December 1935.

SOURCE: F010620, Jewish Historical Museum, Amsterdam.

bastions of decadence and debauchery dominated by alcohol, drugs, and transvestites. "Berlin was a motley crew," one eyewitness said.[4]

The city itself also changed. Once narrow streets were replaced by majestic boulevards and futuristic skyscrapers, and an underground railway was built that provided four million inhabitants access to the new dazzling metropolis. "The old Berlin had been impressive," one historian notes, but "the new Berlin was irresistible."[5] From all over Europe people came to see the "Chicago at the Spree" with their own eyes, and Pool was one of those *Wahlberliner* (Berliner by choice).[6]

Pool and Kramer seemingly enjoyed a blissful life together during the first years of their relationship. They divided much of their time between Berlin and Amsterdam, and they eagerly learned each other's languages. Pool reputedly acquired a Berlin accent while Kramer became fluent in Dutch and even learned some Dutch Jewish expressions through Pool.[7] Like her fiancé, Pool became a *Werkstudent* and probably took courses at Friedrich Wilhelm University while working part time on the side.

What kind of jobs she had is hard to reconstruct. One person remembered she had been a rehearsal pianist for Bertolt Brecht's legendary *Threepenny Opera*.[8] Other eyewitnesses said that Pool worked as an interpreter for the court of justice, while one journalist reported she had worked at a Berlin art trade firm.[9] One friend suggested that Pool had worked at the Institut für Sexualwissenschaft run by the famous sexologist Magnus Hirschfeld.[10] Moreover, one relative claimed she moved in the highest cultural circles of Berlin, and that she once even played piano with Albert Einstein.[11] However exciting all these stories are, it is impossible to ascertain whether any of them are true because archival material on this period is limited. However, many of these accounts may say more about Weimar Berlin's "wild" image as well as Pool's "wild" choice to go there than Pool's life at the time.

It is clear that Pool worked as a Dutch-German translator, at least occasionally.[12] Multiple eyewitnesses also confirmed that she had a job at an antiquarian bookstore, possibly Van Waegeningh, which was just around the corner from the central Potsdamer Platz.[13] The name of the Karl Marx Schule also pops up in various interviews: Pool worked at this progressive school, possibly as a substitute teacher.[14] Pool herself later claimed that she was in touch with the photographer Marion Palfi who was at that time working as an actor at the Theater am Kurfürstendamm.[15] Pool had a deep interest in theater, specifically, according to some friends, vaudeville theater.[16]

Occasionally she wrote pieces about Berlin theater and film for Dutch magazines. In one Dutch revolutionary socialist journal, Pool did not hesitate to sympathize with communist filmmakers (but she was afraid to use her own name, signing the piece with her initials instead). "In the middle of one of the most miserable workers' districts in Berlin there is a large theater," Pool noted. "A beautiful, firm building, which declares its mission in shining letters: Die Kunst dem Volke ["Art to the People"]."[17] Clearly thrilled, she described the *Volksbühne* movement, which offered laborers a means of relaxation and education. Her interest in art was visibly politically motivated, fueled by the idea that art should serve a proletarian revolution.

The extent to which being in Berlin expanded her far-left sympathies is revealed in her admiration for the play 1927 *Kreuzabnahme* (Descent from the Cross) by the controversial writer Ehm Welk. In this play the Russian proletariat needs to liberate itself in order to lose its cross (not only religion but also its enslavement by the capitalists). It was "Lenin's will, Lenin's spirit, Lenin's power" that could awaken the proletariat. "The entire playhouse cheered loudly at the end of the play," Pool reported, when the Marseillaise and the Internationale were played, accompanied by the "heavy pounding of thousands of feet, the advancing red army, the will of the proletariat!"[18] She did not disclose that the play was so controversial that it was shut down—as was Welk's 1926 *Gewitter über Gottland* (Thunderstorm over Gottland). Pool saw great potential in these plays, and she was in awe of what she called the "enormous educational power and propagandist worth of theater plays."[19]

Her taste in films was equally radical. She was impressed by the nonnarrative documentary *Melody of the World* (1929) directed by the abstract filmmaker Walter Ruttmann, which depicts laborers from all over the world and also enjoyed his documentary *Berlin: Symphony of a Metropolis* (1927). But the best movies came from even further east, or so she thought: "A curious phenomenon is happening when we look at the programs of Berlin film theaters," she reported. "Week after week the biggest, most capitalist cinemas show nothing other than Russian films. The *Sovkino* and other Russian productions dominate Berlin film life." And Pool loved these films with all her socialist heart.

One of her favorites was the Russian director Vsevolod Pudovkin, whose innovative and vibrant Soviet montage was a style as well as an ideological tool for bringing dialectical materialism to the masses.[20] Pool was impressed by his silent film *Storm over Asia* (1928) which depicted the struggle of the communist Mongolians against the White protsarist

Russians, although she was less impressed by Pudovkin's mise-en-scène, which she dismissed as "American grotesque."[21] Pool regarded the popularity of Soviet movies in Berlin as a sign that "the public at large slowly also gets fed up with the sugarcoated Hollywood movies."[22] This would be the only time she referred to the United States in her writing during this period.

Political Radicalization

Many regarded expressionist movies as a form of escapism during turbulent times. Berlin started to change rapidly after Pool settled there. The Wall Street stock market crash of 1929 was a turning point for the entire world economy. Despite its image of prosperity, the economy of the Weimar Republic was very unstable, and it didn't take much to push the country into a full-blown economic crisis. The country was now faced with even more unemployment and popular discontent, all of which instigated the growth of radical groups on both the far left and on the far right. The moderate German Social Democratic Party was rapidly losing support, especially among communists, who believed that capitalism was yesterday's ideology. Although there is no evidence that Pool ever became directly involved in German Socialist or communist groups, her letter to Henk Sneevliet is especially revealing (and coincidentally the only piece of correspondence that survived this period).

Henk Sneevliet (1883–1942) was a prominent Dutch communist. His international activism brought him to the Dutch East Indies and China, and he knew Lenin quite well. However, he parted ways with the Dutch Communist Party in 1927 because he opposed Moscow's rigid influence. He moved toward the ideas of Leon Trotski, who predicted a permanent state of revolution, an anticapitalist theory that argued a workers' state was the one and only option. Some regarded Sneevliet a "Trotsky traitor," a radical dividing the Dutch left.[23] Sneevliet did not abandon his convictions, however, and ultimately founded the Revolutionary Socialist Party. As the name suggests, the goal of the party was a proletarian revolution.

It must have been an honor for the twenty-five-year-old Pool to be asked to translate one of Sneevliet's publications. While he was a living legend, Pool was probably still a student when she translated his article that argued the colonial authorities Dutch Indonesia were abusive, a thesis that she seemingly wholeheartedly agreed with. "Dear Comrade!" she addressed him, when she sent him her German translation, adding a cover letter in which she condemned the German Social Democratic government. "It is tragicomic to see the fear in Berlin over the communist riots," she wrote. "Last Saturday/Sunday [there was] a police force comparable to that of 1 May 1929, accompanied by full *Reichswehr* regiments. Some courageous fighters!" she exclaimed mockingly.[24]

Through her Dutch contacts like the poet Jef Last—whom she also mentions in this letter—Pool was probably aware of Sneevliet's critique of Social Democrats.[25] In her letter Pool firmly positions herself outside of her former Social Democrat milieu, perhaps in an attempt to prove to him that she had made the transition to revolutionary socialism as well. Her sympathy for the communist rioters—whether this was lip service to Sneevliet or not—was shared by many of her communist contemporaries.[26] Around this same time she held a recital in the Netherlands at a lecture by Année Rinzes de Jong, chairman of the Association of Religious Anarcho-Communists, a group that was convinced that real politics took place outside of organized government.[27] Pool had thus now moved toward the far-leftist end of the political spectrum.

More proof of her radicalization was her involvement with the Dutch Socialist Youth Union, the youth club of the radical Independent Socialist Party.[28] Her former friends at the Workers Youth Center considered the Independent Socialist Party a "left-wing deviation," and the center banned all party members in 1932.[29] The exiled members then founded the Socialist Youth Union, and Pool turned even farther left after this split. Ideologically she was now closer to Sneevliet's Revolutionary Socialist Party than the more mainstream Social Democrat Workers Youth Center. Yet she never became a hardcore member of the radical Socialist Youth Union. This was partly because her life in Berlin made her an outsider. She was now worldlier and more cosmopolitan than her peers. "She liked to laugh," one eyewitness, a laborer, remembered. But "she was a typical intellectual, which distanced her from me."[30] Such divisions within the left would have disastrous consequences for Rosey Pool and many others.

Anti-Fascist Activism across Borders

During the depression, Weimar Germany's already frail economy simply collapsed: industrial production plummeted, banks failed, and there was a huge rise in unemployment. By the time Hitler came into power in January 1933, one in three Germans were without a job. Poverty went hand in hand with unrest and popular discontent. Many began to lose faith in democracy and looked to extremist parties on the left and the right, which both seemed to offer quick and simple solutions. Unfortunately, the extreme left was thoroughly divided. Socialist and communist groups fought each other viciously in what has been called a "brotherly quarrel."[31] The Nazis greatly benefited from this schism. During the heated German election campaigns in 1930 and 1933 the fascist movement grew and street violence became more common.

Pool and her husband, Gerhard Kramer, openly opposed the Nazis, well before racial theories became a cornerstone of their propaganda. By the late 1920s, Kramer had emerged as a prominent lawyer who delivered public speeches in favor of social democracy. When the Nazi Party aggressively campaigned for the 1930 Reichstag elections, Kramer became even more outspoken, lecturing in Berlin about "the dangers of national socialism" and "the fascist danger."[32] Pool herself also wanted to warn her Dutch compatriots about fascism. In early 1931 she came to Amsterdam to give a talk on fascism in Germany in which she related her own, firsthand experiences.[33]

In September 1932 Pool and Kramer even made a joint appearance, again in Amsterdam.[34] The German elections two months before proved an utter disaster from the couple's point of view: the Nazi Party had become the second biggest party. Slowly the Dutch started paying attention to what was happening in Germany, and the couple found an especially willing ear in the labor movement. The hall of an Amsterdam trade union was packed when Kramer said—in his best Dutch—that the Dutch peace movement was fiercer than its German counterpart. Yet during his time in Holland he had also noticed that many Dutch people did not take Hitler seriously. He warned the audience not to mock the Nazis: "It is not the correct way to pose a challenge. The triumph of the national socialists during the elections and their massive support can be explained not only through the awful circumstances of this time but also by reference to the fact that they don't ask the masses to reason like Social Democrats do. They influence the masses pretty well through hollow phrases and by keeping them ignorant."[35]

Kramer did not criticize Nazi ideals, but for a good reason: "The Nazis have never said what they actually want," he said. And since they did not "have a program, ... it cannot be challenged."[36] Although Kramer was still a staunch Social Democrat—which was the only "reasonable" choice according to him—his early cries against the Nazis were far from mainstream in Social Democrat circles. He evidently set himself apart from the ruling Social Democratic Party, which adopted a "wait and see" approach to the far right.[37] In the years that followed, Kramer maintained his principled stance against fascism, and when the Nazis took power in early 1933 he abandoned his position as a *Staatsanwalt* (prosecutor) and instead became a *Rechtsanwalt* (lawyer). He was now defending the regime's suspects, including the Jewish communist Sally Epstein in 1933–34, who was accused of the murder of the SA brownshirt Horst Wessel.[38] Several years after he and Pool had separated, Kramer became a member of the Nazi Party when he saw no other way to survive, during the 1940s.[39]

Pool's own role in the 1932 Amsterdam event was minor. As a big finale, "Mrs. R. Kramer-Pool," as she was introduced, read from *Opstandelingen* (Insurgents), a classic written in 1910 by the Dutch socialist writer Henriette Roland Holst, and from the German expressionist writer Leonhard Frank's *De mensch is goed* (Man is good).[40] And although audiences generally longed for such "light" entertainment after heavy and often lengthy speeches, Pool was clearly the support act. This was in sharp contrast to a few years earlier, when Pool had been a well-known figure with VARA, the socialist radio station, and her name and photograph were used to attract audiences. Now Kramer stood in the spotlight while Pool had shifted to the background.

To a friend Pool remarked that she merely had had a "supporting role" during her marriage to Kramer.[41] By the early 1930s Pool had become the spouse of a public speaker whose only task was to support her husband in his ambitions by standing next to him. For someone like Pool, who was a widely known performer in the Dutch socialist movement and who had a sparkling, restless personality, this was hard. Yet for a while it seems that she tried to convince herself that this was the right thing to do. In 1930 she translated a poem about the position of women in the labor movement. It encouraged women to support the class struggle by letting their husbands go to meetings after work. "And don't you keep him back when red flags are burning," it said, echoing Pool's own submissive role as an obedient wife.[42] Yet soon Pool became tired of playing second fiddle.

A Peek out of the Closet

The political situation deteriorated rapidly as the 1930s progressed. Street violence between Nazis and communists and attacks by the paramilitary SA against communists, Social Democrats, and Jews became ever more common. The ever-grimmer political climate as well as Pool's strained relationship with Gerhard Kramer led Pool to move in more radical circles, both in Amsterdam and in Berlin. It was during this period she was associated with the Karl Marx Schule in Neukölln, Berlin's labor quarter, where she likely first met Lena Fischer, a Berlin local about whom little is known besides that she was a lesbian.[43] Pool and Fischer started a romantic relationship that probably lasted many years. It was serious between them: they shared an apartment in Berlin, and Pool also took Fischer with her to meet her parents. They were even planning to move to Amsterdam together.[44]

Pool wrote about this relationship in cryptic yet autobiographical poems from the 1940s, some of which are dedicated to "L. F."—undeniably Lena Fischer. "I was deeply connected to her in friendship," one of those poems, titled "Aan mijn vrienden," reads.[45] The word "friendship" was used more often in lesbian circles, which could both mean a "romantic friendship" or an intense platonic one.[46] In another poem, "Aan mijn moeder," she talks about a *gezellin* ("companion"), clearly referring to a life partner.[47] The impact of this mystery woman on Pool's life was perhaps even deeper than the available material suggests: it is possible that this woman was the love of her life. Yet the relationship between Pool and Fischer suddenly came to an end when Fischer was arrested and never heard of again. Perhaps she was sent to a concentration camp, perhaps for political reasons or because the Nazis saw lesbians as "degenerates."[48] In "Aan mijn vrienden," Pool notes that she was "suddenly and cruelly separated" from someone that she deeply cared about, and in "Kwatrijn voor L. F.," she speaks about being deeply connected to an anonymous woman in a dark time: "The nights she lay in my arms. Fear, about what was to come, often holds back sleep."[49] Of all the things that the Nazis did in the 1930s and beyond, this had the greatest impact; they took away the love of her life.

Pool kept her love life largely to herself, and afterward she meticulously covered up this period in her archives. Yet in her private scrapbooks some loose photographs can be found of a woman, dressed in a sexually ambiguous style with short-cut hair and trousers. One of Pool's students in Amsterdam, a teenager, remembered that Pool treasured a portrait of her Berlin girlfriend, "dressed as a man," making it clear she was not aware this was a lesbian dress code.[50] Had this pupil been somewhat older, then she might have remembered the 1930 movie *Morocco* in which Marlene Dietrich wore a suit and tie and kissed another woman, defying both gender and heterosexual norms. Yet many heterosexuals innocently believed that women in male suits were just "modern" or that this was the dress code of liberated "new women." In popular culture it indeed often was, but Lena Fischer's clothing style (figure 6) obviously went further

Figure 6. "Lena F." and unidentified person, circa 1920s, in a scrapbook compiled by Pool in the 1950s.
SOURCE: Rudi Wesselius.

than Marlene Dietrich's feminine tailored pieces. In figure 6, a picture, probably taken around 1927 or 1928, Lena wears androgynous clothes in Berlin's famous Garçonne style.[51] Her blazer and loosely tied necktie leave little to the imagination: she was a part of Berlin's lesbian subculture.

It is unclear whether Pool was a part of the same subculture or whether she visited any of Berlin's famous lesbian establishments, like the Monokelbar at the Kurfürstendamm, the lesbian bowling club the Lustige Neun, or the Toppkeller at the Schwerinstraße. Pool did not seem to adopt Berlin's dress code. She always refused to use the term "lesbian." After the war she even disliked the Dutch word *vriendin* ("girlfriend"); it was, she said, too "piquant" for her taste.[52] Yet there are strong indications that she was indeed part of Berlin's lesbian subculture; she was just less flamboyant and was more subtle in indicating that she was. Her noting in connection with her marriage that she played a "supporting role" was a well-known way of describing lesbian life, referring to the double role many lesbians had to play, as lesbianism was not accepted everywhere.[53] Pool also occasionally wore a pinky ring, which was an insider's signal that she was "one of us."[54] Some of her poems from the 1940s contain overt lesbian references, such as "Sapphic Ode to Emily Dickinson."[55] Of the poems she wrote under the header "Vriendinnen"—then apparently still an okay term—one poem stands out. It describes a woman nicknamed "Bobby N."—a female mechanic who works at a service station and who drinks beer—against a backdrop that is reminiscent of Berlin:

> In leather jacket or blue overalls,
> Not in the dress that vain women wear,
> Short, dark hair in a waveless drop,
>
> On a motorcycle, which
> trembles and shakes like a brute,
> On the fierce shore of the metropolis
> You have led your life recklessly.
>
> Life caught you as in a flame;
> Too bright, too fierce; perhaps your heart knew
> That such glaring would never last long.[56]

The poem is remarkable because it idealizes the overly macho woman who wants to be seen as "one of the guys" in the garage she works at and suggests Pool was aware of and probably personally knew what sexologist Hirschfeld called "sexual intermediaries," individuals who explored the boundaries between men and women.[57] Perhaps such exploration is what friends had in mind when they said that Pool had had a "rather wild youth" in Berlin.[58]

"Who of us dares that!!"

It became obvious during this time when Pool was exploring Berlin and its lesbian subculture with her girlfriend that her relationship with Kramer was doomed. Their lengthy engagement (that had begun in 1927) came to an end in August 1932—not with a separation but surprisingly with a wedding. Perhaps getting married was a final attempt to make the relationship work, or perhaps they made it official so that she could continue to live in Germany. Yet by 1933 they were already separated, although the divorce was only finalized in June 1935.[59] One of Pool's pupils remembered that it was Kramer who initiated the divorce, "probably because she was homosexual," he said, "but the official, public reason" Kramer supplied to the Nazis was "because she was Jewish."[60]

While the evidence for Pool being a lesbian or perhaps bisexual is subtle, it is crystal clear that she was simply too ambitious to accept a marriage and housekeeping as a career in itself, an idea that was deeply rooted in heterosexual life. Pool was a "very emancipated woman," according to one eyewitness: "She was the first and only woman I have ever seen who wore a monocle at home."[61] Pool was seemingly unaware that the monocle was a famous aspect of the lesbian dress code (both in Berlin and Paris); that she wore one shows how her sexuality and her ambition were unconsciously linked together. Further, it is not uncommon for a sexual revelation to occur at the same time as a social rebellion.[62] Often they are both part of a simultaneous transition that compels a more thorough exploration of the inner self. And as heterosexuality was the norm or even silently compulsory, coming out as or even being a lesbian inherently meant distancing oneself from those norms. It was, in other words, an act of defiance against Nazi rule.[63]

In Nazi Berlin, Pool was torn between society's expectations of women and her own mind and ambitions, forcing her to act on "contrary instincts."[64] To find true love but also to find herself, Pool had to resist patriarchal structures, starting with her own marriage. It is possible that Pool preferred an open marriage (not uncommon in Communist Party circles) or at least expected more freedom in her relationship with Kramer. The few sources that discuss his private life suggest that Kramer saw women's place as being primarily in the kitchen.[65] Curiously, he did not think Pool's name was worth mentioning in any of his recollections.

Pool's interpretation of one Soviet film, Fyodor Otsep's 1929 *The Living Corpse* that deals with adultery, is perhaps revealing in this context. An adaptation of Tolstoy's novel of the same name, this movie tells the story of a man whose wife is unsure whether to stay with him or pursue another man, who had also competed for her hand. The husband cannot stand this; he contemplates suicide but instead runs away. After a while, his wife assumes that he is dead and marries the other man. But then her first husband reappears. The woman is charged with bigamy, and a judge rules that she must leave her new husband or be exiled to Siberia. Unexpectedly, her first husband shoots himself, however, and the film ends with the woman shouting hysterically that her first husband had always been the love of her life. The suicide and resurrection theme was not uncommon in Soviet cinema, in which deaths were often represented as the beginning of a new life or the source of a life-changing revelation. Yet the silent film with limited intertitles was ambiguous enough for Pool to have an entirely different reading of the movie that centered on the female experience. Pool noted that the man "knows that his wife loves another, he wants to see her happy, *with* the other, but the church will not approve of the divorce." She also explained that in real life marriage legislation prohibited divorces, which she said was "narrow minded and inhumane."⁶⁶ Pool described in awe how the protagonist "disappears in the darkest corners of the proletarian life," living a life in poverty—all to set his wife free. "Who of us dares that!!"⁶⁷

As she herself was also in love with "another" around this time, the review perhaps ended up being more autobiographical than Pool had intended. A couple of years later Pool finally dared to set herself free, both from her marriage and from heterosexual norms. The city of Berlin was largely responsible for that. Many of her Amsterdam friends had thought of her as "asexual" or even "sexless," but in Berlin Pool finally recognized undefined feelings of "otherness," enabling her to come out of the closet.⁶⁸ More importantly, she no longer had a "supporting role" to play. She again assumed the leading role in her own life.

A Jewish Woman in Nazi Berlin

With the assumption of power by the Nazis in 1933, the Weimar Republic soon became a faint memory. Thousands of soldiers marched through the streets, and Nazi flags besmeared Berlin's architecture. Initially, Pool had observed the Nazis from afar, paying special attention to their songs, as a sort of anthropologist looking at a weird breed or unidentified species.⁶⁹ But soon she had to admit that things were getting out of hand. Germany "was going through a period of major political problems," Pool wrote much later in a dry and distant manner, "which culminated in the burning of the Reichstag building in Berlin in February 1933 and the rise of Adolf Hitler."⁷⁰ But that was of course just the beginning. Through her left-wing network and Kramer's inside information from the judicial system, including that of the notorious anti-Jewish Nuremberg Laws of 1935, Pool was at an early stage already aware of how the Nazis treated their opponents. Still, it was simply unfathomable that the worst was yet to come.

For a Jewish, lesbian, and revolutionary socialist woman, the rise of the Nazis had serious implications. Intimidation of opponents was a key Nazi strategy and within months after the Nazi takeover in January 1933 all opposition was eliminated. The Nazis hunted down "November criminals," which encompassed Jews, Republicans, Democrats, and communists. Pool's life in Berlin almost reads like a Kafka novel, given that the Nazis opposed everything she was and everything she stood for. In 1933 women were barred from the workplace and only rarely admitted to universities.⁷¹ The Karl Marx Schule was closed by the Nazis that same year. Subsequently, lesbianism was denounced as a "perversion." Socialists and communists were declared to be enemies. Moreover, after the Reichstag was set on fire by the Dutch communist Marinus van der Lubbe, all Dutch people living in Berlin were put under house arrest too.[72] All these "anti-otherisms"—as Pool later called them—targeted Pool.[73] The situation became increasingly hazardous.

Her Jewishness, however, was the most problematic to the Nazis. Something she had always seen as a minor element of her life story suddenly defined her. Jews became the scapegoat and were blamed for nearly everything. Pool probably experienced up close the early anti-Jewish boycotts and consequences of legal exclusion. The infamous book burning of 1933 took place only a few hundred meters away from the antiquarian bookstore where she worked and likely included books she read. Soon people were being physically attacked as well, and rapidly violence became commonplace. In a rare comment on her Berlin days, Pool remarked to a reporter that she "saw old men trampled in the streets, killed only because they looked Jewish." That same journalist quoted her as saying that "at this time people were taken from their homes and . . . placed in collective camps simply because they were Jews."[74]

Pool looked for opportunities to leave Nazi Berlin, if only for a short while. She possibly took elective courses at universities in Munich, Paris, and Perugia. Yet she did not leave her new hometown behind entirely, and her name still appeared in Berlin address books of 1936 and 1937.[75] It was probably around this time that she undertook "small" acts of resistance, perhaps helping the underground Communist Party or the International Red Aid. To an American journalist she said that she became "a one-man underground system" in Berlin who "helped Jewish people flee Nazi control" and get to the Netherlands.[76] One of those she helped might have been the Berlin typographer Susanne Heynemann (1913–2009), who married the much older Dutch diamond trader Benjamin Lopes Cardozo (1887–1942), a communist who probably agreed to a sham marriage to protect a comrade.[77] Rescuing Heynemann and other unknown people was the first step Pool took as part of the resistance work she would continue when she finally returned to Amsterdam in late 1938 or early 1939.[78] This was, of course, extremely late. Perhaps Pool had hoped that German fascism was just a temporary fad, as many continued to believe despite all the signs to the contrary. Or perhaps she wanted to continue her antifascist activism, which required that she remain in enemy territory. Unfortunately, she stayed long enough not only to see Lena Fischer disappear but also to experience Nazi violence firsthand. An American friend remembered a meeting with Pool in the late 1950s: "We were talking about a Brecht play—possibly *Threepenny Opera* itself—and Rosey sang a few measures in German with marked vocal flair. I said: Rosey, I didn't know you sang! She said: I played the piano for rehearsals in Germany. I said: I didn't know you played! She said: Oh yes, but the Nazis broke the bones in my hands and I couldn't play any more."[79]

Where, when, or how this alleged assault happened is not known. This memory is just as chaotic as Pool's time in Berlin. In later life she would make shocking revelations like this, often without "a vestige of complaint or self-pity."[80]

Her date of arrival in the Netherlands, in January 1939, suggests that she was still in Berlin during Kristallnacht, a final turning point for Nazi Germany. Also known as the "Night of Broken Glass," this pogrom was defined by widespread mob violence against Jews. Dozens of synagogues, Jewish schools, and stores were destroyed that night. German authorities did not intervene, making it clear Jews were living targets.[81] It was what convinced Pool she had to get out of there, as quickly as possible. There was now no doubt about it: Hitler's regime was a "dictatorship of fear and murder," Pool remarked.[82] She immediately returned to Amsterdam.

Mass Movements, Individual Decisions

Rosey Pool's time in Berlin was a turning point in her life during which she had redefined herself. The political situation shook her deeply: it showed that the labor movement, which she so wholeheartedly supported, stood no chance against nationalistic frameworks that national socialism brought, and the threat of war grew by the day. Yet perhaps what was most painful for Pool to confront was the fact of bystanders who let it all happen out of complacency or out of fear of being the next target and who thereby were an undeniable part of what Pool later called "mass insanity."[83] It shocked her to see how "many German parents and teachers took part in Hitler's anti-Semitic programs," she later said.[84] Race ideology was not the biggest threat, she thought: indifference was. To her, apathy was the exact opposite of solidarity.

Pool believed in actively fighting for the oppressed labor class. It is thus not strange that she later embraced the African American cause, which was by the 1930s known among communists as the cause of the "Negro proletariat." It is nevertheless astounding that there is not a single indication that she showed an interest in African American poetry or culture in this period. In the sixties Pool briefly remarked that there was a protest by

Berlin's Transport Workers Union in 1931 to support the Scottsboro Boys, but she left it unclear whether she was there or not.[85] She did suggest that she knew how common it would be to see a Black actor on a Berlin stage during this period, noting in a 1953 article on Black actors on European stages that "The writer, who lived in pre-Hitler Berlin from 1927 until 1933, can safely say that to her knowledge no Negro ever appeared on the German-speaking stage in straight [i.e., nonmusical] plays."[86]

Pool later claimed that in Berlin she had written a dissertation titled "Die Dichtung des nordamerikanischen Negers" (The poetry of the American Negro), adding that the Nazis had ruined her academic career. "Back in Amsterdam in 1938," Pool later recalled, "I found that the Gestapo had confiscated all my scientific work that I left in Berlin on my rather hurried departure, that they had seized all my papers and destroyed the research material of so many years."[87] The only formal supervisor for this topic would have been professor Friedrich Schönemann, a pro-Nazi Americanist at the University of Berlin.[88] Pool could have studied with him, but her topic would have had to fit in with the Nazi's racial theories that represented Black people as an inferior "race." Although her university enrollment records might have simply gone missing, it is highly unlikely she ever completed a PhD or that she even did a *Habilitation* for that matter.[89] After 1933, Jewish lecturers were barred from universities, and in 1937 Jewish students were expelled as well. Pool did, however, put "Dr." in front of her name in years to come, especially when she was in England and the United States. "I never dared ask her, what kind of doctorate do you have," one Dutch friend shyly recalled, "because I had a feeling that it was something she had merely given to herself."[90] And there was more to come that Pool did not want us to know—starting with her life during the Second World War.

CHAPTER 3

Westerbork, 1939–1945

"**I managed to jump from the death train,**" **Rosey Pool remarked in** the course of briefly describing her war experiences to an American journalist.[1] And no, she told another reporter, she did not know what happened to her parents. "They died in the gas chambers so far as I know."[2] Perhaps she wanted to shock people with her casualness, or perhaps she wanted to prevent herself from emotionally breaking down by taking control of the story. Her life during World War II might have sounded exciting and heroic, even in comparison with that of other Holocaust survivors: teaching Anne Frank, helping Jewish refugees, fighting in the resistance, and spectacularly escaping from a Nazi transit camp. Yet the reality of war was frightening, full of moral dilemmas and irresponsible risks, and the outcome was extremely random. She refused to be seen as a hero. "I was just lucky," she admitted candidly.[3]

The year 1939 heralded a new era for Pool. She left Germany and returned to the Netherlands, moving back in with her parents in the Nieuwe Hoogstraat. This move was motivated by her assumption that her homeland would remain neutral, as it had done before. "We would always be safe" was the general thought at the time, Pool recalled.[4] Nazism was a temporary madness that could not last long, she surmised. Pool nostalgically remembered "those happy days" of the late 1930s when the Dutch enjoyed life "as if there were no Hitler regime across our borders."[5] But it was simply impossible to turn a blind eye to fascism. The Nazi dream of a German *Vaterland* generated a hunger for territorial expansion, while political opponents and Jews were viciously attacked. German Jews tried to flee, and after 1933 about fifty thousand fled to the Netherlands. For many, their stay was meant to be temporary.

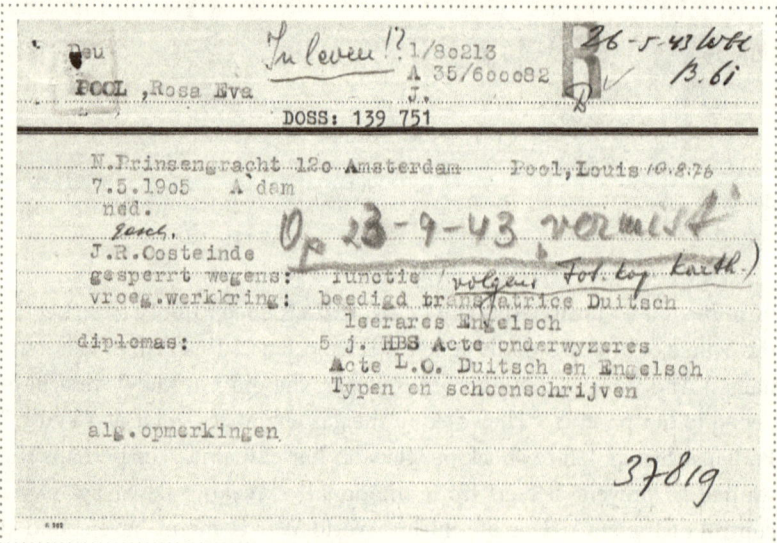

Figure 7. Pool's identification card from Camp Westerbork. It is noted on the card that she went "missing" on Thursday, 23 September 1943.

SOURCE: 278364, Carthotheek Jewish Council, Memorial Center Camp Westerbork.

Pool strongly identified with these refugees, as she herself had also been forced to leave Germany behind. This close identification was one of the reasons she started teaching Dutch and English crash courses as well as holding occasional English evenings at Tehuis Oosteinde, a popular meeting place for German migrants and refugees, primarily Jews.[6] Her students were of all ages and from all walks of life. But they were similar in that they had no prospect of gaining Dutch citizenship, no ability to integrate into society, and no chance of moving on to another country. Pool actively tried to address this demoralizing and hopeless situation by making her classes lighthearted and witty. Many found her attitude inspiring, and one pupil recalled that Pool "brought a light of hope to masses of people."[7] However, being a beacon of light was not an easy task. Pool remembered one gentleman from Germany who wanted to learn English in order to emigrate to America. He became upset when he found out that the English language not only had a present tense but also a past tense, which discouraged him deeply. "Und das alles durch den EINEN Menschen," Pool remembered him saying—and that all because of that one man: Hitler.[8]

Around the same time Pool also started to teach English lessons at the Lloyd Hotel, a refugee center near the eastern docks of Amsterdam. The population of this camp changed continuously. Some refugees only stayed for one night, some a bit longer. But almost all were traumatized by the expulsion from their homeland. Some had been on the dramatic "voyage of the damned" on the MS *St. Louis*, the ship that was denied entry in both Cuba and the United States in mid-1939 and so was forced to return to Europe, eventually landing in Amsterdam where the situation became even more hopeless now that the passengers were out of money as well. Against that desolate and bleak background, Pool was regarded as an inspiration. Two pupils—both of whom had been on the MS *St. Louis*— fondly recalled this "very heavy, friendly Jewish lady" and described her as a "born teacher."[9] As there were no German-language syllabuses available, Pool decided simply to make up teaching methods herself. One pupil recalled an English song they learned in her class, a song about a "little nigger boy" with "woolly" hair.[10] This remembrance indicates that by this time Pool had become interested in African American culture, albeit not in the most sophisticated manner.

Pool's recollection might have been that the neighboring Dutch "welcomed thousands of refugees from Germany," but in reality, Jewish refugees were scarcely admitted by the Dutch government, and in mid-1939 the country closed its borders to all foreigners entirely.[11] Perhaps Pool was remembering her own welcoming attitude toward these refugees, which was shared by the members of the radical leftist circles she operated in. While moderate socialist groups did little or nothing at all, small groups of revolutionary socialists and communists reached out to these Jewish refugees.[12] The majority of the Dutch population was largely passive and silent. Most non-Jews saw these refugees as competitors in the already tight Dutch labor market, which was still recovering from the depression of the 1930s. Yet many in Dutch Jewish circles were not particularly welcoming either because they feared that these newcomers would exacerbate antisemitism in the Netherlands.[13]

Pool's character also drove her to help. Max Gruber, one of her students, remarked that Pool's work with refugees was a "natural outcome" of her personality. "She always took an interest in the oppressed, persecuted, or people otherwise in need."[14] Perhaps this character trait grew out of her having been bullied as a child; perhaps that experience taught her to follow her inner moral values, regardless of what others might think—an important characteristic of many helpers.[15] This desire to do what was right had led her to embrace the ideals of far left, antifascist groups in the 1930s, groups that had already begun resistance efforts against the fascist threat, largely operating underground and actively seeking to help the victims of fascism. Her way of thinking noticeably influenced by Marxist writers and thinkers, such as the evolutionary biologist J. B. S. Haldane who argued that "there is no difference between one and the other kind of people." Pool came to believe that words like "us" and "them" were artificial categories meant to divide people.[16] She became convinced that there was only one category: citizens of the world. So helping refugees did not really feel like a choice to her. Like her other efforts to help people on the fringes of society, helping these refugees was a duty, a responsibility she felt she owed herself and humankind.

The "Race Madness" Spreads

Pretending that the Nazis were harmless was a daydream from which the Dutch were rudely awakened on 10 May 1940. On that day Nazi Germany invaded the Netherlands, and after a short amount of fighting and disastrous city bombings, the country was occupied. Soon, however, most people returned to their daily lives and the new circumstances became almost frighteningly normal. An attempt to normalize the occupation was part of the Nazis strategy in the Netherlands: the Dutch were seen as part of the Aryan "master race" and were therefore treated more or less the same as

Germans. But Pool quickly came to see that she was not included in this conception of the Dutch; she also knew how the Nazis treated their opponents, and through her antifascist networks, it is likely that she heard at least rumors about murders and the systematic persecution of Jews.

She started to get rid of her paperwork, much of which was never to be seen again. By June 1939 she had donated some of her materials to a socialist archive in Amsterdam, including a book on the Russian revolution and even a printed speech by Adolf Hitler—another sign of her antifascist activism; she clearly wanted to undermine this enemy by studying its tactics and arguments.[17] Like many other radical leftists, Pool destroyed all of her letters and papers shortly after the occupation, as they could have put anyone mentioned or addressed in them at great risk.

Now that the country was occupied she started to "think three steps ahead."[18] Anyone who was "not unmistakably one of us" was "our enemy until he has proved the contrary," she later recalled.[19] Her activist experience, her time in Berlin's lesbian subculture, and even her public performances as recitist and speaker made this "double life" mentality easier for her to adjust to, preparing her to assume different identities just about everywhere she went. Yet the war brought a completely new, never-ending alertness. "You looked around to see if somebody was spying," Pool recalled. "You were not even free in your own home."[20]

The use of real names during the war was often avoided, and Pool once claimed that her nom de guerre was "Harriet Tool," after Harriet Tubman, her "personal hero."[21] Tubman had played an important role in mid-nineteenth-century America, facilitating the escape of enslaved African Americans to the free North. Pool later also noted that her "underground group against Hitler" was "named after Harriet Tubman," although at the time she "felt that we had hardly the right to do so."[22] The absence of sources makes it impossible to verify these claims, but secret coded messages were a crucial part of the underground resistance. Also, the Underground Railroad would play a crucial role in Pool's survival later on.

The first, relatively peaceful period of World War II ended in early 1941 as Nazi repression went from bad to worse. Through numerous decrees Dutch Jews were targeted, a process that was carried out in a bureaucratic and distant manner. Jews were "sent to special schools," Pool later recalled. They "couldn't use parks, couldn't show themselves outside."[23] Each separate measure seemed initially trivial, but taken together they were catastrophic. Jews were increasingly cut off from Dutch society. The faint hope that the hatred toward Jews came only from one man, the *Führer*, also faded away. Now even Dutch citizens began taking initiatives

Figure 8. World War II–era sign: "Jews not wanted."
SOURCE: 216370, Huizinga collectie bord voor Joden verboden, NIOD Institute for War, Holocaust and Genocide Studies, Amsterdam, Wikimedia Commons.

to bar Jews. By late 1942 "No Jews" signs were almost everywhere, often put up by local municipalities or shop owners themselves (figure 8).[24]

This development was to have dramatic consequences for Pool herself, who was according to Nazi race laws a *Volljude*, "full Jew." One of the most tangible measures was the yellow star, a cotton Star of David that Jews were forced to wear in public after May 1942. This was necessary "to distinguish us from the so-called 'Herrenvolk,'" the "master race," Pool wrote.[25] Although Pool had never really felt "Jewish," she did not resist the anti-Jewish laws at first. On the contrary, she tried to make the yellow badge her own. "I wore it like my shoes, like my skirt," she states in one of her poems, titled "Het teken." "[I did] not feel insult or resentment." This changed, however, when she saw a child "walk[ing] alone with that yellow stain, which besmeared him like stinking slime."[26] It was only at that moment that it finally hit her what kind of "race madness" the Dutch had so quickly grown accustomed to.[27]

Observing Anne Frank

Pool witnessed up close what happened to Jewish children when she started to work at the Joods Lyceum in Amsterdam, probably as a substitute teacher in English. This "Jew school"—as Pool called it—was for children from the age of twelve to eighteen and had opened its doors in October 1941 when Jewish children were barred from the Dutch school system.[28] Despite the threat of war, the Jewish Lyceum was a school like any other. There were exams, and children stared out of windows and played games on the schoolyard. One pupil remembered that during Pool's English classes they often made fun of her because of her posh British accent. "Oh, she was always so dramatic." She orated histrionically: "'No sun, no moon.'... We couldn't stop giggling. Yes, we were never serious in class, we were very mean!"[29] Pool herself tried to lighten the mood as well by giving extracurricular lectures on humor in literature and reading parts of plays in her classes.[30] Like many of her colleagues, Pool felt morally obligated to ensure that these children's lives were as normal as possible.

Behind the scenes Pool adopted a more serious approach, however. Together with a colleague she worked on a formal recommendation to prioritize Hebrew and English in the curriculum in order to prepare the children for their emigration to Palestine, a suggestion that was quickly dismissed by the Jewish Council, the institution founded in 1941 on Nazi orders. Her colleague wrote disdainfully that the reason the proposal was rejected was that the council "did not want to give the Germans the idea that the Dutch Jews wanted to emigrate."[31] Fear muffled any type of open resistance. Through happenstance Pool's influence grew. In the last few weeks of the school's existence, Pool was appointed *rectrix* (female principal) of the school, and in this position she tried to help. Every day children were either "taken away or went into hiding," she recalled, and the school became ever emptier.[32] Around May 1943 a talented, bright pupil called Hajo Meyer, who had just received a call for deportation, caught her eye. Pool bafflingly urged the *rector* (male principal) to give this student "a list of his achievements of the written exam" to take with him on the train to the East.[33]

At this moment in time nearly all Jews were being deported from the Netherlands, and so Pool's insistence that the student be given a list of his accomplishments seems naïve. Was she trying to keep his spirits high? Or is it proof that Pool knew little about the Final Solution? Considering her own background, it seems highly unlikely that she was naïve about the deportations. She had witnessed herself in Berlin how the Nazis not only physically attacked Jews walking on the street for no reason but disappeared political opponents, including her own beloved Lena Fischer. Contemporary sources also reveal that most of the teachers at the Jewish Lyceum thought the deportations meant certain death, and so they encouraged children to disobey deportation orders, even though it was hard to do.[34] Pool likely shared these ideas, and it seems possible that Pool wanted to create a paper trail for the boy. Hajo Meyer remembered that after taking his final exam, he visited a man he had never met before who then led him to a hiding place.[35] Most likely then, Pool's letters to the rector were merely a cover, just in case the Nazis decided to research the case.

Children who were not as bright received far less attention from Pool. One child she did not notice that much was a young girl called Anne Frank. Pool recalled her as being "your ordinary, pleasant girl to have in the classroom" but "not frightfully brilliant."[36] Pool gave private English lessons to Edith, Anne Frank's mother, and occasionally went to the Frank family's home. Anne Frank would "scrutinize the visitor" who entered their home "with a pair of large eyes."[37] Pool always thought of her as "well, a little bit awkward." She was even a bit annoyed by her curiosity and keen observance, which she said not all adults always liked.[38]

She also remembered that Anne Frank had a "weird talent for impersonating people," including Pool herself.[39] Once at school, Pool overheard a noise in the schoolyard. She climbed on a table to peek through the window to see what was going on. There she saw how Anne Frank did "an excellent and hilarious impersonation" of the teaching staff.[40] Pool was amazed how the girl meticulously caricatured her colleagues and finally Pool herself as well, mimicking "every gesture and intonation."[41] Whether Anne Frank did this or not, Pool's anecdote about it shows that she had a sincere interest in these children.

Forging Papers and Rescuing Children

Shortly after the beginning of the war Pool had become involved in a resistance group that had been established through Tehuis Oosteinde, a refugee center for German Jews. The Nazi invasion had caused great alarm among the Jewish refugees in Holland. Many feared a repetition of the pogroms they had experienced in Nazi Germany. Yet some of the refugee center's visitors decided to actively defy Hitler and resist. A number of these, including Alice Heymann-David, Nathan Notowicz, and Ernst Levi, already had experience carrying out illegal work for the Communist Party and now organized themselves into a bastion against Hitler. This group became known as the Van Dien group, a randomly chosen name. They were far less arbitrary when it came to choosing its members though. With care these three picked out "the good ones," and Pool apparently was one of these.⁴²

In many ways Pool was a perfect candidate. They already knew her from the refugee center, and she spoke fluent Dutch and German. Moreover, all of her teaching jobs were part time and her private classes at people's homes enabled her to move around freely without raising much suspicion. But most importantly, her desire to help refugees was sincere, fueled by personal experiences and backed up by a firm ideological belief. In Berlin she had helped German Jews to get to the Netherlands, and so it was a no-brainer for her to accept the invitation to join this underground group. Pool saw "nothing brave" in that.⁴³ It was simply something she had to do.

Although the majority of the Van Dien group was Jewish, most saw themselves as antifascists who fought fascism in any form.⁴⁴ One eyewitness dryly remarked that at the time the term "antifascist" was simply used as a cover-up word for "communist."⁴⁵ And indeed, there were leaders of the exiled German Communist Party among the leaders of the Van Dien group. Yet while both factions targeted fascism, the Van Dien group differed from the exiled party in that helping Jews was its top priority. Both the German Communist Party and the Dutch Communist Party announced its solidarity with Jews. The party had organized the famous 1941 February strike to oppose anti-Jewish measures, and in their illegal newspaper it repeatedly wrote about the "mass murder" that was taking place.⁴⁶ Yet it also took selective action. Since socialism was only the logical outcome of history, such artificial walls between people would soon become outdated, it believed.⁴⁷ Sadly, Jewish antifascists largely fought their own battle. Throughout the war, the Van Dien group helped dozens, possibly even hundreds of people. Pool recalled, again casually, the kind of resistance work this group did: "We just did things like finding hiding places for small Jewish children and Jewish adults, getting documents and microfilms from the Germans, kidnapping people sometimes and leading people on escape routes out of the country."⁴⁸

Later on Pool said she and her group "kidnapped children off death transports," specifying that they "took seventy-two children into safety," an oddly specific number that is impossible to verify.⁴⁹ She also forged identity papers, which required a good eye for detail. She cooperated with Martin Löwenberg, who belonged to the group of leaders of the German Communist Party in exile.⁵⁰ Löwenberg, a resolute communist from Hamburg, arrived in Amsterdam around 1935 where he started a letterpress printing business. This became the perfect place to duplicate identity papers. Like any resistance fighter, Löwenberg understood that accuracy in the process of forging was absolutely crucial. In early 1942 he looked for four months for a particular gray linen paper that matched that used in original identification cards.[51] In his search for a specialist and trustworthy printer, Pool likely assisted him, as she had a wide cultural network. Duplicating identity cards were small acts of resistance, but these small acts had a great impact. Soon she would take greater risks, however.

Probably around this same period, somewhere in 1942 or 1943, Pool had started working for the Jewish Council, seemingly as a secretary. As a result of holding this position as well as her teaching at the Jewish Lyceum and Tehuis Oosteinde, Pool became one of the happy few to acquire a *Sperre*, an exemption from deportation. This gave her relatively more freedom in these fearful times, or at least the illusion of more freedom. Pool also secured work for both her brother and her father at the Jewish Council, which likewise provided them with a much coveted *Sperre*.

To this very day the Jewish Council is a controversial organization that arouses fierce debates among historians. Its attempts to follow Nazi orders, guided by the thought that in so doing it would prevent worse, sadly became a fatal mechanism in the Dutch community's undoing. Its efficient implementation of Nazi decrees enabled the swift deportation of the majority of the 140,000 Dutch Jews as well as the German Jewish refugees.[52] In hindsight it completely underestimated the true intent of the enemy. And the system of exemptions (*Sperre*) created confusion, division, and false hopes in desperate times, which became the subject of intense debate after the war.

Pool's personal affiliation with the council brought her suspiciously close to collaborating with the enemy. Afterward Pool never spoke to anyone about this work, although she once equivocally admitted that through her job at the Jewish Lyceum she was indirectly and inadvertently employed by the Nazi regime.[53] Her work can be interpreted in multiple ways. By doing this job she acknowledged and thus accommodated the Nazis.[54] Perhaps she was pushed to take temporary and part-time jobs like this one simply because she needed the money. And then there is another possibility: by working her way up in the enemy's ranks she was able to exert influence and perhaps help people. Seeing as she had more often concerned herself with the victims of the fascists, it is not unlikely it was a conscious choice of hers. Yet if so, it was a bold and risky strategy to adopt to fight the fascist enemy. Although after the war Pool belittled her own work in the resistance, all of it entailed great risks. A number of the risks she took were outright irresponsible or even utterly insane; around this time Pool even set foot inside a Nazi transit camp.

In the Lion's Den

It was probably in 1942 that Pool occasionally set out to Camp Westerbork, about two hours northeast of Amsterdam, then still a refugee camp for German Jews. Pool went here to teach the children in the camp. Yet Pool was accompanied on those travels by Löwenberg, a clear sign that the Van Dien group was exploring enemy premises and possibly assisting resistance fighters who operated inside the camp.[55]

The situation changed drastically in July 1942, when the Nazis took over the refugee camp and turned it into a *Judendurchgangslager* (Jew transit camp). They started to deport the Jews from the camp two weeks later to what they misleadingly called "labor camps" in places with odd names like Auschwitz. These deportations of hundreds of people daily were chaotic and emotional. The paper work was done by the members of the Jewish Council, who had their hands full with registering new "residents" of the camp. The council temporarily transferred some of their Amsterdam employees to the camp to assist as well. Pool, with certificates as Dutch-German translator and even a diploma in calligraphy and typing, was considered for a job, and she started working inside the camp in the summer of 1942.

In an anonymous poem that clearly bears her style and even the signature "Rosa" (her official and possibly German name), Pool mocks her administrative duties. She had to type dozens of letters, translate documents into German, clean her boss's bed, and—one of her key tasks—type lists "with about a hundred names!"[56] What she was doing is obvious: she was duplicating deportation lists. Yet the cavalier style of the poem seems to suggest Pool hardly realized that these chores were facilitating the Final Solution. But how could she have known this? What we now call the Holocaust, the systematic extermination of Jews, was unprecedented in human history and therefore hard to even imagine. Accounts warning about mass murder and even the use of gas were dismissed as paranoid horror stories. The poem could thus suggest that although Pool was a fierce antifascist activist at this point, she did not seriously consider the worst-case scenario as a full-blown reality. However, it is more likely that the concept of "choiceless choices" provides a better explanation. Her forced choices in these abnormal times were not conscious "choices" but rather desperate acts of a person who had no viable alternatives.[57]

In these hazardous times, it thus remarkable that Pool still showed signs of agency. While she worked in the camp administration, Pool received exemption requests. The Van Dien group, for example, almost immediately tried to get their own people out of the camp, and it was probably through Pool's intervention that both the prominent scholar Kurt Baschwitz and the resistance fighter Bruno Ast were released. Baschwitz's card went missing, very likely through Pool's interference.[58] So it appears that she had another, secret reason to be here: to spy on the enemy and to sabotage it.

Sadly, Pool received far more requests than for just these two people, most of whom she was unable to help without raising more suspicion. She did, for example, not succeed in getting the sixteen-year-old Cilia Jacobs and her forty-nine-year-old mother Martha Jacobs-Gast off the deportation list. They were deported to Auschwitz, where they were murdered.[59] Whatever Pool believed these "labor camps" were, she was faced in Camp Westerbork with a moral dilemma. In order to help people, she had to continue her work, which included copying deportation lists of the trains leaving for Auschwitz. This made her an accomplice to whatever happened in those camps in the east. The longer she stayed, the more people she could help, but that also meant she was helping put more people on the trains. She had to apply a "selective ethics" in her "choiceless choices," in other words: helping some while disregarding the fate of others.[60] Luckily for her, this harrowing situation did not last long and her job at Westerbork was temporary. By the end of that year, 1942, she was back in Amsterdam.

Westerbork, the Portal to Hell

When she returned to Amsterdam, she moved back in with her family—her parents, Louis and Jacoba, as well as her brother Jopie and his wife Anna Frank (not to be confused with Anne Frank)—on Nieuwe Prinsengracht 120, in the middle of Jewish Quarter. By the end of that year the district was visibly emptier owing to deportations. Jewish men, no longer allowed to work, were asked to "voluntarily" turn themselves in for "unemployment relief work" in Germany. If these instructions were not followed, the Nazis turned to more aggressive measures. Pool told an American reporter she was "arrested by the Germans for underground activities." In an attempt to break her during her interrogation, her parents were taken hostage. "They had many ways to loosen my tongue," she sadly said, "but their torture of my parents was the worst."[61] She was put in solitary confinement and communicated with other prisoners by knocking the rhythm of the Dutch national anthem on the heating pipes to let them know she was "one of them."[62] Apparently she was released shortly afterward.[63]

Pool was arrested again on 26 May 1943. After she and other Jews failed to report for a "voluntary" call for deportation, the paramilitary Waffen-SS, the German Grüne Polizei, and Dutch police teamed up and invaded the Jewish Quarter. Not even Pool's "never-ending alertness" had foreseen this raid.[64] "Heavy boots passed by the house," Pool remembered in a poem titled "Amsterdam," and then someone pounded on the door.[65] She had to gather her belongings in an instant and leave the house immediately. Outside her house a crowd had gathered along the canal side, their belongings hastily stuffed into bags, a "sad row of people," that was forever burned into her brain.[66] A group of three thousand people were ordered to walk to the nearby Muiderpoort train station. After a long wait a freight train arrived. They were forced on board and taken away.

When the train doors opened again, she stepped out with her parents, her brother, and her sister-in-law. The sight was sadly not unfamiliar to Pool: she again found herself at Camp Westerbork. Yet this time she was on the other side, a prisoner. After she was assigned a bunk bed, she started to find her way in this new environment. "Believe it or not," she wrote to a friend much later, "I tried to make my so-called 'bed' something of a home."[67] After a few weeks even the watchtowers and barbed wire fences became familiar. Some recalled that the camp felt like a "village."[68] There was a school, a synagogue, a hospital, and a camp cabaret. People married and babies were born. And it did not feel like a real prison, as everybody still wore their own clothes. This all was, of course, a conscious strategy on the part of the Nazis to make the camp appear as normal as possible. In reality Westerbork was the portal to hell.

Situated in the northeast of the Netherlands, Westerbork was a desolate place. Camp Westerbork was always in transition. About four to ten thousand prisoners lived there, "depending upon how recently the death trains had come by," Pool stated.[69] Every other Monday a nerve-wracking ritual turned the camp upside down. On the "Boulevard of Misery," the strip in the middle of the camp, all prisoners were lined up for the reading aloud of the deportation list for the next morning to Sobibór and Auschwitz.

Most prisoners did not stay long; they were generally forced on the first departing train to the east. Pool's loved ones were among those who were rapidly deported. After only two weeks in Westerbork, on 8 June, her parents were put on a train to Sobibór, while her brother and his wife were deported three weeks after that, on 29 June 1943, to Sobibór as well. All of them were killed almost instantaneously upon arrival. Pool was left behind, terrified, alone, but also desperately waiting for any sign of life from her family. In a poem that she likely wrote inside the camp, she asks, "Friend, Parents, Brother, is life still bearable over there[?]"[70] This hopeful poem suggests that despite her leftist activism and personal experiences, she did not know about extermination camps. It would be one of the few remarks she made about her family for the rest of her life. Years later Pool said that "the human mind is not able to grasp the horror of the Nazis."[71] Indeed, perhaps even now the Holocaust remains stranger than fiction. And even for the people that did believe all the "paranoid" stories that were going around, there was no choice: escape was impossible. Or, in the case of Pool, almost impossible.

A Not So Great Escape

While most of the prisoners only stayed for a few days in the camp, at the most two weeks, Pool had been in Westerbork for over a month.[72] Possibly she worked at the school within the camp, which exempted her from deportation. This offered her enough time to connect with the Alte Kampinsassen—the "oldies" of the camp, German Jews who had been there since 1939 when the camp was built as a refugee camp. This controversial group became the "camp establishment," and they were in control of almost everything. They had the best and most important jobs, which temporarily exempted them from the transports. Among those jobs was compiling each week's deportation list, which not so coincidentally rarely included any of the German "oldies." It seems easy to judge them, but in reality they had been corralled into the divide and conquer mentality that the Nazis pushed to run the camp. The Alte Kampinsassen were more or less the "permanent inmates" of Westerbork, and any contact with them could greatly extend one's stay in the camp.[73]

Pool's contact with Werner Stertzenbach was especially decisive. This Jewish communist from Düsseldorf had arrived in the camp in 1941 and had since then become a central figure not only in the camp's organization but also in the camp's resistance. Although he was trained as an accountant, Stertzenbach became a bricklayer in the camp and so he was able to go beyond the camp gates. Shortly after his arrival he and other prisoners formed an "anti-Hitler coalition" that consisted of Social Democrats, communists, and, above all, people who had "experienced the persecutions, prisons, and concentration camps of the Nazi regime firsthand," Stertzenbach recalled.[74] It became the core of one of Westerbork's most successful resistance groups.

Pool quickly became good friends with Stertzenbach. She likely stood out because of her charismatic personality, but Stertzenbach would also have recognized the vital importance of her outside contacts. Stertzenbach was surprised to find out she closely knew family members of his girlfriend, Stella Pach, who still lived in Amsterdam.[75] From other prisoners he also learned about the work Pool had done for refugees and her work with the Van Dien group that had brought her to Westerbork before. One of her former pupils from the Lloyd Hotel, Max Gruber, had also become a member of Stertzenbach's group, and he may have given a glowing recommendation. Gruber later explained that he was deeply impressed by Pool's "fighting spirit and her courage" in Westerbork: "If she did something she did it fully, irrespective of the circumstances," he said. "One could always count on her."[76] Recommendations like those were essential preconditions of her eventual escape.

Of the more than 100,000 people that were deported though Westerbork, only 210 were able to escape, mostly through organized resistance groups within and around the camp. Each of these escapes was a miracle, considering that they were "in the claws of the SS," as Stertzenbach said.[77] They had to be careful, but they were also forced to make impossible choices. Rescuing one person often meant that another person had to be "sacrificed": if one person's name was taken off of the deportation list, another person had to take his or her place. As escape options were limited, Stertzenbach's group had to make strategic choices and save people based on whether they were "useful" in the sense that they could do resistance work after a possible escape. It was Pool's excellent antifascist track record that convinced them that they needed to get her out of Westerbork.

The resistance group started to look for opportunities to get her out, which were few and far between. Transit camp or not, Westerbork was a highly secured prison with barbed wire fences, a canal, and security dogs that guarded the camp both day and night.[78] There was no standard procedure to get people out, and the risks were high. So the group chose for the least dangerous option. On 9 July 1943, Pool requested to be put on the emigration list for Palestine, one of the few countries that accepted Jewish refugees, albeit on an extremely limited basis. Pool had never been a Zionist or even felt very Jewish, but it was worth a try in order to get out of the camp. One day later the request had already been denied by the Jewish Council. This was a major setback. Luckily, Stertzenbach had a few more tricks up his sleeve. He just needed help from outside.

Stertzenbach's group was able to communicate with the outside world through the post room and couriers. Five days after the Palestine rejection, Pool requested to send a message to Nathan Notowicz, a resistance fighter of the Van Dien group. Notowicz was still operating on the ground in Amsterdam for now, but time was quickly running out. The systematic deportations continued relentlessly, and in the summer of 1943 almost all Van Dien resistance fighters went into hiding themselves. So Pool's message needed to be clear and yet not raise the suspicion of the camp guards who could check messages, both incoming and outgoing. So Pool asked for the musical score for the song "Die Eisenbahn" (The railroad), which she "needed for teaching" in Westerbork.[79] That was a blatant coded message. Pool had told the other members of the Van Dien group at Tehuis Oosteinde many times about the Underground Railroad. When the message arrived in Amsterdam, Notowicz immediately understood what was really meant: Pool needed help from outside to get out.[80]

Just as the resistance fighters in Westerbork and Amsterdam were working on a plan to get Pool out of the camp, the news of Mussolini's defeat reached the camp and for a moment dispersed the dark clouds over Westerbork. "The end had come," Pool recalled, remembering the joyous feeling inside the camp. "To-morrow Hitler would retire.... Our nightmare was over."[81] Perhaps the resistance group did not need an elaborate escape plan after all, and there now seemed no particular rush to get Pool out. Yet disaster struck on one Monday evening in early September: Pool's name was announced for the 7 September 1943 transport to Auschwitz. As there were only a few hours left and the deportation lists were final at that moment, there was little to be done. So the resistance group turned to their last resort, which had no guarantees, but had worked before. Occasionally the group would take people off the train just before its departure, hide them, and smuggle them out of the camp at dark. The SS then thought the train had left with the required amount of people, and escapees would not be hunted down afterward. It was tricky, but it was the only option left.

After a sleepless night, it slowly turned morning. Pool went to the middle of the camp, where the deportation train was already lined up. Forced by the Waffen-SS and the Ordnungsdienst, almost a thousand people entered the carriages, with their luggage, as if they were just going on an ordinary journey. Pool also stepped in a cattle car, cramped together with dozens of others. Yet, as Pool later explained, just "as an S.S. man was about to seal the door" she stepped out of the carriage and said to the guard that she was "on transport duty," pretending to be of the Ordnungsdienst.[82] Her fluent Berlin accent probably made the story viable, and her acting skills did the rest. When the guard remarked that she had no armband to prove her rank, she improvised: "Oh, I must have lost it in the bustle." The SS guard replied, "Don't let it happen again" and ordered her to go back to her barrack.[83] As Pool returned, the train's whistle blew and the train set off on a three-day journey to Auschwitz, with 987 people on board. Only eight of them would survive: most were immediately killed in the gas chambers, and others were worked to death. Some women on this train were separated from the rest, designated as subjects for medical experiments by the newly appointed "physician" at Auschwitz, Josef Mengele.[84] Pool escaped a gruesome and painful death in the blink of an eye.

Yet those fortunate moments also created new problems. Her unexpected meeting with an SS officer meant she had been noticed, and so her name was taken off the deportation list and her card put back in the card index. Now she could not be smuggled out of the camp without being reported as missing. The resistance fighters had to look for another way. Then a chance suddenly popped up: the Red Cross announced it was going to visit the camp for an inspection. Wanting to give a good impression, Westerbork's German camp commander decided that the camp needed to be neat and clean. Perhaps it was the *Alte Kampinsassen* who convinced him that a library would look good and who told him that they knew a person who could fill those empty shelves: Rosey Pool.[85] She could quickly obtain free books from the Jewish Lyceum and possibly also Tehuis Oosteinde, which were both deserted by then. The camp commander agreed and gave her permission to leave the camp.

Pool was allowed to leave the camp for two days, together with a man called Jakob Hermann Bier, a former civil servant who had been a vital organizer at Tehuis Oosteinde before his deportation to Westerbork in the summer of 1943.[86] Such business trips were rare but not unheard of. Occasionally prisoners were sent out, usually to buy luxury products for the camp commander.[87] However, the only people who were selected for such "holidays" were trustworthy inmates that would not run off, almost exclusively *Alte Kampinsassen*. Using this option as an escape route would surely mean that the Stertzenbach group would never be offered this privilege again and would lose an important line of communication to the outside world. Freeing her this way would severely limit their further resistance possibilities within the camp and could also have serious repercussions for all camp inmates. It is possible that this plan was not designed as an escape but rather as an outside mission through which Pool could secure information. In any event, at the last minute Bier refused to accompany her. So Pool left on her own on Sunday 19 September 1943, rather unspectacularly. She was probably escorted to the train station and then left curiously free to do as she pleased.[88]

At first it seemed that Pool just went on to fulfil her duties. She went to collect some books, possibly from the empty buildings of Jewish Lyceum or Tehuis Oosteinde, but she certainly went to the city of Utrecht to visit Gijsbertus Martinus van Wees, a bibliophile and publisher. Pool had met this shy and rather unexceptional looking man in late 1940, when they were introduced to each other by theater director Max Ehrlich. Ehrlich was now also a prisoner in Westerbork and director of the camp theater. Yet before that imprisonment, van Wees had provided him several hiding places until he had been discovered. Pool appears not to have gone to van Wees for a hiding place but just to get books for Westerbork. Van Wees, shocked, told her to go in hiding—he had even already arranged a place she could go to. Yet Pool did not give in immediately: somehow she was determined to go back. Van Wees persisted: "I maintained that she had to go into hiding now that it was still possible." In order to convince her, he called in the help of two members of the Van Dien group, Susanne Heynemann and Alice Heymann-David, who came rushing to the scene to persuade Pool as well. "After a conversation that almost took all night," van Wees remembered, Pool finally changed her mind and decided she would not return to Camp Westerbork.[89]

She made this decision just in the nick of time. A few days after Pool's escape, the Netherlands were declared "free of Jews" by the Nazis. With no new prisoners arriving in the camp, now also the "permanent inmates," including the *Alte Kampinsassen*, were put on transport, although some of the resistance fighters of the Stertzenbach group were able to flee the camp just in time.

A Literature Snob in Hiding

A few days later, van Wees took Pool to Baarn. In this small town midway between Amsterdam and Utrecht a surprise was waiting for her. The hiding place appeared to be a comfortable room in a classy guesthouse, run by three women—An and Aaf Bronkers and Pool's own grandniece, Marie Jessurun—about whom little is known except that they were all former teachers. Another person was also in hiding: Pool's cousin Joost Jessurun, then still a teenager. Pool's new room overlooked a pretty garden and a nearby water tower, which presented a sharp contrast with the mud and watchtowers of Westerbork. In Baarn, Pool was slowly able to become her old self again: a cultivated citizen of the world. She again taught English, now to her cousin. Her room, "first a little bit barren and impersonal, changed visibly," her friend Susanne Heynemann remembered: "She again had books around her, personal things."[90]

The importance of literature to Pool's well-being cannot be overestimated. Luckily for her, van Wees was a bibliophile who completely understood Pool's intellectual hunger. Every week he came by to drop off fresh books. Even after September 1944, when checks were increased sharply, he kept coming to Baarn from Utrecht, now on his bicycle. This took over an hour and always involved the risk of being caught near the Soestdijk Palace, "where Krauts were always roaming and frequently held inspections," he recalled.[91] By then it became extremely dangerous for men to go out on the street; they could be arrested and sent into forced labor or even deported. The only reason van Wees was never caught was probably because he looked so unassuming that no one thought he could be a resistance fighter.[92] And apparently he thought these risks were worth it. After all, was life really worth living without art?

Despite these distractions during those first months in Baarn, Pool mentally hit rock bottom. Her time in the camp had kept her mind busy with activities, plans, and possibly resistance work, all of which prevented her from overthinking too much. Yet in Baarn her world became small and her anxieties began to spiral out of control. She partially poured this whirlwind of thoughts and emotions into the poetry she wrote during this period. She wrote that even the rustling of the trees set off thoughts about her family. "The suffering that I banned from the day," she writes in "Stacheldraht VII," "at night, ... blows up walls and tears down the room."[93] She was alone, only accompanied by feelings of guilt and shame about her behavior.[94] Had she done the right thing? Could she have done more? She found herself in deep isolation, cut off from the world, in "the tower of a lonely country house."[95]

However, although she might have felt lonely, in reality her existence was less lonely than one might expect. Hiding is generally a collective enterprise that required the help of dozens of people, both directly and indirectly.[96] And even in Baarn Pool had many contacts with the outside world. She communicated with other Van Dien resistance fighters with the help of messengers. They even had their own illegally printed newsletter, the *Mitteilungsblatt der Interessengemeinschaft antifaschistischer*

Deutscher in den Niederlanden.⁹⁷ Pool also received personal visitors. Her main contact person, van Wees, came by every week to bring food, money, and, of course, books. Susanne Heynemann brought some of Pool's possessions from her old home on the Nieuwe Prinsengracht and also frequently came by with food and coupons.⁹⁸ She received visits from a mysterious German soldier who brought food.⁹⁹ Also her distant cousin Rudi Wesselius remembers that he occasionally visited the place when he was just a child. An early recollection was how he and his mother Eva (Pool's cousin) first had to talk with the "old bats" downstairs before his mother could see Pool.¹⁰⁰ And van Wees introduced Pool to a Catholic priest named Baks who went to see her regularly. Although Pool was "an agnostic in those days" or, as she noted, she at least called herself one, she was deeply impressed by the underground work and bravery of this priest: "He forged identity cards, stole ration books, [and] lied to the authorities until they believed the sun was . . . the moon."¹⁰¹ These visits enlarged her world and offered her much-needed distractions, all from people she barely knew or did not know at all before the war.

Despite everybody's good intentions, Pool fell into a deep depression. Several months into her stay in Baarn she was "in such bad shape," van Wees remembered, "that I proposed she stay with me for a couple of weeks in Utrecht."¹⁰² Pool immediately accepted the offer. She left Baarn behind, again risked her life by traveling to Utrecht, and stayed with van Wees for a while in the city center, where he had a three-room guesthouse. They celebrated Christmas there, and Pool ended up staying until mid-January 1944. She felt so much better after this "sleepover" that the visit was repeated five more times that year, "each time for a period of two to four weeks,"¹⁰³ until the famine in the winter of 1945. It is not unthinkable that Pool occasionally strolled around the city of Utrecht, especially since her resistance group had provided her with a fake identity card, possibly with her fake name "Harriet Tool." These trips gave her a small taste of life before the war.

The visits to Utrecht allowed her to flourish again. Ever since her deportation to Westerbork she had lived in an intellectual desert. Once she was ordered to clean a SS barrack. When she saw a German magazine, she eagerly started reading. Yet when she found out that it was about "salads and flowers and plants" she tossed the magazine away.¹⁰⁴ The Nazis deprived her of many things, but not of her snobbery toward popular magazines. And this was exactly why literature and poetry became so important to Pool during her period in hiding; she was finally able to again decide what she read. She started to work on English and French translations of works by Joost van den Vondel, William Shakespeare, and Voltaire, most of which dealt with freedom. She committed some works of Emily Dickinson she knew by heart to paper—"a good thing to have a rather reliable memory," she wrote—and with the help of van Wees and Susanne Heynemann, she even published some of these translations with clandestine presses, including the bibliophile Five Pound Press in Amsterdam, often using her own name.[105]

She took large risks in engaging in these activities. After all, she was still a wanted fugitive. Yet few considered these activities to be "real" resistance. Many thought it was an "elitist waste of paper" or at best "underground snobbery."[106] To Pool, however, literature was essential for her emotional well-being. Literature kept her going. In desolate and horrific times like these, books were a window on the world but also beacons of hope and a way to sustain the self-identity that the Nazis so viciously tried to destroy. This "illegal snobbery" was one of the few ways Pool could symbolically defy Nazism.[107] The Nazis had taken away the love of her life, her family, her freedom, her identity, and even her name. "I always had a name," Pool later wrote. But with the Nazi occupation "I lost my name, received a number, and was addressed as Jewess."[108] So she clung onto those things that the Nazis could not forbid with legislation: independent thought, a free mind, and a will to survive. It was a sign that she had not given up.

Real Resistance and Women's Work

The "longest five years" of Pool's life ended at last with the liberation on 5 May 1945.[109] It was finally over, although Pool would "constantly" question why it all happened. "It is very difficult to say why [the massacre] ended the lives of my parents and . . . my brother," she said in a BBC interview in 1962. It also puzzled her why she was still there, of all people, "why with a little bit of luck and a bit of pluck I came through."[110] It was indeed a combination of random coincidences and an astonishing boldness that she slipped through this disaster. In the eyes of postwar Dutch society, however, her "pluck" was hardly heroic. Compared to someone like Etty Hillesum—a writer who was put on the same train as her to Auschwitz (Hillesum probably even dropped by to say hello shortly before the departure)—Pool had made some "selfish" choices.[111] Hillesum was also in close touch with Werner Stertzenbach, and he offered to help her to escape from the camp as well. Yet Hillesum refused and decided to go with the transport to Auschwitz, because she wanted to "help the helpless." Stertzenbach thought that was "naïve"—yet "honorable."[112] Comparatively, Pool's actions, including the copying of deportation lists and her so-called escape from Westerbork, were far less honorable. Pool must have felt shame, disgust, and denial, especially as the Jewish Council was widely and fiercely denounced after the war.

Pool decided to remain silent about most of her resistance work after that. She never profiled herself as a resistance fighter in a Dutch context. Partially this was because of the narrow definition of "resistance" that soon became dominant. "Resistance?" one friend of Pool said in surprise during an interview. "No, she wasn't in the resistance." When the interviewer insisted that Pool brought children in safety, he replied: "Oh yes that may be, if *that's* what you mean, but not *real* resistance, sabotage or anything."[113] In the eyes of many Dutch people, Pool merely did "illegal work," which was much less valued than "resistance work." Because her work was not deemed to qualify as resistance work, she hardly talked about this period of her life, making it difficult to verify the bits and pieces she relayed about what she did along the way. It remains unsettled, for instance, how much she knew about the Holocaust. From her antifascist activism, her time in Berlin, and even her visits to Camp Westerbork she should have been prepared for the worst, yet her poems indicate she still hoped for the best. She published a book of poems immediately after the war titled *Beperkt zicht* (Limited sight), which refers to "the time in which these poems originated." It suggests she indeed had a limited view of what was really happening.[114] In general, it seems that she did realize what the dangers were but that she could not imagine the systematic destruction of a people as a whole.

After the war, she awoke from this "nightmare" and decided to take her destiny in her own hands.[115]

CHAPTER 4

Amsterdam, 1945–1949

Of the 110,000 Dutch Jews who were deported to concentration camps, only 5,000 returned to the Netherlands.[1] Many of these survivors encountered an atmosphere that one eyewitness called "cold, bureaucratic, formalistic, and above all repellant"—a "small Shoah," another traumatic experience on top of the Holocaust itself.[2] At times survivors were even met with hostility or antisemitism upon their return. Pool herself did not receive a warm welcome when she came out of hiding in May 1945. She went back to her former home at the Nieuwe Prinsengracht, only to find out that the house was now occupied by a member of the Nationalist Socialist Movement in the Netherlands who had thrown away most of her books.[3] Much had changed since her deportation to Camp Westerbork, two years earlier. She had lost many friends and family. Holland's laughter had been "extinguished in the gaschambers," she soberingly commented two decades later.[4] The city of Amsterdam did not feel much like home either. "Between the ruins I look for children's dreams," she states in one of her poems titled "Thuiskomst," possibly referring to her own childhood, "and in front of the remains of a house I sobbed."[5] Every canal and every street evoked painful memories. In "Amsterdam," she lamented that not only the people of Amsterdam but the city itself had betrayed her.[6]

In a picture from this period we see Pool standing alone in a field, and as if the camera was set to take a family picture, the void around her depicts the emptiness in her life. Most of the people in her prewar network—mostly in left-wing, avant-garde, and Jewish circles—were simply gone, killed in Nazi death camps or shot for their resistance activities. The most casualties were among those who were closest to her: her family.

Figure 9. Pool, visibly overweight, sitting behind her desk, probably at Paletstraat 14, Amsterdam, circa 1947. On the wall hangs one of Nola Hatterman's drawings.
SOURCE: F010624, Jewish Historical Museum, Amsterdam.

The life she had before the war was gone, and it seemed she no longer wished to be reminded of it. The past was behind her, or so she told herself. It was not until 1950 that she received a final confirmation from the Red Cross that her parents and brother were dead.[7] Until then she was in limbo, and looking for people who might have survived was a heartbreaking and exhausting exercise.[8] Whenever she met an old acquaintance, the conversation one way or another always went to "And where were you during the war?"[9] And this was just something she did not want to talk about. So she focused her attention on people she met that she was not acquainted with rather than being on the lookout for people that she had known before 1940.

Someone she randomly encountered while walking on the street was Otto Frank, who immediately asked her if she wanted to read the diary of his daughter, Anne Frank. Pool later boasted that she was "the second person ever to read it," although that turned out not to be true.[10] She also claimed, years later, that she discouraged Otto Frank from publishing the diary because, "I mean, who'd . . . be interested?"[11] What she did not mention was that she produced an English translation of the book in 1946 or 1947, perhaps because it was never used. Otto Frank thought her translation was not good enough, although he never directly told Pool that. He simply avoided the issue by not responding to her letters. "I never told Mrs. Pool but paid her," he admitted to his publisher.[12] Pool's manuscript was sent back and forth to people whose opinion was sought of the diary, including the writer Meyer Levin, but the manuscript is lost.[13] At the time the incident was a small bump in the road for Pool, one of those what she called insignificant "bread-and-butter" jobs. She got rid of her papers and cleaned her desk, like she did after so many projects. After all, she carelessly remarked later, "nobody would ever have thought that this unremarkable child would become known worldwide."[14] She quickly shifted her attention to other projects.

After a short period of recovery in Baarn and Utrecht, Pool moved back to Amsterdam. The graphic designer Susanne Heynemann, her fellow resistance fighter who had persuaded Pool not to go back to Westerbork after her "escape," offered Pool her own attic space in Amsterdam as a place to live. Through Heynemann and with help of the other members of the Van Dien group, Pool started to reestablish her life. One of her first jobs was teaching Dutch language skills to German and formerly stateless Jews who decided to stay in the Netherlands.[15] She also contacted the Dutch military government to urge it to allow German antifascists to return to Germany if they wanted to.[16] She also, as I have noted, published a book of autobiographical poems titled *Beperkt zicht*. Hardly a best-selling book, Pool did not explore a career as writer any further.

In the first months after the liberation she relied heavily on her antifascist resistance group network. It was probably through these comrades that she met the Dutch artist Nola Hatterman, whose exuberance occasioned a turning point in Pool's life. Hatterman had been a professional painter of Surinamese people living in Amsterdam. Her ex-husband was Jewish, while her new partner had been active in the resistance and the underground German Communist Party. Hatterman later remarked that it was not a surprise that "there was immediately a big understanding between us."[17] Both found inspiration in Black culture, and their leftist backgrounds likely also created an ideological bonding that was quietly understood. But it was certainly their utterly personal approach to the "race question" that made them click. Pool told Hatterman about the time she asked schoolchildren—possibly at the GICOL, a public school set up for Jewish orphans after the war—to write poems about racial discrimination. She saw that in their poems many imagined themselves to be Black, sometimes even writing in the first person. This struck a deep chord with Hatterman: "When I heard that," she said, "I thought, my god, that is what happened to me."[18]

Pool's meeting Hatterman was instrumental in her turning her attention to the Black cause. Their mutual enthusiasm created a synergy that would last until 1953, when Hatterman left for Suriname. They organized cultural events together, Pool held recitals at Hatterman's art exhibitions, and Hatterman illustrated an article that Pool wrote titled "The Art of the Negro" for the former resistance newspaper *Vrij Nederland*. Hatterman also produced illustrations for poetry that Pool translated from the American poets James Weldon Johnson and Countee Cullen.[19] The women inspired each other and deepened their understanding of their joint interest in the oppressed and in Black artists. More importantly, they shared ideas on how to communicate their passion to the outside world.

In April 1948 in Arnhem, Hatterman exhibited drawings "with and about Negroes," while Pool recited poems by African Americans that one journalist found "moving in their simplicity." Although attendance was low, he saw it as a significant event: "What Mrs. Harriet Beecker [*sic*] Stowe did in her book 'Uncle Tom's Cabin,' two voluntary ambassadresses of the black race, namely, Rosey Pool and Nola Hatterman, try to do in our time."[20] This was an apt observation, because Pool and Hatterman were certainly not the first "voluntary ambassadresses" or patrons of the Black cause. There had been white women before who fought for the rights of Black people, often in an effort to provide a moral compass to society and above all to show that they were "ladies."[21] Pool's and Hatterman's efforts placed them in that tradition, while also enabling Pool to define her own public identity.

Before the war, Pool "did not know one single Negro," but that changed after 1945.[22] Probably through Hatterman, she met many Surinamese people living in Amsterdam, including the anticolonial activist and Communist Party USA founder Otto Huiswoud (also spelled Huiswood) and his American wife, Hermie Dumont, who had worked for the NAACP back in the 1920s.[23] Although Pool was very fond of Hatterman, she disapproved of her "almost complete identification" with the Black race. Eventually Hatterman tried to cross the color line by tanning herself, wearing an "afro wig," and eventually ending her seventeen-year relationship with her husband because he was "white," while she had become "more and more 'Negro' inside," making it, according to Hatterman, "a mixed relationship."[24] Pool found this "absurd" and said it could only lead to "a psychological 'impasse.'"[25] As the years went by, though, Pool's identification with the Black race also became stronger. Later in life she would talk about having a "black soul" and say that the yellow "Jew" badge had taught her "to think black, to live black, [and] to suffer with all people oppressed on account of their race."[26] Both Pool and Hatterman turned their activism into a full-time profession shortly after the war. Pool's old life lay in ruins, but her new life had just started.

A "Consciously Living Jewess" on the Run from Herself

Pool also started working as a teacher of English at the GICOL. Although this was not a specifically Jewish school, most of the pupils as well as the staff were Jewish (figure 10). While Pool was ambivalent about her Jewish background throughout her life, at times reducing it to an insignificant element of her family's past, on other occasions it became the center of her existence, and one of her former GICOL pupils, Meijer van der Sluis, described Pool as a "consciously living Jewess."[27] Pool was redefining herself and this new world she was living in.

The GICOL was also the first school where she took her passion for African American poetry into the classroom. Many students agreed she was not an everyday type of teacher with her "revolutionary" teaching methods.[28] Her use of African American spirituals was especially unconven-

Figure 10. All teachers of the GICOL, together with two children, in front of the train station in Baarn, 10 July 1947. Pool is the fourth adult standing from the left.
SOURCE: Mink van Rijsdijk, *Reünie op papier: Joodse oorlogskinderen kijken terug op hun jaren aan die "wonderlijke school"* (Weert: Van Buuren, 2000), 37.

tional yet nevertheless highly appreciated. She once invited the famous actor Enny Mols-de Leeuwe to the school to recite poems by Langston Hughes and Countee Cullen.[29] Such events and Pool's deeply felt stories about African American poetry and literature were an inspiration and comfort to the students, most of whom had just survived the Holocaust and had almost nobody. Apart from teaching the students, this school had another important goal: to make them feel human again. Pool was particularly successful in empowering these pupils. "She was more a sort of therapist than a teacher of English," van der Sluis later remarked.[30]

Although Pool's interest in the Black cause may not have specifically been associated for her with her status as a Jew, her zest to help others and relentless fight against injustice perhaps was. After 1945 Pool embraced *tikkun olam*, a concept in Judaism that literally means "healing the world."[31] Although she never used that term, her actions reflected this ideal, and Pool eagerly went about trying to make the world a better place. Pool's postwar list of publications shows an unprecedented work ethic. Heartbroken but determined to live life to the fullest, she held poetry recitals, translated literature, and compiled poetry anthologies, while also working as a teacher. Yet in her efforts to heal others she ignored one person: herself. Perhaps as an attempt to avoid dealing with her recent trauma, she worked almost day and night on the Black cause and African Americans in particular.

A Transatlantic Black-Jewish Alliance

In the mid-1940s, Pool was working on an anthology of African American poetry, and she contacted a number of African American writers to gather material. Between 1945 and 1948 she corresponded with Melvin Tolson, Richard Wright, Ann Petry, and Langston Hughes—all now well-known African American writers but who were then quite obscure, especially in Europe. In these letters she used her own life story to explain her view on interracial solidarity. She told Tolson, for example, that she had little African American literature in her collection because "nearly all the books I ever possessed on the subject were taken by the Germans."[32] To Hughes she wrote that she knew what persecution, discrimination, and "modern slavery" meant, as she herself was "one of the millions that were put into concentration camps by the Germans."[33]

Dutch postwar society often deemed such comparisons "sentimental" or an ahistorical overidentification. But among these African American writers, who were less burdened with the specific details of the recent Nazi occupation, she found a willing ear. Her requests fit in perfectly with the Double V campaign that at the time dominated African American newspapers, which argued that the victory over fascism in Europe should be continued with a victory over Jim Crow at home.[34] Perhaps African Americans also understood Pool's letters in terms of the broader tradition of what was called the "Black-Jewish alliance," the idea, popular both before and after the war, that African Americans and Jews shared a historical bond and should support each other.[35] These new friends and her transatlantic letters introduced Pool to what would become an extensive American and also transnational Black Atlantic network.

On the other side of the Atlantic Ocean Pool found encouragement and warmth. Tolson, a poet and educator, wrote that he was "very much interested" in her poetry anthology and thought it was "a fine contribution to our One World."[36] Of the at least four African American poets she approached, three sent back material to her, including poems, clippings, and books. Langston Hughes was one of the most generous of all. Perhaps that owed to the subtle name-dropping of the Dutch writer Jef Last in her first letters, a mutual acquaintance who had translated Hughes's work back in the 1930s. This was a sign that Pool and Hughes were part of a similar cultural vanguard that was left oriented and whose members were now forced to redefine themselves publicly in the face of the Cold War. The rhetoric of the old left was no longer useful, but the old networks and international kinship that had accompanied it were. Hughes immediately asked his secretary to send books across the ocean and poems by Black World War II veterans that had been published in the *Pittsburgh Courier* between 1945 and 1946.

Pool was pleasantly surprised by the countless poems that compared the South's "senseless traditions" with the "Nazi gloom" and the "anti-ism" that had fueled the late war.[37] One poem that made a particular impression, however, was written by a white woman from Georgia, who thought it was odd that Americans liked to point fingers at Hitler for his "killing, rape and torture of the Jews," while also justifying the "Segregation, Discrimination, [and] Hatred" at home, in "a land where—'All men are created equal.'"[38] Pool treasured all of these poems, which she arranged neatly in scrapbooks, and together with the other materials that these writers sent her, she built up an extensive library. One eyewitness recalled how amazed he was when he first visited Pool's home and got to see books from Langston Hughes and works like Countee Cullen's *Caroling Dusk*—"material which I only knew about by hearsay . . . way back in 1947."[39] Within a matter of a few months, Pool had become a connoisseur with a growing reputation in Amsterdam and beyond.

I, Too, Am America

The timing of Pool's new interest was perfect. Despite antisemitic upsurges, the Dutch saw themselves as tolerant and antiracist and regarded Black Americans as a group that had suffered as well.[40] Pool stressed the similarities between Jim Crow and Nazi Germany not only to condemn the racism of the past years but also that of the present, not only in the United States but also at home in Holland. Pool did not think that the Dutch were as tolerant as they believed themselves to be. To Pool it was obvious—Nazi Germany and Jim Crow exemplified the same "race madness," and the Dutch had been infected by this virus that was far from gone. She had seen the passivity of the Dutch during the deportations. And she thought it was not the indifference of the Dutch that was worst but their silent consent. Since words such as "racism" or "Holocaust" were not yet in use, and as Pool had to be careful not to offend her audiences, she danced around the issue creatively. "The race-madness that went over

Europe," she wrote in an introductory letter to Melvin Tolson in 1946, "has, alas, not died with nayism [sic]."[41]

However, the suggestion that the Dutch were partly responsible for the Holocaust did not go over well in the Netherlands. When she was preparing her first anthology of African American poetry in 1945, negotiations with Querido broke down after Alice von Eugen, the publisher (who happened to be Jewish), demanded that the introduction be rewritten "without drawing parallels between the sorrow of Jews and Negroes."[42] Pool was deeply offended and complained to Langston Hughes that Querido found her approach too direct and "aggressive."[43] However, Pool was also pragmatic, and she decided to drop the comparison and focus solely on the African American situation. To Richard Wright she wrote that she consciously wanted to address the "terrible inheritage [sic]" of Nazism in the Netherlands "by the example of a people far-away"—African Americans. In this way she could make her point without insulting her Dutch audience: "It never hurts so much when you see how somebody else cuts himself in the hand," she said, translating a Dutch proverb in English.[44] Although the anthology with Querido was never published, Pool had certainly learned her lesson: in her future Dutch endeavors she made the Black/Jewish argument implicit instead of explicit.

In mid-October 1945 she arranged "I, Too, Am America," a poetry program titled after a poem by Langston Hughes at the Concertgebouw as part of an event being held by the underground paper *De vrije katheder* (figure 11). The African American cause was in line with the Dutch zeitgeist, as the Dutch had also faced a vicious oppressor.[45] The program was so popular that it was repeated five times in 1945 alone and then reprised in 1948. Among the poets whose poems were recited were classic Harlem Renaissance authors like Claude McKay, Waring Cuney, Countee Cullen, James Weldon Johnson, and of course Langston Hughes. The program bore a primitivist and orientalist stamp, much like Nola Hatterman's programs. The accompanying apinti drums by Surinamese artists were described by one reviewer as pulsating with the spirit of "the African motherland."[46] All reporters agreed that an "injustice" was being done to Black Americans, and the former resistance newspaper *Het Parool* added that the discrimination against African Americans could be understood by the Dutch through the "Jews forbidden" signs from the occupation.[47] Tellingly, the Germans were blamed for those signs, and not the Dutch. Such discrimination was seen as antithetical to the Dutch tradition. Pool's mission to force the Dutch into self-reflection was a tough job.

Figure 11. Program of "I, Too, Am America," Vrije kathederclub, Amsterdam, 13 and 14 October 1945.
SOURCE: SxMs19/10/1/2, Rosey E. Pool Collection, University of Sussex.

On top of the Dutch reluctance to face up to its ugly past was another challenge, namely, to make the claim that facing it was a necessity sound not too leftist. Although the Soviets had helped liberate Europe, Communism had rapidly become suspicious again in Dutch society.[48] The Americans were "good," the communists were not. The African American struggle for equality had already been a theme in Popular Front movements before the war: Pool simply took those ideas and stripped them of their "isms." She no longer used the phrase "Negro proletariat" or the term "imperialism," but the ideas remained largely the same. Her tacit references to communism were perhaps accepted or at least tolerated in cosmopolitan Amsterdam, but in provincial areas this was certainly not the case. When Pool repeated the program in Dordrecht one critic remarked that Pool had mentioned the Philadelphia Transit Strike of 1944, yet "forgot to mention that most of those harbor laborers were . . . communists!"[49] Although this was not true, it does show how carefully Pool had to choose her words to get her message across.

A Heavy Burden

Starting in 1946 Pool wrote a series of articles almost in a frenzy about African American culture and literature, many of which were published in former resistance papers such as *Vrij Nederland* and *J. M.* ("Je maintiendrai," I will maintain). Her arguments were consistent and straightforward: she asserted that Black Americans were limited by "race madness, social prejudices, and neglect" but also that this discrimination paradoxically gave rise to an "intense and soulful" artistic inspiration.[50] Occasionally her criticism was fiercer; for instance, she decried the United States, challenging the idea that it was the "land of the free," when she described Jim Crow laws as the "dark side of democracy" and an unacceptable hypocrisy.[51] Such statements were not at all controversial to Dutch listeners: most had a love-hate relationship with America, seeing it both as a promised land and the cradle of "vulgar mass culture."[52]

Focusing on the United States was a game changer for Pool. Her life before the war had been centered around Germany—the heart of civilization. Although Pool was still "fond of the German language," and she would speak German on a daily basis with her future life partner Isa Isenburg, she was never able to travel to Germany "just for pleasure" ever again.[53] Pool only returned once to Germany, in 1948, "for the first and only time after 1945," she wrote.[54] She was hired as an advisor in the American zone on how to denazify the German education system and to reeducate its teachers.[55] But when she stood one morning outside the railway station in Frankfurt, she had a relapse of trauma while she watched the commuters: "To me every single one wore an invisible uniform. I heard myself asking myself: who of you were my prison guards and torturers, who of you pressed the button of the gas-chamber in which my parents were murdered, who of you shot my brother at Buna [Monowitz-Buna or Auschwitz 3] where he was a slave-labourer ... I had to fight down the strongest urge to take the next train back, home."[56]

The Nazi era had forever smeared Germany for Pool. Not only did she want to have a focus other than Germany—she simply needed to. And that focus became the United States.

Soon a central part of Pool's narrative became her story of how she "discovered" African American poetry. She dated that interest back to 1925, when she had just turned twenty years old and was a student at the University of Amsterdam. "I went to the University library and flipped through the card-index," she recalled. "There was nothing under 'A,' American poetry." So she proceeded to "B" and then to "C," where she saw that there was a book called *Color* by Countee Cullen. "When I asked for it, the book fell open at the poem Incident," she said.[57] The poem hit her like a "sledgehammer," she would relate countless times to audiences all across the world.[58] In the poem a young Black boy smiles at a young white boy, but the latter pokes out his tongue and calls him a "nigger." Pool was deeply moved by the short but powerful poem. Surprisingly, this was not because of her Jewish background, she said; rather, it struck her because she had been "an exceptionally fat child."[59] She believed that her struggles with her weight enabled her to appreciate the suffering of others: "My own childhood experiences opened the door to the understanding of my darker brethren," she explained.[60]

In reality there is little evidence that Pool's passion for Black poetry dated back to the 1920s. Although some Amsterdam libraries owned works by Countee Cullen by 1930, it is rather unlikely that the book *Color* was available in the year 1925, the year it was published.[61] Pool did, however, mention *Color* in a letter shortly after the war, in the summer of 1945.[62] It thus seems that the year 1945 was replaced by 1925 in her recollections. It is also quite possible that antedating her experience was an inventive way to circumvent any accusation of being a communist, as the story was personal and nonpolitical. Perhaps she did know Countee Cullen's poetry before the war, but it acquired a whole new meaning after it. In part she deeply identified with the poem because she had gained an enormous amount of weight when in hiding. Despite the food shortages and the 1944 "hunger winter" she was bigger than ever. Her weight remained a lifelong struggle that she blamed on an insatiable appetite, which she thought was typically Jewish, but also biological issue, mainly "a faulty link" in her metabolism.[63] It remains puzzling why she gained so much weight, especially in such austere times. Perhaps it was her forced idleness, perhaps it was her severe depression, which is linked to overeating.[64]

Her size made her an easy target in a postwar society that was remorseless and that did not consider the possibility that stress or trauma could be the cause. Given that antisemitism was on the rise in Dutch society and that Dutch people tended to be insensitive toward and ignorant about survivors, people she encountered may have asked her how one could have become so heavy (morbidly obese, we would now say) during the war, whether she betrayed her family for food, whether she stayed in some kind of luxurious concentration camp, or whether she collaborated with the Germans.[65] Pool's physical appearance belied the (emotional) starvation she experienced during the war. As in her childhood she again felt excluded and left out. This period was very difficult, as it brought back her original trauma when she was at an all-time low in her life, making it hard for her to process her suffering.⁶⁶

Just how traumatic the postwar period was for her is indicated by how she linked her weight problem to her activism, as she made her body a part of her argument: because she was "an exceptionally fat child," she reflected later on, she spent her time "mostly with black writing, black thought, black people."⁶⁷ This logic might seem inappropriate and insensitive to contemporary readers. Is it possible to compare obesity to skin color? For Pool, being overweight was not a choice; despite her many diets she never got rid of it. Still, obesity was frowned on and was generally seen as a failure of will.⁶⁸ One acquaintance even bluntly remarked that Pool's appearance made her look less intelligent.⁶⁹ Although this still does not compare to the racism African Americans faced, nevertheless, throughout her life Pool had to face moral judgments and prejudices.

In her "conversion narrative" on how she became so passionate about African American literature, the Holocaust was absent. This is not as surprising as it might seem; Holocaust survivors faced a "conspiracy of silence." People from "outside" were reluctant or unable to listen to what victims had experienced, so survivors were forced to keep their traumatic stories to themselves. Pool thus decided to tell another story. Like other genocide survivors, she replaced the sorrow and pain she could or did not want to talk about with another person's dramatic story, using it as a metanarrative of her own life.⁷⁰ She repeated the story so often that it came to function as a CV: her personal correspondence with Countee Cullen and Langston Hughes became more important than the PhD she claimed to have earned on this topic.

The serendipitous story of her encounter with Countee Cullen's poetry also became the perfect explanation why a white, European woman ended up becoming so deeply interested in the African American struggle. Additionally, the conversion narrative gave her the chance to take back control over her own life.⁷¹ She and no one else would decide what or who she was. She quite literally rewrote her life story. She stated that she corresponded with African American authors back in the 1920s, a claim that was largely fabricated. She even went as far as to quote from letters that other people wrote to Countee Cullen, willingly plagiarizing in order to create historical evidence on which to build her new life.⁷² She ensured that the past would not haunt the present or future.

The Thin Line between Passion and Obsession

The year 1945 was a "year zero" for Pool, and it felt as if she had returned from the dead. If any good could come out of the war, it was that she could start anew. No longer did she have to drag the burden of her past behind her (a failed marriage, an unfinished PhD). Like many other socialists and humanitarians, Pool turned to "other" oppressed peoples.[73]

Her resilience after the war went hand in hand with an unprecedented work ethic. Friends were amazed that she only needed four hours of sleep daily and that she seemed to work the other twenty hours.[74] All this extraordinary activity was instigated by both her newfound passion and the restless feeling that she had to accomplish something important. Many Holocaust survivors suffered from insomnia or nightmares, and so Pool's four-hour night's rest was perhaps also the result of her trauma.[75] Occasionally Pool would write about her flashbacks: frightening memories intruded on her thoughts and brought her back to the war.[76] She also had dark thoughts, "a scorching hot hatred," as she writes in "Aan mijn moeder," when her mind drifted toward what possibly had happened to her mother.[77] There thus was a thin line between a bustling ambition and an unhealthy compulsion. Work became a way to banish her thoughts, and she could be obsessive about Black poetry, doing the work of many people simultaneously. She "actually was two, three different people at once," her friend Albert Mol, a Dutch television presenter, remarked.[78] Black poetry became the perfect vehicle for her to work through her own troubling experiences and to distract herself from her invasive thoughts in the process. The years after she turned forty would be the busiest of her life.

CHAPTER 5

London, 1949–1971

"Yes indeed *Black Nativity* is all over Piccadilly Circus," Pool wrote to Langston Hughes. Although he had written and composed this Black retelling of the classic nativity story, without Pool reporting to him about how the 1963 European tour was going he would have been left largely in the dark. She telegrammed him with information about box office sales, reviews, and news about the opening night: "We're taking a party of fifteen friends," she wrote, "among them Shirley Graham and if the doctors will permit W. E. B. [Du Bois]."[1] Pool had become a central figure in Black Atlantic networks, all from her tiny apartment in London.

The reason Pool ended up in London was because she had begun to feel like a stranger in Amsterdam after the war. Luckily, she found another city nearby where she could start over and where she felt at home almost instantly: "London has gained warmth through the presence of decolonized immigrants," she wrote.[2] After a couple of short visits, Pool migrated to England in 1949 and moved in with Ursel ("Isa") Isenburg (1901–87), a friend from her Berlin days. Isenburg was a German Jewish radiologist, who had left Berlin in 1933 and ended up in London via Paris in 1936, together with her mother and sister. "She was a gaunt, Prussian lady, brusque and angular," one friend recalled. She wore "tailored suits," had "short hair," and was skeptical "in all matters."[3]

Isenburg owned a small one-bedroom apartment in the north of London that used to be a servant's home. It was forty-five square meters, and soon every spare inch was filled with books and memorabilia. It was not quite the "penthouse" that Pool later liked to brag about. The apartment, on the top of a seven-floor modernist building, nevertheless offered a breathtaking view both to the east and to the west of the metropolis. The

Figure 12. Nigerian sculptor Justus D. Akeredolu with his family and Pool in the background, on the balcony at 23a Highpoint, London, circa 1960s.
SOURCE: Rudi Wesselius.

friendship between Pool and Isenburg gradually developed into a love affair, albeit an ambiguous one: Pool described Isenburg as her "best friend and house-mate" and only occasionally as her *vriendin* (female friend or girlfriend).[4] Apparently, they always had separate rooms, with Pool sleeping in the bedroom and Isenburg on the living room couch.[5] They also had different professions. Isenburg had a career at London's Royal Free Hospital, while Pool set out to become an "expert of Negro literature."[6]

London became a creative and postcolonial magnet, attracting people from Britain's former and still existing colonies. England had been important to people of the African diaspora since the late eighteenth century, when the country supported white abolitionists. The imperial capital of London was at the center of this. By the mid-twentieth century the city was playing a critical role in increasing awareness of the global Black community. England, and London in particular, never failed to make an impression on Black visitors. Famous Black Londoners included the American opera singer and actor Paul Robeson and his wife, Essie Robeson, the Trinidadian pan-Africanist writer George Padmore, and the Trinidadian journalist and activist Claudia Jones.[7] The people that visited Rosey Pool at 23a Highpoint thus not only visited her but also came to see the city they had often dreamt about for years. Yet many of those who visited were shocked by what Britons euphemistically called the "colour bar." It was actually a stripped-down version of American segregation.[8] Many had problems finding accommodation or venues that welcomed nonwhite people. This discriminatory atmosphere rapidly united people of color, turning London into a center of a global Black awareness.

Pool was determined to be a part of this movement. As soon as she had settled in London she vigorously set about achieving this goal, going to places like the West African Arts Club and the International Language Club in Croydon—hotspots with mixed metropolitan crowds from all over the globe, including Burma, Demerary, and the Gold Coast.[9] Simply by going to theater shows with all-Black casts and hanging around afterward, Pool became acquainted with the Caribbean singer-actor Edric Connor, the American but London-based singer Elisabeth Welch, the British actor Cleo Laine, the African American and soon-to-be London-based singer Muriel Smith, and the African American actor/playwright Vinnette Carroll. With her vast knowledge of Black culture, Pool bridged the divide between Black artists and writers from around the globe, including the United States, the Caribbean, and Africa. Many recalled her talent for memorizing poems, plays, and even entire operas.[10] Gordon Heath remembered the time he met Pool backstage at Wyndham's Theatre in 1947, after a performance of the "race play" *Deep Are the Roots*. He was astonished by her in-depth knowledge. "How did this roly-poly Dutch lady," he asked, condescendingly referring to her size, "who had never set foot in America come by her firmly-held opinions, her acute perceptions, her formidable intuitions, her informed passions?"[11] They talked for hours about Black theater, poetry, and art, continuing their conversation that night at Pool's house.

Starting in the early fifties, Pool and Isenburg began organizing dinner parties at their house. They even had a tiny storage room on the ground floor, a former servant's room that Pool now offered to friends and travelers alike. They transformed their place into a "salon," and guests would drop in at every hour of the day. Most of her guests came from the London area, but Americans were a close second. The first thing most visitors would do was to ogle Pool's small library, and her collection never failed to impress. With classic books by Sojourner Truth and Booker T. Washington, Harlem Renaissance writers like Melvin Tolson and Claude McKay, and more contemporary writers such as Gwendolyn Brooks and James Baldwin, her bookshelves eliminated any doubts that her white skin might have raised. To visiting African Americans 23a Highpoint felt like a homecoming; many referred to it as "a second home" or even "23a Paradise."[12] Langston Hughes described Pool lovingly as "a Dutch bonbon," meaning white on the outside but Black on the inside.[13] With her open house, contacts, and reputation, Pool thus soon became an intermediary for Black Londoners and Black visitors alike.

While Pool had been a radical socialist in the years before the war and her resistance group against the Nazis had included many Communist Party members, she was quiet about this old left past, especially once the Cold War began in earnest. She even seemed a bit conservative in her public appearances. Yet the genuine radical could easily reappear, depending on who dared to scratch the surface or to knock on her door. Pool and Isenburg's "salon" attracted many left-wing activists, writers, and actors, some white, some Jewish, some Black. Unintentionally, their place bore an uncanny resemblance to the famous Paris salon of art collectors Gertrude Stein and Alice B. Toklas of the 1920s and 1930s. Pool and Isenburg were also Jewish, they were also partners, and they also lived in voluntary exile. Heath explicitly compared them to this illustrious lesbian couple: Isenburg "was the vertical one against Rosey's spherical spontaneity—the Toklas to Pool's literary Stein persona," he remarked.[14]

And as at the Stein salon, the personal was political at 23a Highpoint, and it was no coincidence that many "closet gays" came by, including not just Langston Hughes, Earle Hyman, and Gordon Heath but also the poet and playwright Owen Dodson—all African Americans—as well as the writer Jef Last and actor Albert Mol, both Dutch. Many visitors faced a double burden of disadvantaged sexual and racial identities, much like Pool and Isenburg themselves, and this shared intersectional bond seemed instrumental in creating mutual understanding and solidarity, especially as the Cold War raged on outside. Communists, homosexuals, and Black people were equally targeted during the 1950s, and it is not a coincidence that this salon became a sanctuary that attracted so many individuals from those marginalized groups. In short, 23a Highpoint was open to people that were "different," and here they were united by their "otherness." And, as it turned out, meeting likeminded people could turn personal disillusionment into activism or desire for change.

Black and Unknown Bards

Initially Pool served as an intermediary, acting solely behind the scenes. She briefly worked as a talent scout for a Dutch copyright company called SEBA (later renamed Buma Stemra).[15] But she had bigger plans. The idea of publishing a Black poetry anthology had lingered in her mind since at least 1945, when Dutch publisher Querido rejected her collection of African American poetry because it included too many "simple verses" that were "soaked in a feeling of social injustice."[16] But this was exactly what Pool had wanted: she had carefully selected poetry that explained injustices in an accessible and compelling way, and she had chosen poems with easy rhymes that would make them easy to memorize.

It is apparent that her literary taste was deeply influenced by the interwar idealism of Dutch socialists who celebrated "labor poetry." This form of poetry was able to express grand ideas through concise verses, and could bring theory-laden ideology to the masses. Pool never abandoned this approach or the passion for the African American cause that she developed immediately after the war, even during the 1950s when interest in African American poetry hit an all-time low, both in Europe and the United States.[17] Pool got through this period by juggling various jobs. She translated radio dramas for Dutch radio, wrote biographies for young adults about Frédéric Chopin and George Gershwin, and taught Dutch evening classes at London's Holborn College of Languages. By 1953, however, most of her time was consumed by Allways Travel Service, a travel agency that she ran together with Isenburg, where her job was to make travel arrangements and occasionally act as a tour guide. Yet even then she was still writing about African American literature, poetry, and social issues and frequently about African and Caribbean literature as well. Black art and literature clearly remained her one and true passion. By the end of the decade the tide finally seemed to turn in her favor. The Montgomery bus boycott in 1955–56 and the desegregation crisis in Little Rock, Arkansas, in 1957 generated a worldwide interest in the African American civil rights struggle. So she returned to the idea of an all-Black poetry collection.

After several rejections from Dutch publishers, Pool started looking for possibilities in her adopted home country. Pool found an ally in Erica Marx, a Jewish woman who had fled Germany in the 1930s. From her new English hometown in Aldington, Kent, Marx founded the Hand and Flower Press with one single goal: to produce well-printed fine poetry books.[18] Marx's first encounter with Black poetry came through a meeting with Eric Walrond. This Afro-Caribbean writer had had his share of fame in the 1920s during the Harlem Renaissance, but his career had gone downhill after that. After he moved to England in the 1930s, he wound up becoming a jack of all trades but rarely did anything that was related to literary writing. It was through the activist and heiress Nancy Cunard that he was introduced to Erica Marx. Together they came up with the idea of bringing Black poetry to British audiences through a theater evening. Walrond got a free hand to make a selection. Unfortunately, owing to financial problems and his deteriorating health, Walrond was unable to complete the task. So, Marx brought in Rosey Pool as an additional coordinator for the event.[19]

Pool had long loved Walrond's classic novel *Tropic Death* (1926), and she was thrilled to get the chance to work together with this Harlem Renaissance cult hero.[20] She embraced the project wholeheartedly but also quickly made fundamental changes. Perhaps anticipating a larger public, she narrowed the focus to American poetry, dropping all the Caribbean and African works that Walrond had gathered and replacing them with the material of her original 1945 collection. The result, a performance at the small but charming Royal Court Theatre in London in October 1958, was so well received that the selection was printed with Marx's Hand and Flower Press. *Black and Unknown Bards* was the first of several other anthologies edited by Pool, published in England and eventually in the Netherlands as well, including *Ik zag hoe zwart ik was* (I saw how Black I was) (1958), *Beyond the Blues* (1962), and *Ik ben de Nieuwe Neger* (I am the New Negro) (1965). In hindsight these anthologies were early examples of the renewed interest in African American poetry and a precursor of the Black Arts Movement of the 1970s.

Many of these anthologies featured up-and-coming poets, for instance Audre Lorde, Amiri Baraka (formerly known as LeRoi Jones), Margaret Danner, and Dudley Randall, who were barely known on either side of the Atlantic. For many of them it was the first time their work appeared in a book, a noteworthy moment in their careers, as book publication was more valued and more prestigious than magazine and journal publication. Moreover, in many cases their work was appearing years before they were finally able to publish in the United States itself. Langston Hughes had pointed her in the direction of a number of poets, others were "discovered" by Pool herself during her travels. "From her beautiful apartment in Highgate to the rural corners of Alabama," one poet eloquently wrote, Pool was "aiding, teaching, [and] encouraging young black students to write."[21] The styles and topics varied, but all were Americans of African descent. The choice to put together all-Black anthologies was part of a mission, Pool explained in the late 1960s: "I've been asked so often: why do you publish segregated anthologies.... My answer: I'll quit as soon as Negro poets who are Americans will find fair representation in anthologies of American verse and fair publication opportunities if their talent deserves it. No matter what they write about."[22]

However, it did matter what these poets wrote about. Her selection reveals as much about Pool herself as they do about the contemporary Black poets she included. In a 1966 interview Pool explained that the titles of her anthologies that had appeared between 1958 and 1965 not only spoke to the emancipation of African American poets in this period but also reflected changes in her own perception of Black writers.[23] At first, they were "Black and unknown bards," ready to be admired, she explained. This celebration of Blackness was often cloaked in primitivism, such as in one poem by the young poet Leslie M. Collins:

> When you cry,
> Do you think of Africa—
> Blue nights and casual canzonets,
> Creole girl?[24]

The poem seems to espouse the idea not just that African Americans were to be pitied but also that their connection to nature was more primal and direct than that of white people. In *Ik zag hoe zwart ik was*, the next anthology Pool edited, the "ik" ("I") in the Dutch title signals a shift toward a Black perspective and also toward the idea that Black poets had become aware of themselves as well as of the hatred and pity behind the white gaze. The young writer Calvin Hernton addresses this in his poem "The Distant Drum":

> I am not a metaphor or symbol.
> This you hear is not the wind in the trees,
> nor a cat being maimed in the street.
> It is I being maimed in the street.[25]

Poems like these spoke to the formation of Black consciousness as well as the reclamation of power. Four years later Pool concluded that African American writers were "beyond the blues"—meaning that they had moved past melancholy and self-pity. This collection showcased poets who assert a newly found self-esteem and confidence without too much despair. The activist Julian Bond unmistakably takes a humorous approach in a poem that echoed a recent Ray Charles hit:

> Look at that gal shake that thing . . .
> We cannot all be Martin Luther King.[26]

Pool's publication was undeniably inspired by her recent visits to the United States, where she had scouted for new talent, both in her classes and pamphlets and movement publications. Another poem by Julian Bond, for instance, titled "I Too, Hear America Singing," had been published in the Student Nonviolent Coordinating Committee journal *Student Voice* in June 1960.[27] But the real shift only came in the mid-1960s with Pool's anthology *Ik ben de Nieuwe Neger*, in which more militant voices dominate, again emphasizing personal, autobiographical experiences captured in verse. Pool had by this time come to see African American poetry as "protest poetry." Her belief that Black and Jewish experiences were similar is highlighted in this publication, the cover literally spelling out the book's focus on *verzetspoëzie*, "resistance poetry." The use of the word *verzet* unambiguously references resistance against the Nazis during the Second World War.[28] The choice to use this word was partly a conscious strategy intended to give more gravitas to the African American freedom struggle and also to present these barely known authors as significant and authoritative actors of opposition to brutal regimes. Some poems are outspokenly confrontational, like one Naomi Long Madgett had written after Pool's visit to Alabama:

> They said, "Wait," and I waited.
> For a hundred years I waited . . .

And some said, "Later."
And some said, "Never."[29]

That these authors were prepared to start a revolution is self-evident, and Pool had framed their cause in such a way that it appeared just, similar to that of Dutch resistance fighters during the war. With this 1965 anthology, Pool wanted to show that now Black writers themselves were defining who they were and demonstrating that they were in control. As good as that may sound, there were still power relations that Pool seemed to forget. Pool failed to see that it was she, a white Jewish woman, who controlled the selection and framing of those books and occasionally even the poets themselves.

At times, Pool suggested that the poems needed some "working on here and there," while at other times she suggested that words be deleted or, when there was an urgent deadline, even adjusted poems herself.[30] Remarkably, she encountered little opposition from the authors. On the contrary, most admired her fortitude and force: "An elevation of spirit overcame me as a result of your kind words of encouragement, and, far more important, appreciation," the aspiring poet Sarah Webster Fabio wrote to her after her poems were selected for publication.[31] Even to older and even semiprofessional poets her encouragement could be instrumental. "Strange," Dudley Randall wrote to her in 1963, "a year ago I thought of myself as a person who occasionally tried to write poetry. Now, I think of myself as a poet. A lot of that you are responsible for, by your encouragement."[32]

Yet that these poets praised her does not mean that they agreed with everything she said. Rather it just underscores the highly unequal relationship Pool had with them, as they were largely dependent on her, since most American presses never published anything by Black writers.[33] Pool did not really seem to notice this dependency or maybe she wanted to pretend it didn't exist. But she even actively reinforced it by calling these writers "her" poets and, a bit oddly, describing herself more than once as a "grandmother."[34] She thereby vicariously claimed ownership over these individuals by paradoxically claiming to give them agency. This inequality was further emphasized by the fact that it was not their names that appeared on the cover of these anthologies but most often hers.

This brought her uncomfortably close to the controversial white patrons of the Harlem Renaissance, who also encouraged and financed the work of Black artists, often in a mentor-and-apprentice relationship.[35] Pool is even described as a "patron" in the finding aid of one of her archives.[36]

Pool's vocabulary was also problematic. Her writings are peppered with the word "Negro" and also statements such as that "the black man's soul" had preserved poetry, rhythm, and music.[37] Her choice of words has become so outdated that it tends to distract one from Pool's presumed intentions and her notable racial sensitivity for her day and age. Her comments on whiteness, for example, which scholars now define broadly in terms of power relations, are likewise surprisingly contemporary.[38] For instance, she pointed out that "in our world white still is a symbol of the pure and the good," while "black symbolizes the evil and impure." She also thought it was outright ridiculous that biblical figures were "pictured with light skins [sic] and blue eyes," all because "white men were the masters" and controlled much of the wealth and power in the world as well as the history books.[39] Black and white were thus not just skin colors to Pool but referred to values, ideas, and power structures.[40]

Nevertheless, despite Pool's nuanced theories about race and "anti-otherisms," in practice she perpetuated many primitivist and racist tropes. Back in the interwar period white people both in the United States and in the Netherlands often harbored an essentialist vision of Black people and Black culture. They tended to see Black people and culture in either an orientalist way as "wild" and "childish" and—quite contradictorily—as hypersexual and a danger to white women or in primitivist terms as "exotic" and "closer to nature."[41] Although these ideas increasingly came under fire as the fifties and sixties progressed, Pool's exoticism was so tenacious that it was still apparent in her anthologies from the mid-1960s. These never failed to mention palm trees, jungles, and other tropes that sound uncomfortably racist to contemporary ears. Take for example one poem by the Detroit-based poet Margaret Danner that appeared in *Ik ben de Nieuwe Neger*:

> Over the warts on the bumpy
> half-plastered wall
> just recently slapped with peach-
> colored calcimine,
> Carter the artist curved tan
> mahony chalk African women, tall
> and arched with a swaying grace.
>
> He then conjured nine
> green palm trees and three Egyptian
> perfume urns,
> so that those whom some might call
> after tippling their cheap, heady

> drinks, could discern
> the palms, waving cool, green, shady,
> over the (dancing now) African ladies.[42]

The use of such stereotypes and racialized tropes was not just dictated by the market but was often demanded by Pool herself. Her collaborator Paul Breman, with whom Pool had edited *Ik zag hoe zwart ik was* before Breman started his own publishing house, said he absolutely "hated" the first half of their book. He was furious about some of the "lousy poetry" Pool wanted to include and that he accepted in order to compromise, "all of them weeping about the poor oppressed gay little barge-loading shoeshine boys (and girls)."[43] Although there is truth in his assessment, over time Pool did adjust her views and come to attribute more power to Black writers themselves. However, she was still the final arbiter on what would be included and what not, blurring the line between helping and patronizing.

"Everyone knows Rosey"

With these anthologies, Pool became influential in the realm of world literature. By midcentury the written word was still the primary way people spread ideas, and intellectual communities were forged through the publications that likeminded people read and supported. Black Atlantic intellectuals from the United States, Africa, and Europe were no exception, constituting a distinct transnational community that communicated through Black literature.[44] Pool tried hard to curate her own corner within that community. She aimed to make Blackness a matter of global awareness, which through its transatlantic connectedness would be empowering to all its members. Her selections brought people together, establishing a "school" to the outside world.

Occasionally these publications did lead to the formation of groups, such as the Boone House poets in Detroit: "It was Rosey Pool's *Beyond the Blues* that first brought us together," one member of that group recalled.[45] Pool's impact was by far the most tangible in the greater Detroit area, where she had worked, teaching at Wayne State University. A breakthrough was when *Beyond the Blues* was turned into a TV series by Vinnette Carroll in February 1964, yielding an Emmy award.[46] Naomi Long Madgett, a Detroit poet who became a member of the Boone House group, named Pool as "the catalyst for a significant period of literary activity."[47] Even years later Madgett acknowledged Pool's role in bringing

Detroit poets together in a poem that she dedicated to her titled "Poets Beyond the Blues (in memory of Rosey E. Pool)":

> We were like particles of metal dust floating on stagnant air,
> visible only in our separateness, until you rose among us
> with a solar clarity that magnetized us
> with your sharing of our pain.
> Then we looked around
> and saw that we were not alone.
> We were one. And we were strong.[48]

Almost echoing Pool's own poem from 1926, which she wrote for the Workers Youth Center, Madgett's poem gives voice to the exciting synergy and togetherness of a collective rather than individuals. Pool's anthology *Beyond the Blues* led to several other meaningful encounters. As she was walking around the campus of Wayne State University in late 1962, Danner saw Pulitzer Prize–winning poet William Snodgrass reading *Beyond the Blues*. She slowed down and asked him where he got the book, and they got to talk.[49] The synergy that came out of such meetings was so powerful that the poet Oliver LaGrone, perhaps overdramatically, called Pool's *Beyond the Blues* "one of the first guns in the cultural revolution" that swept America in the 1960s.[50] Although this is perhaps a bit of an exaggeration, Pool's anthologies did not just become passive objects sitting on library shelves. They were often passed around among students and activists and made an impact.

Pool's anthologies also drew many writers to Pool's house at 23a Highpoint. One extraordinary visit was that of the Alabama poet Julia Fields, whose career was about to take off. Pool had first met Fields in early 1960 at Knoxville College, a small Black college in Tennessee, during her lecture tour through the South. Pool was immediately impressed by the poetry of this twenty-two-year-old student, perhaps because it reminded her of the work of Countee Cullen, Langston Hughes, and Waring Cuney, all poets from Harlem who understood the power of concise verse. Pool never lost her taste for short poetry: "The mere fact that poets have to economize means that they are more honest," Pool believed.[51] And Fields shared this tendency to "economize." Fields wrote to Pool: "I really want to write THREE good poems. No more. No less. . . . Do you think that I could do this in less than a lifetime?"[52] Pool published Fields's poems in *Beyond the Blues*, and soon Fields's work began appearing in major African American journals and other anthologies, including Langston Hughes's significant overview work *New Negro Poets: USA* (1964). It was a meeting at Pool's house that decisively changed Fields's career.

In the spring and summer of 1963, Fields stayed for a couple of weeks at 23a before setting out to a summer school program in Edinburgh. At the same time, the South African writer Richard Rive was also passing through the city and was able to meet Langston Hughes, one of his idols, who also happened to be in London. Rive described how he had dinner with Hughes before he was dragged to 23a Highpoint: "Did I know Rosey? Everyone knew Rosey. I must meet Rosey. So we took a taxi afterwards to the apartment of Dr Rosey Poole [*sic*]."[53] That's where he met Julia Fields. Rive immediately fell in love with this "strikingly beautiful, statuesque Black girl." But she was so thrilled to meet the great Langston Hughes that she barely noticed Rive, who was a bit shy. Nevertheless, there was plenty to talk about. Pool soon found out that Rive spoke Afrikaans, a language derived from seventeenth-century Dutch. They even had a small conversation in Afrikaans/Dutch. Hughes watched the whole scene with his mouth open and said: "My God, now I've heard it all. A goddamn nigger speaking Dutch."[54]

Later on, Rive continued his attempts to woo the beautiful Julia Fields but was unable to "break through the cold barrier." That was until she asked: "Do you know a writer from your country called Richard Rive?" He responded: "I *am* Richard Rive" (Hughes had introduced him as Dick Rive, so she had not made the connection).[55] The ice was finally broken, leading to the sharing of more personal experiences. Fields went on and told him both excitedly and in disgust about the time when she worked as a teacher in the American South. One time "white racists were cruising in cars around her segregated school shooting into the classrooms," he remembered her telling him. While they were hiding under the tables, Fields tried to calm her pupils by reading them stories—and one story she read was Rive's "The Bench," a short story about a Black South African who decided to sit down on a bench reserved for "Europeans only" in Cape Town. The existence of the apartheid regime was eye opening to these young Black children in Alabama, as was its parallels with the Jim Crow system.

Sharing of this story must have chilled all the attendees in Pool's home that night. Chance meetings like these between Black people from different parts of the world were among the highlights of Pool's dinner evenings. They contributed to the transnational identification of a global Black consciousness, which was crucial in this period of Black freedom struggles in Africa and the fight against racism in the United States. Most attendees kept in touch afterward, although there is no evidence that Rive and Fields ever became romantically involved.

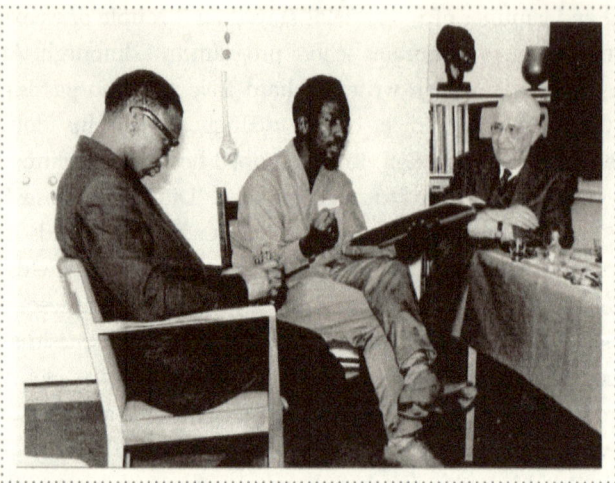

Figure 13. From left to right: Bloke Modisane, Frank Parkes, and Arthur Spingarn at 23a Highpoint, London, May 1962. In the background is an artwork possibly by the Nigerian sculptor Justus D. Akeredolu.
SOURCE: Rudi Wesselius.

Another notable visitor was NAACP president Arthur Spingarn. It was once again Langston Hughes who coaxed him to visit Pool, in May 1958. Pool intended to win him over and carefully arranged an evening with various friends. The meeting was a tremendous success: "I loved him from the moment I saw him," Pool wrote to Hughes afterward.[56] What undoubtedly helped was that Spingarn and Pool were both secular Jews who shared an interest in Black emancipation. Whenever Spingarn came to London in the years to come—which was usually every year, for business—he visited 23a Highpoint.

Perhaps his most memorable visit, however, took place in May 1962, when Pool invited him to meet the Ghanaian journalist Frank Parkes and the South African writer Bloke Modisane at her house (figure 13). Parkes read "very long subject poems," perhaps relating to decolonization struggles in Ghana.[57] It is likely they also discussed each other's experiences, work, and tactics, including Pool's recent lecture tour in the American South with the United Negro College Fund (UNCF). On her tour, she had repeatedly compared southern racial segregation with Nazi-occupied Europe. Bloke Modisane listened carefully, and when he went on an almost identical tour in the South, also sponsored by the UNCF, he called Jim Crow and apartheid similar systems of "pigmentocracy" (a system based on skin color or pigment).[58]

By sharing experiences, Modisane might have learned about the extent of public antiracism around the world, and it seems to be no coincidence that both he and Pool referred to their own homelands instead of directly attacking the system. Moreover, Modisane's experiences also gave Pool new insights, who afterward occasionally described the Jim Crow system as "American Apartheid," probably realizing that Western public opinion was turning against the apartheid regime by that time.[59] Pool's house at 23a Highpoint was in the 1960s a place where visitors could grapple with new perspectives on world politics and activist repertoires. The discussions that were held in this cramped apartment resonated far beyond that small living room, both on and off paper.

Spider in a Black Atlantic Web

Pool's apartment was always open to traveling minds from the Black diaspora. It is where they could meet in an informal setting. It thereby became a hotspot of the Black Atlantic: both a meeting place of Black cosmopolitan intellectuals, writers, and artists and a place where, as Paul Gilroy describes the Black Atlantic more generally, "the structures of the nation state and the constraints of ethnicity and national particularity" could be discussed, challenged, and transcended. Her anthologies were a crucial part in that process, as they enabled her to establish contacts and gave her authority at the same time.[60]

Yet she was far from perfect. Whether it was her self-proclaimed role as "grandmother" or her meddling with materials that poets provided, it seems that her well-meant intentions were also manifestations of a deeper need to be in control of people and to wield power. Despite these authoritarian tendencies, her contribution to the promotion of African American poetry was profound. Her encouragement was of particular importance. The poet Robert Hayden, for example, remembered Pool's visit to Nashville in detail, when she read his poem "Runagate Runagate." "Now I hadn't dared look at this poem for years," he wrote, "and as Rosey read it I was amazed and gratified to discover that most of it was much better than I'd thought." It was only then that he "realized the poem was worth saving."[61] Some scholars have rightly claimed that Pool's greatest contribution was that she showed greater respect for Black artists than the U.S. cultural establishment did at the time.[62]

The international contacts she established in 1945 had by the 1950s and especially 1960s grown into an extensive network. Her strong ties to people like Langston Hughes and Arthur Spingarn provided her with additional contacts and would open doors to her that would remain closed otherwise. Yet she also had weaker ties to aspiring authors and received occasional letters from celebrities like Ira Gershwin, Léopold Senghor, and Aimé Césaire. All these types of contacts provided her with social capital, which was needed in order to get such publications off the ground. She was a powerful spider in the Black Atlantic web, with its ties, friendships, and alliances that were already there before she arrived on the scene. As a white spider in that web, her position was also incredibly precarious and could not be sustained forever.

Pool was nevertheless a pioneer, whether it was with her publications or her ideas that never came into fruition. Immediately after she had sent *Beyond the Blues* off to her publisher, she already had a new idea: an anthology of Black female poets. This idea, she admitted to Shirley Graham Du Bois, was tied not only to her old left sympathies but also to "old-fashioned" feminism. "So far I call it: 'Against Three Odds,'" she wrote, "namely the odds of being Negroes, Women, and Workers."[63] This idea predated the second feminist wave of the late 1960s as well as Black women's poetry anthologies, which began to appear much later, in the 1970s and 1980s. It shows once again that Pool was ahead of her time and had a fine sense for the spirit of the times. It was the same intuition that led to her involvement in a new medium that appeared in the 1950s: television.

CHAPTER 6

Hilversum, 1958

It was the summer of 1958, and Gordon Heath was practicing his Dutch pronunciation in his Paris apartment. The African American actor had just accepted a one-time role for Dutch television in a TV play titled *Advocaat pro deo*. His friend Rosey Pool had daringly convinced him to take the part, and, in a moment of temporary insanity, he said yes.

The 1950s often tend to be overlooked, and the Dutch 1950s are no exception. With its housing shortage, segregation of society according to political beliefs or religion, and black-and-white television, it is generally seen as one of the dullest and unremarkable periods in contemporary history. Yet if we look beyond its gray image, we can see that large-scale changes often associated with the "swinging sixties," including democratization and social rebellion, were already under way in the 1950s.[1] The transformations that were happening were especially visible on Dutch television, a brand-new medium that was introduced to the Dutch in 1949 by a bold vanguard from Dutch theater and radio.

Throughout the fifties, there was only one TV channel available, which broadcast only about twelve hours per week from Hilversum, the media capital of the Netherlands. The media landscape was, like Dutch society, clustered in different "pillars" or segments. Each group—Protestant, Catholic, liberal, and socialist—had its own political parties, schools, trade unions, and of course broadcasting organizations. As a student in the 1920s, Rosey Pool had been a pioneer with VARA, the socialist radio station. Later she occasionally worked for the neutral AVRO, the cosmopolitan Wereldomroep, and the Catholic KRO. Pool adopted a pragmatic approach and simply went to whatever broadcaster was willing to give her an outlet for her message.

Figure 14. "Dutch in 5 Lessons," an unknown magazine, circa September 1958.
SOURCE: SxMs19/13/6, Rosey E. Pool Collection, University of Sussex.

In London, Pool tried to break into mainstream media, far from the radical socialist media outlets she contributed to before the war. In England she set up poetry readings for BBC radio, such as *Calling West Africa* (1951) and *Negro Poetry* (1952, rebroadcast in 1953). These programs fit in well with other programs in this period through which the BBC sought to engage with Black British authors and writers. Perhaps most memorable was the radio series *Caribbean Voices* (1943-58), which featured many West Indian literary talents. However, the BBC was a bit too proper to Pool's taste. It especially horrified her that program makers had to "take their place in the queue" and wait, in true Briton-style.[2] It had taken three long years of pitching, lobbying, and revisions to produce these two programs at the BBC, which both barely lasted half an hour. The bustling Pool did not have the patience for this, and she also believed that her topic, the "race question," was far too urgent for this kind of bureaucracy. So she shifted her attention to other projects that could be carried out quickly. She wrote reviews about plays, taught Dutch at a London evening school, wrote books for young adults, and translated poetry and radio plays. She also started working for the BBC Dutch Service. A continuation of the London-based exile radio station Radio Oranje (1940-45), the BBC Dutch Service (1945-57) also broadcast in Dutch, both in the United Kingdom and in the Netherlands.[3] In 1955, Pool launched a series of radio programs for the Dutch Service that covered a wild variety of topics about daily life in Britain as well as theater.[4]

However, the real turning point in Pool's television career came in 1953 when she met the thirty-five-year-old Jack Dixon, a Dutch actor turned director with Scottish roots who came to London for a crash course in television production. Like Pool, Dixon had a love for theater and was also an Anglophiliac. They both took a pragmatic, commercial approach to the new medium and had a taste for the rebellious. In the years that followed, Dixon gained notoriety in the Netherlands for taking on controversial topics, bringing Dutch versions of international plays and novels about adultery (*Brief Encounter*, 1956), the moral implications of war (*All My Sons*, 1958), and the hypocrisy of contemporary Christianity (*Christ Recrucified*, 1959). With only one TV channel, his reach was enormous. In 1954 Dixon directed a broadcast about the Jewish community of Amsterdam in which he paid special attention to Anne Frank, and he explained to a journalist that his interest in this topic had come out of his personal experiences when his parents had helped hide Jews during the war.[5] Only after the war had ended did it dawn on him just how outrageous the war actually had been, and he had grown "ashamed" of the "attitude of the Dutch during the war."[6] In his political engagement as well as his desire to have an impact, Pool had finally found her match in Dixon.

The transition from theater to television was not so seamless as it now may appear. Dixon's work for TV soon made him an outsider to his old friends. "Some intellectual friends still say: television? Oh right—my maid has one of those things," he told a reporter.[7] Such condescending remarks only seemed to fuel his inventiveness, which was further encouraged by a playful yet masculine rivalry with other TV directors. His colleagues were without exception all men—women who worked there were either TV announcers, script girls, or secretaries.[8] It may thus seem surprising that the almost fifty-year-old Pool thrived so well in this environment, but she easily won people over with her enthusiasm and had a "strong personality," VPRO producer Joes Odufré recalled. On rare film footage she indeed comes across as a charismatic and talkative host who is able to hold audiences spellbound, a quality that she had demonstrated in classrooms and on stages and that she now displayed on television.[9]

Her charm was either simply irresistible or utterly obnoxious—there was no middle ground. One Dutch reviewer described her somewhat condescendingly as "the voluminous, likeable, London teacher Dutchwoman," while another one compared her voice to a "circular saw."[10] Although women in the public sphere of the 1950s were expected to be demure, Pool defied that expectation with a bravado that was typically reserved for men only.

Her collaboration with Dixon lasted for over a decade and led her to the liberal protestant VPRO. Because she was so witty, likeable, and big mouthed, she was attractive to the VPRO, whose directors continuously tried to push the limits of television. At first sight it was a strange brew: a former radical socialist working for a protestant Christian broadcaster. However, VPRO was very progressive, and its nonconformism had made it a haven for freethinkers during the 1950s. Pool, more than a bit unconventional herself, felt immediately at ease. VPRO also had a humanitarian agenda, producing progressive programs on Third World issues and, occasionally, on provocative topics that no other broadcaster dared to touch, such as American racial discrimination. In 1957, for example, it aired a radio series called *White on Black* about race relations in the United States.[11] Pool tried to carry on this tradition with a travel show on the upcoming civil rights movement, but unfortunately there was not enough money for that. "She knew so many people over there," one producer later recalled. "The historical importance of such footage would have been enormous."[12]

Pool then opted for the next best thing: to invite international guests to Holland. In 1957 Pool and Dixon brought the Nigerian musician Ambrose Campbell to VPRO studios, and one year later they invited the British-Chinese dancer Chin Yu together with a Surinamese women's orchestra.[13] Pool was prominently featured in those broadcasts as a host. Although she lived in London, she once again became a part of the Dutch cultural vanguard. She frequently appeared on VPRO television, often together with paragons of Dutch literature. She participated, for example, in a TV fundraiser opposing South African apartheid alongside Simon Carmiggelt, Jan Wolkers, and Harry Mulisch.[14] This put her in a position to initiate projects herself as well. So when in 1958 she suggested the TV play *Advocaat pro deo* to Jack Dixon, she got his full attention.

"We were both out of our minds"

Written by the Jewish Canadian but London-based playwright Stanley Mann, *Advocaat pro deo* (originally titled *For the Defence*) tells the story of a fictional court case in which a white teenager is prosecuted for attacking a Black teammate. After his arrest, the white teenager is randomly assigned a pro bono lawyer, who happens to be Black. The original 1956 broadcast on BBC television was only mildly successful, but then the script was reworked into a radio play in early 1958.[15] It was probably then that Pool realized its potential. "*Advocaat pro deo* is the only play I know," she wrote, "that fully explains the attitudes and moral dilemmas of both parties, white and brown."[16]

She became determined to take it to Dutch television as well. When she pitched the play to Dixon, she came up with another wild idea: to hire the original American actor to play the leading role in Dutch as well. And by sheer coincidence—of course—she happened to know that actor: Gordon Heath (1918–91). Dixon gave her two thumbs up, probably foreseeing yet another television sensation. Pool immediately called the actor in question. Gordon Heath later remembered the phone call: "Rosey got on the phone calling me in Paris from London: 'Would you play it for us? I'll teach you the Dutch. You'll have to play it 'live' of course. I'll make a tape of the dialogue tonight'! It was a very expensive phone call. I laughed for five minutes to begin with. Then I said, 'Yes. OK.' We were both out of our minds."[17]

Pool had met Gordon Heath some years before in London, when the young African American actor had performed in Arnaud d'Usseau and James Gow's 1945 protest play *Deep Are the Roots*. "She was a sparkling conversationalist and a great listener," Heath remembered. "She indicated that we ought to be friends and, after ten minutes, I agreed."[18] He also immediately understood Pool's "anti-otherisms" thesis that saw a commonality between anti-Black racism and antisemitism. Heath was already convinced that "the Negro and the Jew in America had more in common than the history books dealt with."[19]

An affectionate friendship followed. Pool regularly visited him in Paris, where he owned a café together with his life companion and musical partner Lee Payant. Pool visited Paris frequently anyway, largely because her partner, Isa Isenburg, had lived there from 1933 to 1937 and had fallen in love with the French ("I don't understand why she left there," Pool wrote to a friend).[20] This was another thing that brought Heath and Pool closer to each other: both were in a same-sex relationship at a time when both lesbianism and especially homosexuality were a criminal offense in most Western countries. Facing similar intersections of oppressed identities they found solace and solidarity with each other.[21] And, perhaps even more importantly, they just clicked. "She and Isa . . . loved my partner, Lee," Heath remembered.[22] At this time, Heath was hoping to make it as an actor. He had performed in British theaters in *Othello* (1950) and in TV plays like *The Emperor Jones* (1953) and *For the Defence* (1956), and he had narrated the voice-over of the 1954 animated film *Animal Farm*. Still, his acting career had not taken off quite as planned, and the café and his music remained his main sources of income.

Perhaps Pool saw it as a cry for help when Heath wrote to her around 1953, saying "I seem to have sung my way through these last four years" and sadly concluding that acting remained peripheral and "non-existent as a source of livelihood."[23] Pool refused to see such talent go to waste. Heath was, in her opinion, the real deal, an actor, poet, musician, and reciter with a voice "well near perfection."[24] She appointed herself as his unpaid "impresario," set out to find jobs for him, and involved him in her own projects.[25] She secured him a place in the BBC radio poetry reading *Negro Poets* in 1953, together with Aubrey Pankey and Muriel Smith, and also included him in the 1958 "Black and Unknown Bards" program, which also featured Pearl Connor, Cleo Laine, and Earle Hyman. She included Heath's poetry in her 1962 anthology *Beyond the Blues* and also on the accompanying twelve-inch LP, along with Brock Peters, Vinnette Carroll, and again

Cleo Laine. Heath even made a brief appearance on Dutch television in July 1956. A replica of his café in Paris was built as a décor, with the help of Jack Dixon. And just as in Paris, Heath sang songs together with his partner, Lee Payant, on guitar.[26] As always Pool made sure there was a formal role for herself in such events as well, whether it was as translator, writer, or presenter—basically anything that would pay the bills.

Still, Pool was on the lookout for something with more gravitas. Theater had been one of Pool's first and biggest loves, especially political theater. Back in the 1920s she had come to believe in the "enormous educational power and propagandist worth" of theater, a medium that brought theory-laden socialist ideology to the masses in an appealing form. Although her love for Lenin had waned, her confidence in theatrical persuasion had not. She believed it was simply easier to catch flies with honey than with vinegar. And now that the struggle against racial prejudice had become her mission, she saw great promise in "race plays"—social protest plays about the race issue. By immersing themselves in the lives of Black people depicted on stage, European audiences—predominantly white—could walk a mile in someone else's shoes. Pool believed that plays like these were crucial in dissolving "the fog of prejudice" that hovered over the Western world.[27] And with television, now thousands or even millions of people could be reached all at once. Pool believed Heath brought a perfect mix of artistic talents and political convictions, and she praised him as "a fighter for his race."[28]

But as in theater, opportunities for Black actors in television were extremely limited. In general, most Black actors in the Netherlands were only hired for highly stereotypical roles: servant, musician, chauffeur, pimp, drug dealer, slave, or bad guy.[29] Yet by the late 1950s, slight progress had been made, and a turning point in the entertainment industry seemed imminent. Just one year before *Advocaat pro deo*, in 1957, the TV series *Pension Hommeles* (Pension trouble) had started airing with African American actor Donald Jones in a nonstereotypical Black role, speaking Dutch. The show made him overnight a star in the Netherlands, partly because of his thick American accent. Although Pool probably did not see *Pension Hommeles* herself (it was only broadcast in the Netherlands), she would have been aware of the show. She was friends with the producer, Wim Ibo, and Pool had also collaborated with the famous writer of this show, Annie M. G. Schmidt.[30] She probably saw in Donald Jones's rapid rise to fame an opportunity to introduce more Black actors. After all, each contribution to clearing the "fog of prejudice" was helpful.

Audrey Hepburn

After Heath was officially cast, it became a challenge to find suitable actors for the other Black roles in the play. There were simply not that many professional Black actors in the Netherlands. So Pool looked around her own network, casting friends with zero acting experience, including Hermie Dumont Huiswoud, William Spaarndam Johnson, Paula van Wijk, and Django Sterman. "When back in the day they needed a Negro actor," Donald Jones remembered, "there were three professional Negroes. Otto Sterman, Marius Monkau, and me."[31] Pool thought Sterman was unfit for the leading role because of his West Indian accent, which she found "almost incomprehensible," although he did end up being cast a Black father.[32] And Marius Monkau was too young to play the lawyer, so he was asked to play the Black teenager.

For some reason Donald Jones was not cast. Maybe this was because he was known as a comical actor, and this was a serious play. But more likely, it was probably because Pool was such good friends with Gordon Heath that she turned to him. And it would perhaps be a bit odd to have two African American actors, both speaking Dutch, together in one play. So Donald Jones was snubbed, and in press releases Gordon Heath was erroneously presented as a unique case of a Dutch-speaking American. This message was so convincing that even Heath himself remembered years later that he had been asked because there was "no one" in the Netherlands "to play the lawyer."[33] Yet TV audiences certainly compared Heath to his fellow countryman. One journalist even described him as a "Donald Jones with a moustache."[34] The true reason why an American rather than Dutch Black actor was hired was because an American one would simply attract far more viewers and generate much more interest in the "race question" than a Dutch one owing to the fact that at that time the Dutch found American culture simply irresistible.[35]

In the weeks before the broadcast both local and national newspapers wrote about *Advocaat pro deo*, turning the event into "almost a happening" throughout the country.[36] Journalists were eager to report on the strange case of the American who was learning Dutch for one single occasion. Most found it highly entertaining that his foreign language lessons and personal coaching had resulted in an inexplicable German accent. Heath told a reporter that he practiced his lines with the Dutch actress Hetty Blok and that he now not only had a German accent but also a French one.[37] He decided to make an extra effort and started studying Dutch grammar.

More headlines appeared when the rumor spread that Heath had practiced his pronunciation with the Belgian-British multilingual actress Audrey Hepburn, when they were both on the set of the movie *The Nun's Story* in the Belgian Congo. Yet Heath said that although they had certainly met, the story was grossly exaggerated: "That's nonsense, she was far too busy. She saw me walking with a Dutch grammar [book] under my arm and called: 'What are you doing with that?!' She didn't give me lessons, but she wished me all success."[38] With only six weeks to rehearse his part, Heath memorized his lines largely phonetically with an audio recording that Dixon had made and a translation tailor made by Pool.[39] Heath fondly remembered Pool's private pronunciation lessons and, even more importantly, her confidence: "She never doubted for a minute that it would work," he said.[40]

An Intimate Dinner with W. E. B. Du Bois

In the meantime, Jack Dixon looked around to fill the rest of the TV evening, which was gradually turning into a theme evening that focused on race. He landed an interview with John Thivy, Indian ambassador to the Netherlands, who came to speak about Malayan minorities in his home country. And at the last minute another interview was added with the famous African American scholar W. E. B. Du Bois, another suggestion from Pool, after she found out one week before the broadcast that Du Bois was visiting Holland for a public speech.[41]

This visit was purely coincidental, but the timing was great. It was Pool's protégé Paul Breman who had invited the older scholar, who had led an isolated life for many years. He had appeared in front of a McCarthy committee in 1951 and although he was not convicted, his passport had been confiscated. Now, eight years later, he had finally regained his passport and was able to travel again, and almost immediately he was on his way to Moscow to be honored with the Lenin Peace Prize. This showed that the old radical had not been tamed by eight years of isolation. To Breman's surprise the Du Boises accepted the offer. Breman explicitly did not inform Pool. They had had "terrible trouble" in their collaboration for the poetry anthology *Ik zag hoe zwart ik was*. Somehow either one of them chose poems that the other one did not like.[42] But their disagreement went deeper than that, as Breman especially despised Pool's Black/Jewish comparisons. Eventually it was what he called Pool's "'I was Anne Frank's teacher' number" that created a "lasting estrangement" between the two.[43] He was trying to break free from Pool's influence and so largely organized the Du Boises' six-day program all by himself.

It was only when his plans to hold a large meeting at the Hague as part of the program fell through at the very last minute that Breman called in help from others. And even then he did not want to call his former meddlesome tutor and instead contacted Otto Huiswoud, president of Ons Suriname, and his wife Hermie Dumont Huiswoud. "Fearing a total fiasco, Paul called in our help," Dumont Huiswoud recalled, "the day before the DuBoises arrived."[44] But as Dumont Huiswoud had a guest role in *Advocaat pro deo*, Pool soon found out anyway and swiftly took over. She arranged an intimate dinner with Du Bois and his wife, Shirley Graham, together with *Advocaat* actors Gordon Heath and Otto Sterman, who were deeply honored to meet the ninety-year-old sociologist, Niagara Movement leader, and NAACP founder. The choice of an Indonesian restaurant in the center of Utrecht for dinner was likely a conscious one on Pool's part, designed to spur conversations about colonialism among this crowd and to situate the TV evening in the wider context of antiracist and anticolonial activism.

One day after the cozy dinner, Du Bois gave a speech at the Hague, during which he shocked friends and foes alike when he called President Roosevelt a "socialist." Moreover, he claimed that "the new science of psychology so effectively and fatally used by Adolf Hitler to make Germany attribute all its woes to Jews" was now also used by "big business in America to make America prepare for total war against the Soviet Union."[45] It was music to Rosey Pool's ears, who sat spellbound in the audience that night. But Du Bois estranged almost everybody else with his talk, even Social Democrats. It appears that only the communist newspaper *De Waarheid* supported him. One conservative journalist was wildly outraged by this "open propaganda for Moscow," demanding to know whose fault it was that this evening had gotten so "completely out of hand."[46] This anticommunist reaction to Du Bois's explicit sympathy for the Soviet Union was a sign that the Cold War was heating up. America's racial segregation had been a target of communists since the 1920s, often referred to in order to reveal the hypocrisy of American capitalism.[47] So anyone who wanted to address the American "race question" publicly ran the risk of being called a communist, resulting in their message being dismissed immediately.

The creators of *Advocaat pro deo* obviously wanted to avoid such accusations no matter what: excessive criticism of the United States would estrange various viewer groups and undermine their message of equal rights. Perhaps this was why the preceding programs had focused on former British colonialism in India and not on Dutch colonialism. Pool had learned after the war that the Dutch did not like to be confronted with their own racist past, nor their colonial wrongs. That became especially clear one year before, when a television broadcast (again from the VPRO) thoroughly divided the nation. Commemorating a 1933 mutiny of Indo-Dutch soldiers near the Dutch Indies (current Indonesia), the broadcast was widely condemned as "inappropriate" and "antinationalistic."[48] The only support came from the far left and communists. It was clear to Pool and other members of the team that Dutch colonial history was off limits if they wanted to reach a general audience.

Likewise, television reports of the civil rights movement focused solely on "acceptable" types of protest. In recent years, activists had embraced a new approach to challenging segregation. Peaceful protests like the Montgomery bus boycott, the integration of Little Rock Central High School, and nonviolent protests led by Martin Luther King Jr. had shown that the violence only came from one side: white racists. These protests turned the race issue into a mainstream one: suddenly the subordinated position of African Americans was seen as an injustice by Dutch leftists, moderates, and conservatives alike.

Coverage of the civil rights movement in the Dutch media was so extensive that one journalist spoke of a "hype" and a "fad."[49] American news was often covered by Dutch media outlets. The United States had a certain irresistible appeal, and even the dark side of this world power spoke to the imagination. The fact that the January 1957 radio series *White on Black* was broadcast on primetime, at 9 p.m. on a Friday says a lot about the popularity for the subject.

Dutch newspaper articles from the weeks before the broadcast reveal just how timely *Advocaat pro deo* was. Media from all denominations extensively covered the escalation at Little Rock Central High School, a white school that was being desegregated. The Black students that tried to enter the school were viciously attacked and spat on, creating a public outcry across the Western world. Another hot case that spurred outrage was that of Jimmy Wilson, a farmworker from Alabama who had stolen $2 and had been sentenced to death by an all-white jury. Dutch journalists from all backgrounds were appalled by those stories, finding them "startling" and "absurd." Perhaps that is why an extremely brief excerpt of an interview with Du Bois was broadcast in which he condemned the situation in Little Rock but not segments in which he mentioned Hitler or Roosevelt. Many Dutch viewers approved of the eloquent and elder statesman-like scholar, and his remarks on the situation of African Americans helped frame the TV play an example of "a personal tragedy of the Negro."[50] Like American civil rights activism, *Advocaat pro deo* presented an sanitized plea for equal rights to mainstream audiences that was almost impossible to disagree with.

High Expectations

After weeks of preparations and rehearsals, the moment finally arrived on Wednesday, 10 September 1958: live from Studio Vitus in Bussum, *Advocaat pro deo* appeared on television screens all over the country. It told the fictional story of a North American white teenager who has a disagreement with one of his teammates, a Black teenager, after a game of basketball, which then quickly escalates into a fight. They roll over the ground, fighting, when the white teenager screams: "Nigger, dirty nigger. . . . Nigger, dirty nigger!"[51] Embarrassed by their behavior, both teenagers want to forget the whole thing and move on. Yet the father of the assaulted Black boy is convinced there was a racist motive and pushes his son to press charges, which he does. The white teenager is arrested, and since he comes from a poor working-class family and can't afford to pay for a lawyer, he is assigned a pro bono one named Frank Wilson, a Black man. "The drama," Gordon Heath explained, was "in the lawyer's tactics to convince the parents and the [white] boy that he is on their side."[52]

His character sets out to do his job but meets opposition from all sides: from people who think he has a moral obligation to his race and from people who question his objectivity because of his skin color. In one key scene the lawyer is visited by the Black father, who is clearly desperate:

> THE FATHER: You are a Negro, Wilson, and you have suffered for that just as much as we all did. You can't stand up and prosecute someone of your own race because of a race-obsessed white man. . . . What do you want, Wilson? Do you want to show the white people that you are willing to attack your own race? Prove that you are superior to the race problem?
> THE LAWYER: I am a lawyer, just like all other lawyers. I have a lawsuit that I need to fulfil. That's all that matters.
> THE FATHER: Of course. You are a lawyer. A wonderful lawyer you are. Selling [out] his own people as long as they say he's a fine lawyer. You only want to impress white people. You are the meanest type of Negro there is. A traitor . . .[53]

Notwithstanding these threats, the lawyer continues his work, determined to succeed. But things do not go smoothly. Even his own client, the

Figure 15. Gordon Heath (portraying lawyer Frank Wilson) and Pool (portraying legal advisor Janet Morrison) on the TV set of *Advocaat pro deo*, 10 September 1958.
SOURCE: F010643, Jewish Historical Museum, Amsterdam.

white teenager, starts to question his objectivity: "Who can assure me that you won't feel sympathy for Edison, when he stands in front of you," the boy asked. "I don't know how you feel towards whites. Maybe you hate them. I don't know."[54] The lawyer starts to lose his self-confidence and sureness about the case, and he begins to doubt whether he is truly doing the right thing.

But then he goes to see Janet Morrison of the Association of Legal Advisors, a character vividly portrayed by Rosey Pool (figure 15).[55] *Advocaat pro deo* was her debut as an actor, although she was no stranger to performing different roles, both off and on stage. Pool wrote in an op-ed piece that her own character represented the essence and "the principle of the piece," and which suggests just how closely this TV play represented her own personal beliefs.[56] It also seemed to be no coincidence that this role reflected her own character as well or at least how she wanted to be seen by others: "A sophisticated, idealistic woman," Pool described the character in her translation, "who has had and still has a lot on her mind."[57] The lawyer comes to her and asks her if he can drop the case because he finds it simply impossible to "defend a client who hates him." But she thinks the problem is not that the boy hates him: "That boy is scared, Frank," she tells him, "and fear and hatred are often very similar." She pushes him to continue with the case.

Still unsure, the lawyer decides to give the case a final chance and returns to his client, albeit reluctantly. When they again discuss the upcoming defense, he suddenly comes to see how he can present the case. The white teenager explains that he does not understand his own violent behavior either: "I swear... that I wasn't myself. That wasn't me, who said that. Those words just came out of my mouth and when I heard them I became even more furious." The boy argues that he did not really do it but that it happened—"it happened to ME, of all people."[58] It is a revelation to the lawyer, and his doubts disappear: he is not representing a racist after all, or so he thinks. Now fully convinced of the boy's innocence, they go to court. Near the end of the trial, after each side has made its case, an unexpected plot twist occurs: without a decision being made by the judge, the play suddenly ends, and the television screen goes black. "I have never looked so flabbergasted at my television set," one journalist wrote.[59] Numerous viewers called VPRO to report a technical error. However, it was not an accident. The sudden ending was intentional, Dixon told one bemused reporter: "[I]t would have been easy to write three additional sentences and explicitly show that the [white] boy was found innocent. But that was not the issue at all. Then the people would have said: well, that ended well. They would have turned off their TV set and would have gone to bed. I know now that many people not only extensively discussed the ending of the play but also the race problem."[60]

Pool concurred, explaining in an interview that the open ending would extend the "discussion about the true problem... in the living room."[61] According to TV reviewers, the play indeed gave "food for thought." The confrontation between the Black father and the Black lawyer especially made an impression. "Suddenly the performance was made of flesh and blood," one journalist wrote.[62] Unsurprisingly, most sympathized with the handsome and fair lawyer, who exemplified a moderate position, engaging as he did in a "decent" struggle for equal rights. The Black father was seen as the complete opposite, and was described as an opportunistic villain who exploited the situation for his own (financial) benefit. One newspaper even described him as the *blankenhatende vader* ("white-hating father"), which was hardly the intentions of the play.[63] Most reviewers, in other words, did not critically reflect on larger issues from a metaperspective. The appearance of a Black lawyer might have been a groundbreaking moment for Dutch television, but the Black father suspiciously bore out dominant stereotypes of Black people playing the bad guy.

With the same insouciance the violent white teenager was excused as a harmless rascal. Dutch reviewers squarely projected the country's prejudices about whiteness and innocence on this character. No matter his deeds, the white boy received the benefit of the doubt. Even when he screamed the n-word he remained innocent. He was rather a victim of the system than a true racist. Some journalists compared him to James Dean or Marlon Brando, who were also brazen, misunderstood, and innocent characters. Review articles that connected the play to real-life events, usually to Little Rock and the case of Jimmy Wilson (perhaps because the name of the Black lawyer was coincidentally also "Wilson"), arrived at similar conclusions. One journalist wrote: "On the same Wednesday evening on which a Negro—who had committed a two-dollar robbery—was sentenced to death by the Court of Alabama, the American Negro Gordon Heath offered the Dutch TV public a compelling piece of culture."[64]

This reference revealed as much about the play as it did about the self-image of the Dutch, who liked to see themselves as a tolerant and colorblind nation.[65] This idea dominated the Netherlands for several decades and remained the only acceptable narrative for nonwhite actors who sought to explore the race issue in the country. Donald Jones confirmed this Dutch complacency when he said in interviews that he had escaped American discrimination and had come to the Netherlands because he felt free here.[66] Tellingly, Gordon Heath received a fan letter from a young woman who wrote: "I cannot understand that there are people that have something against someone else just because their skin has another color," adding in relief that "luckily this is not the case here."[67] This comment also suggests that the broadcast mainly confirmed the self-image of the Dutch: Gordon Heath's presence in *Advocaat pro deo* itself proved that African Americans had more freedom in the Netherlands than in the United States. Donald Jones's role in *Pension Hommeles* proved the same. Their presence was evidence that the Netherlands was a progressive and tolerant country.

Sadly, this was not what Pool wanted to argue. On the one hand she wanted to show that there were still remnants of the "race madness" that the Nazis had spread in Dutch society, assuming both negative and benign forms. If the Dutch were so innocent, how did it happen her entire Jewish family had been deported and murdered in gas chambers? Moreover, Pool also hoped that the presence of African American actors on Dutch television would encourage participation in and, hopefully, a deeper understanding of the civil rights struggle. She hoped Dutch people would come to see Black people in more complex ways than they were used to, that white viewers would go beyond the simple, one-dimensional view that many Dutch had of Black people. "'Advocaat pro deo' pleas for all," she wrote, and she expressed the hope that this play would compel people to judge others by their actions, not by their skin color.[68] In private letters and other documents she repeatedly made this point. In her scrapbook she systematically cut off all headlines that mentioned the word "Negro" in the title and only included clippings that called Heath "American." The message was self-evident. These were the news clippings that showed that her mission had been successful: Black people were seen as people.

Black Emancipation and White Innocence

Featuring a Black lawyer as the protagonist in a traditionally "white" role, Stanley Mann's *Advocaat pro deo* seemed to be ahead of its time. It predated more well-known international plays and movies like Lorraine Hansberry's *A Raisin in the Sun* (1959) and James Clavell's *To Sir, With Love* (1967), both featuring Sidney Poitier, as well Robert Mulligan's much more well-known *To Kill a Mockingbird* (1962), another courtroom drama that dealt with racial prejudice. This seemed to be a sign that white people too finally came to embrace Pool's vanguard ideas in the 1960s.

However, the impact of *Advocaat pro deo* is difficult to assess. On the one hand the reach was enormous: there was only one network, and probably millions of people saw the broadcast. The effect on Dutch thinking about race, however, is impossible to determine, as the play both reflected popular conceptions of Black people while also challenging prejudices. All in all, the innocent self-image of the Dutch remained firmly in place. The simple fact that this play was accepted and broadcast seems to be a proof of that.

Although Gordon Heath described the broadcast as "a triumph," which to him it certainly was because he received ƒ1,250 for one single broadcast (about $4,400 in today's money) and later that year performed the play on Belgian television, this time in French, *Advocaat pro deo* did not structurally change the job prospects for Black actors in the Netherlands.[69] After this broadcast Black actors continued to struggle with stereotypical and one-dimensional roles. Still, *Advocaat pro deo* did contribute to the visibility of nonwhite people on television, both in a nonstereotypical role and in multiple support roles as well. It thereby had a modest effect on normalizing the presence of nonwhite actors on Dutch television. For many Dutch viewers the broadcast certainly brought the African American struggle for equality—literally—closer to home. As for Pool, however, immediately after the broadcast she went back to editing anthologies and then finally was able to go where the action was: the U.S. Deep South.

CHAPTER 7

Up North / Down South, 1959–1960

Rosey Pool was received like a rock star when she traveled across the United States in 1959 and 1960. In eight months' time she passed through twelve states, delivered over eighty lectures, was interviewed on radio and television, posed for photographs, and handed out signatures. Her trip to the United States was a dream come true for her. For a freelancer like her, the transatlantic passage was simply too expensive, so when the Fulbright Foundation started to offer scholarships for humanities scholars in 1959, Pool immediately applied.¹ Although the Dutch Fulbright committee thought the fifty-four-year-old Pool was "a gifted and dynamic woman," she was a bit of an oddball in the applicant pool, quite different from most of the esteemed professors that applied. Moreover, she was about to get disqualified because she no longer lived in the Netherlands but in London, despite her Dutch nationality. Luckily for her, some other applicants withdrew, so she received the fellowship anyway.²

Around the same time, in early 1959, a movie came out about one of Pool's former pupils, Anne Frank, released in cinemas across the United States and Europe. *The Diary of Anne Frank* was based on the play bearing the same name, which had been a Broadway hit four years earlier. In both versions, Anne Frank's experiences in the "secret annex" were transformed into a coming-of-age story that presented her as an almost all-American teenage girl who falls in love with a boy also in hiding named Peter. This universalized version of the story captivated American and other Western audiences, and Anne Frank became an international symbol of not just the Holocaust but also of injustices at large.³

Because Pool had produced an English translation at the request of Anne's father that he ended up not liking, she was unpleasantly surprised

Figure 16. Pool being interviewed for television by an unidentified man, possibly near the Hampton Institute (in Hampton, Virginia), circa February 1960.

SOURCE: SxMs19/14/1/4, Rosey E. Pool Collection, University of Sussex.

by the publicity surrounding the diary and tried not to think about it too much. So the appearance of another English translation in 1952 that deeply moved audiences worldwide was painful for Pool, to say the least. Yet perhaps even more embarrassing was that the girl that she had barely noticed back then was now becoming a symbol of the fight against oppression of all kinds.[4]

By the late 1950s, though, Pool had pulled herself together and realized that she could also benefit from the momentum surrounding the success of the diary. This sounds a bit opportunistic, and yet it is simply impossible to separate Pool's personal life, her career, and her activism, as they often blended together in most of her projects, as we also see with *Advocaat pro deo*. Her life exemplifies the philosophical question of whether altruism is possible because although she wanted to fight discrimination she also needed to pay her bills and wanted to feel important. In her fight for justice she always relied on the power of storytelling, which she believed "moved more people and opened more eyes than big learned books."[5] The story of Anne Frank was perfect in this sense because, as Pool said to one reporter, the diary "made the tragedy of war more of a reality than most more mature writers have been able to do."[6] One of Pool's main strengths throughout her career was using personal stories to present moral dilemmas and social issues in bite-sized chunks to the masses. It was also apparent to her that she had to act as soon as possible, because it was likely that the Anne Frank hype would soon be over. So although she was meant to focus on African American poetry during her Fulbright tour, both for ideological and commercial reasons she instead highlighted the diary, becoming known as "Anne Frank's teacher." "She knew her own worth," Gordon Heath said about Pool, "and she was not unaware that her experience would have enormous value on the open market."[7]

Up North

Pool's market value soon manifested itself, after she arrived in Detroit in October 1959. She would stay there until December before heading to Atlanta for another two months.[8] There was little time to relax. The Fulbright grant might have sounded glamorous, but in reality it only covered travel to the United States and back.[9] Pool needed to work to pay her living expenses and accommodation. Luckily Pool already knew some people in the Detroit area, but it was Professor Marion Edman who would play a decisive role. Pool had met her in Germany's American zone shortly after the war, where they both worked to denazify the German educational system. Edman offered Pool free accommodation at her own home.[10] Through Edman, the first bookings started to roll in, creating a snowball effect throughout the Detroit area. Pool spoke about a great variety of topics, including African poetry, education in Europe, and, occasionally even marriage guidance, which was quite an ambitious challenge for a divorced lesbian woman.[11] But especially in rural and suburban Michigan, most Americans were eager to hear more about Anne Frank.

Through these lectures she easily reached thousands of youngsters. When she spoke at elementary schools, children from neighboring schools also often came in, multiplying audiences to many hundreds. She liked these schools, as she had noticed that young teenagers often identified themselves with Anne, which made it possible to make a more direct connection.[12] The charismatic and talkative Pool usually explained what Anne Frank had been like and how she had gotten to know her before making an appeal to the children. "Please don't let . . . her down a second time," she said at different occasions to various audiences of schoolchildren.[13]

After her lectures pupils were asked to write about what they had just heard in a short report or in a letter to Pool. Some of these reports were painfully direct and honest. The name "Anne Frank" might have rung a bell, but the majority of these children admitted that they had never read the diary itself.[14] One pupil from Detroit wrote in a report that "Ann [*sic*] Frank was a famous person. After Ann Frank [*sic*] mother had died Ann Frank locked herself in her room."[15] Not quite true, obviously, but it does demonstrate the imaginative ways Pool's talks were interpreted. On the plus side, their lack of knowledge meant that these children soaked up Pool's words like sponges. One of the most eloquent listeners was a pupil from Detroit, who solemnly wrote that "the terrors of Nazi imperialism was left firmly embedded" in his mind after he had heard Pool's talk.[16] Another pupil, from Highland Park, Michigan, wrote: "The story of Anne and her family; the horror of Nazi terror; the work of the Dutch underground; and the wave of anti-Semitism all made me actually feel how the Jewish populace felt and their atrocious treatment by the Nazis."[17]

These reports often literally echoed Pool's opinions and terminology, demonstrating the parrot-like quality that Pool thought many "bright children" possessed.[18] That these reports address the perspective of a Holocaust victim is significant, because in this day and age the Holocaust was hardly commemorated on the massive scale it is today. Pool's talks predated the notorious Eichmann trial and Raul Hilberg's seminal book *The Destruction of the European Jews*, both of which date to 1961 and drew massive attention to the genocide.[19] Although millions of Americans saw the movie about the diary that year, knowledge of the Holocaust remained diffuse, largely transmitted via representations (whether written or visual) and rarely from direct witnesses like Pool.[20] Pool's talks thus not only shaped American perceptions of the Holocaust but also provided the vocabulary for these American children to process the calamitous events of two decades before.

Pool's visit was extremely timely. Many schools were working on productions of the Broadway adaption as a school play, and Pool received invitations to give these teenage cast members a firsthand account of what war in Europe had actually been like.[21] Many asked her how accurately Anne Frank was portrayed in the adaptions. Yet to a reporter from Ypsilanti High School, Pool explained that she had not seen them. "I am completely unable to go and look at a portrayal of things still so much a painful reality to me." Maybe she would watch it, "someday, perhaps, but I am not yet ready."[22] Still, she came quite close to seeing a production a couple of times: "The nearest I've ever got to the play was at a college near Detroit where the set for the play was set up on the stage on which I spoke to the assembly and among them the people who were going to act the play."[23]

In Wyandotte, a suburb of Detroit, a local theater group was just rehearsing the play. The organization thought it would be touching to "stir memories in the heart of Dr. Rosey E. Pool" by presenting her with an Anne Frank look-alike with the words: "Dr. Pool, may I present Anne Frank."[24] Both the reporter and the audience of two hundred seemed a bit disappointed that Pool did not burst out in tears. This was not the only time such surprises came her way. Pool met two other "Anne Franks": one in Detroit and, incongruously, a blonde one in Kalamazoo, although "neither of them" looked in "any way like her," Pool remarked in shocked relief (figure 17).[25] The actor from Kalamazoo who was playing Anne remembered that Pool was very "reserved" when they briefly met. "We didn't have much in common other than Anne."[26] By now Pool had come to understand that the Anne Frank story was a convenient way to get her foot in the door. But showing American society what she thought was important remained a challenge.

Part of the problem was that Pool's name did not bring in audiences, but the name Anne Frank did. "Dear Doctor," one pupil from Ypsilanti bluntly wrote: "I can not say that I am a long time admirer of yours, nor can I claim to be an ardent fan. I have not even read any of your books. The truth is that I hadn't heard of you before today."[27] The ambitious Pool became frustrated that people only came to see "Anne Frank's teacher"

Figure 17. Pool (middle) together with an unidentified man and Priscilla Koestner-Swiat, a freshman at Nazareth College in Kalamazoo, Michigan, at the time who played Anne Frank in a local production of the Civic Players in March 1959. The book they are holding is possibly *The Diary of a Young Girl*. The photograph was probably taken at Kalamazoo College on 16 October 1959.
SOURCE: SxMs19/10/1/5, Rosey E. Pool Collection, University of Sussex.

and not her. "You came not to hear me speak," Pool said in Kalamazoo, Michigan, in October 1959, "but to hear a person who knew a child who means very much to you. It is still a miracle to me."[28]

One might expect that Pool would say that Anne Frank was brilliant and that her own classes had been crucial in the girl's development. But playing second fiddle to Anne Frank did not bring out the best in Pool, and so instead she shocked her audiences by saying that she barely remembered that "unremarkable child."[29] And from there on her recollections became even more unflattering and unkind. "I don't think the diary is an artistic work," she was often quoted as saying, while she also remarked that Anne had been of "average intelligence," that she "wasn't charming" or "pretty" and that she was also "catty."[30] Some remarks were unnecessarily cruel, like that Anne Frank was "a little imp" or that her "head was large for her body."[31] On numerous occasions Pool also stressed how jealous Anne Frank had been of her sister, Margot, who was "everybody's darling," while Anne was the "ugly duckling."[32] Such statements may be partly accurate, but they say something about Pool herself too. As remembering takes place in the present, people adapt versions of the past—which change with every recollection—to suit present circumstances.[33] What these comments suggest is that Pool envied Anne Frank the most.

Anne Frank's story continued to mutate, mostly at the hands of Hollywood, and Pool seems to have simply felt the need to give a more down-to-earth account of her. Her mean remarks thus also had a purpose: she wanted to offer a more realistic picture of Anne Frank in an attempt to make her more human. Pool said that she refused to ascribe a quality to the "now immortal Anne that isn't there," including the saint-like quality attributed to her because of her suffering.[34] She was not a saint, she was an ordinary girl, Pool kept repeating. There had been many who lived just like her and died the way she did.

But Pool also could be found defending Anne Frank, making her appear as a sort of Jekyll and Hyde. Most of Pool's memories in fact seemed to have been derived from the diary itself. Or, rather, from American readings of the diary. Pool said that "sunshine, not poison[,] comes from the pages" and that Anne Frank "never uttered a word of hatred," contradicting her claim that she had been a catty child, and also belying the contents of the diary itself, since as the first translator she knew that the diary abounds in sneers toward almost everybody in the secret annex.[35] Yet as her tour progressed, Pool's choice of words became suspiciously consistent with the forgiveness that the young girl had come to represent in the United States. Perhaps she received too much criticism about her initial approach, or perhaps it was the positivity of most Americans that changed the way she viewed Anne Frank, but after one month in Detroit she suddenly remembered one incident from Amsterdam during the early 1940s: "We were to have a particularly difficult lesson one day, and I thought it best to separate the little classroom gangs. I remember saying to my assistant: 'Now when the Frank children come in, you put Margot in front so everyone can see her—and I'll put Anne in back where she can see everyone.'"[36]

Pool's own recollections thus gradually became intertwined with the movie version of Anne Frank: observant, quirky, and innocent. And yet such memories, whether true or not, also shifted the attention toward her. "If she had one obsession," Paul Breman, her erstwhile and disgruntled collaborator, scoffed, "it was to always be centre-stage in a spotlight."[37] However spiteful Breman may have been, there is truth in his claim. Pool liked to be the center of attention, but to her credit, she was fighting for a good cause, although perhaps not in ways consistent with contemporary standards.

Ultimately, Pool believed that if there were one message in Anne Frank's diary, it was that "suffering is not a virtue. It is no one's privilege to suffer."[38] Pool's message was mostly targeted at white audiences. Probably in an attempt to make her own story more "universal," Pool did not position herself as Jewish. In fact, she often, puzzlingly, outright denied being Jewish. Perhaps she did not want to be categorized as a Jewish speaker, but she also believed that "race" was an artificial construct and she refused to be boxed in by it. One of the few times Pool addressed a Jewish-only audience was when she spoke in early December 1959 at a Chicago chapter of Hadassah, a women's Zionist organization. Her talk was part of a fundraising event for shelters for young children in Israel. Coincidentally it was also the only event that was endorsed by Anne's father, Otto Frank, who wrote that the cause would have had Anne's "wholehearted championship, I am certain."[39] Whether Pool liked it or not, these Jewish organizations were perhaps her most welcoming audiences. On another occasion at Temple Beth Emeth at Wilmington, Delaware, a tape recording of her talk was made, which was afterward used "almost daily" in meetings.[40] But she was preaching to the choir here while she wanted instead to focus on issues that provoked. She came to believe that the real problems in the United States could not be found in the North, but in the Deep South and that she would have to go there to do her work.

Down South

Shortly after New Year's Eve 1960, Pool continued her U.S. journey in the South, the cradle of African American culture. With the money she made with her northern talks—$1,220, a little over $10,000 by today's standards—she was now at liberty not only to mobilize public opinion on her own terms but also to scout out aspiring Black poets for a new poetry anthology. This is how the idea was born of her touring a series of historically Black colleges and universities (HBCUs), schools that remained de facto segregated, even after the 1954 Supreme Court decision that segregation in public schools was unconstitutional. Arranging such was easier said than done, however, as most of these colleges had extremely limited budgets.[41] So when Pool started to contact colleges from her London home, she offered them guest lectures with an optional fee, as long as they could provide accommodation and arrange for her travels.[42] Her friend and one of her Fulbright contact people, Professor Mozell Hill from Atlanta University, advised her to contact the UNCF.[43] This fund oversaw dozens of private HBCUs in the South and could thus perhaps help arrange for her to visit far more colleges than she could manage to set up by herself and maybe even cover some of her travel costs.[44] The answers she received exceeded her expectations: a three-month trip to twenty-two colleges in ten different states, fully sponsored by the UNCF.

The scope and length of this college tour was unprecedented and unparalleled in the history of the UNCF.⁴⁵ From January to March 1960 Pool zigzagged through the South. The order seems illogical—she flew from Tennessee to North Carolina and then to Mississippi before again returning to Tennessee. Yet it does make sense through the lens of American traditions of philanthropy, altruism, and fundraising.⁴⁶ Both the UNCF and its associated HBCUs were largely dependent on gifts from governmental institutions, charities, and individual donations, and so her visits no doubt were set up to coincide with fundraising events and appeals for financial support, which provided financial stability to UNCF colleges.⁴⁷ Pool's tour included no less than fifteen domestic flights, which must have cost a fortune. Yet the UNCF probably saw it as an investment in the future that would outweigh the costs in the long run. The UNCF not only tried to reach African American but also white and Jewish audiences.⁴⁸ After each talk UNCF pamphlets asking for donations accompanied by return envelopes were distributed, all in the hope of raising money from organizations and individuals alike.⁴⁹

The UNCF chose visiting scholars based on ideology. Its fellows ideally broadened the worldviews of their students and also supported its ideals of racial equality and emancipation. Pool was the perfect speaker with her interest in both African American poetry and Anne Frank. The UNCF probably hoped that "Anne Frank's teacher" who criticized segregation would be an instant success, and the many headlines she made indicate that that hope was realized. Pool's visits were also used to produce more lasting PR materials. The colleges were asked for photographs that "show Dr. Pool chatting with students in an informal setting"; these requests were often accompanied by meticulous instructions: "Please . . . not more than five or six students with Dr. Pool" (figure 18).⁵⁰ Such visual material retained its missionary value, long after Pool had left.

Pool was warmly welcomed in the South, and both her talks about Black poetry and Anne Frank were well received. Yet the context of racial segregation obviously gave an entirely different meaning to her message. Although Pool was well prepared, as she had heard a lot about the South and had also extensively read about it, the level of segregation nevertheless deeply shocked her. "It's in everyone's minds, on everyone's lips. One just can't get away from it," she wrote.⁵¹ The "whites" and "colored" signs instantly reminded her of the "race madness" she had experienced herself in Nazi-occupied Europe. In hindsight those signs had only been a precursor to something much worse: the systematic destruction of European Jewry. Pool thought it was not unlikely that the U.S. South would follow

Figure 18. Pool with unidentified students at Talladega College in Talladega, Alabama, late March 1960.
SOURCE: SxMs19/14/1/4, Rosey E. Pool Collection, University of Sussex.

that same trajectory and that it was already in a shockingly advanced phase. "Prejudice doesn't only hurt," Pool said. "It can kill."[52] Referring to the Holocaust she exclaimed: "It can happen here!"[53]

Pool found the situation in the South to be far more desperate than up North, and she used both her own life story and that of Anne Frank as wake-up calls, as tools to get people to see the necessity of resisting any kind of "anti-otherism," whether at home or abroad.[54] Although Pool was not the only one who suffered from a kind of "resistance fighters' syndrome," a compulsion to fight for the discriminated and the oppressed— her urge to defend others dated back to her youth.[55] Whether it was her efforts to advance the career of the Dutch blind poet Frits Tingen when she was just twenty-two years old, her help to German Jews when she was in her thirties, her resistance work during World War II, or her teaching of children after they came out of hiding, standing up for the marginalized and oppressed was a recurring theme in Pool's life. Her commitment to helping others grew out of her being bullied as a child herself, when her peers made her feel diminished and vulnerable.[56] This experience had fueled her activism ever since: she wanted to be the helping hand she had so desperately needed when she was young.

Her desire to help others did not prevent Pool from falling into altruistic pitfalls, including overidentification with the victim and attempting to work out problems of the past in the present. Another danger for do-gooders is that they may engage in masochistic or even narcissistic behavior to keep going, behavior that is often marked by an often unconscious desire to stay in the helper position and thereby keep victims dependent.[57] Pool no doubt sincerely wished to help African Americans, but she also very much wanted to play the role of savior.

Little did she know that soon she would find herself greatly disempowered and made a victim herself as a result of concerns raised over the trustworthiness of Anne Frank's diary. Despite the ever-growing popularity of Anne Frank, by the late 1950s, people were beginning to have questions about the story. American playwright Meyer Levin's lawsuit against Anne's father significantly contributed to the doubts about the veracity of the story even though it only concerned who owned the rights in the play.[58] Right-wing extremists seized on the case as evidence that the Holocaust was a hoax and supposedly part of a Zionist conspiracy to control the world's finances. During the 1950s, American Holocaust deniers started to openly question the existence of extermination camps and claimed that the number of six million murdered was a gross exaggeration. Although these bogus narratives were initially only found among fringe groups, they slowly worked their way into the mainstream.[59] The *Diary of a Young Girl* became one of the deniers' most popular targets.

Pool never directly encountered Holocaust deniers. Yet she certainly met people who were influenced by negationism. For example, after her talk at Xavier University, a predominantly Black college in New Orleans, reporters from white newspapers asked her to confirm rumors that the diary was actually written by someone else, which she refused to do. "I can vouch for every word of it," she answered. "I made the first English translation of Anne's notes."[60] Another argument made by Holocaust deniers, namely, that the writing was far too advanced for a teenage girl, had also found its way to these reporters, who confronted Pool with this supposed fact. Again, Pool forthrightly defended the work by saying that "Americans fail to realize that children in Western Europe are far ahead of American children in education."[61] Pool further explained that "war was to Anne very much like a hot-house is to a plant. . . . She matured very rapidly."[62]

Such attacks on the veracity of the diary were not an exception. Pool said that "too often" she bumped into people who doubted Anne wrote it. In Mississippi she rebutted the idea that Otto Frank "was pushing Anne's book for the money," a rumor that emanated from antisemitic prejudices about "greedy Jews." "This is far from true," Pool said, claiming that all the revenues went to charities and Israel, which was indeed partly the case.[63] She was forced to defend the diary far more often in the South than in the

North. Perhaps this was because in the South antisemitism always lurked just below the surface.[64] This sentiment at times spoke to a southern resentment against northern establishments, but often it simply reflected a lack of knowledge, among white and Black people alike. People did not grasp the nuances of the story unless they were particularly interested in European history. Most of the people Pool encountered had only vaguely heard about a lawsuit against Anne Frank's father. Some had only heard that there was a play and a movie and even sort of assumed that Anne Frank was a fictional character.

Pool was constantly debunking myths and fighting misinformation. One Black journalist from Atlanta described Pool as the "world famed author" whose "best known book is diary by 'Anne Frank.'"[65] Having to devote time and effort to challenging such inaccuracies seriously jeopardized her underlying goals for her tour: to convince African Americans to resist the "race madness," so that they would not make the same mistakes Europeans Jews had made.

Yet there were also triumphs in her attempts to fight prejudice, most notably at Fisk University, a Black university in Nashville, Tennessee. There her talk "Anne Frank and Her Friends" inspired Professor Robert Hayden to write a poem called "Belsen, Day of Liberation (for Rosey Pool)." Hayden somewhat sentimentally describes a young girl who witnessed the liberation of Bergen-Belsen by African American soldiers: "They were so beautiful, and they were not afraid," Hayden imagines the girl saying.[66] Pool's talk also inspired students and staff to perform the Anne Frank play at Fisk; "we wished," one professor wrote to her, "to capitalize [on] the inspiration and enthusiasm your visit brought."[67]

Pool suggested that she influenced civil rights activists as well, as her tour coincided with the sit-ins that were slowly spreading across the South in the first months of 1960. For example, in Greensboro, North Carolina, a sit-in was taking place at a local Woolworth store just when she arrived. Pool said she "vividly" remembered discussions on the campus as to "whether or not direct action could indeed help the cause of the black man."[68] As Pool's life story demonstrated that direct action did work, she happily and conveniently concluded that she had had a "small share in acting as an alarm clock to the great awakening," by which she meant the civil rights movement.[69]

Her comparisons of Nazism and the Jim Crow system was what stood out most in her wake-up calls to African Americans. On numerous occasions Pool said that the Nazis introduced "segregation, persecution and racial discrimination" in Europe—her choice of words was no coincidence.[70]

William Fowlkes, an African American journalist working in Atlanta, Georgia, was particularly inspired by Pool's analogies. As managing editor for the *Atlanta Daily World*, Fowlkes extensively covered civil rights activism and also Pool's seven-day stay in Atlanta in February 1960. In an article entitled "Author Pool Notes Similarity of Nazi Oppression, Segregation" he quoted Pool as saying that she was frankly "surprised to find so many people in their right mind, living under oppression." In another piece he quoted her as saying that a repudiation of "southern ways" was long overdue given that Hitler had been crushed.[71] Fowlkes recognized in Pool an ally and moral authority whose provocative comparisons exposed the hypocrisy and injustice of racial segregation. They allowed readers to comprehend racial oppression at home more fully, he believed.

However, African American audiences did not tend to see parallels between themselves and Anne Frank. Unlike white newspapers, Black newspapers rarely wrote about her, nor does it seem that the play was often performed on Black campuses (the production at Fisk was a notable exception). Although Anne Frank wrote in her diary that the transports of Jews reminded her of the "slave hunts of olden times," this single reference was insufficient to create a meaningful Black/Jewish identification.[72] Perhaps despite its supposed universality, the story was too far removed from the experience of Black southerners Pool encountered, especially after Anne Frank had been "white washed" and de-Judaized by Hollywood.[73] The biggest stumbling block, however, was that the story was not one of triumph. Yes, she had kept to the moral high ground, but how could that be of use to African Americans in a time when direct action activism was on the rise?

If any lesson was to be learned from the diary, it was that passive resistance did not in fact work. Especially revealing in this context is the way Pool was meticulously remembered by Fisk student Julius Lester, who also saw a basis for solidarity but not equivalence: "As I listen to her talk of a child hiding in an attic, . . . I understand her accented words, but they do not make sense. I do not know how to live with the knowledge of such evils and such suffering. . . . I think about gas chambers and furnaces into which human beings were shoveled like waste paper. . . . Being forced to ride at the back of a bus is not in the same realm of human experience."[74] Not only did Lester fail to discover inspiration in Anne Frank's story but he also acknowledged that her story and that of other European Jews could trivialize the daily oppression of African Americans. Whatever discrimination they may have faced, they had never faced gas chambers. A Black/Jewish comparison could easily lead to arguments over which was "worse" and could thus undermine the cause of Black emancipation.

Both metaphorical and literal connections between colonialism and the Holocaust could be made, as theoreticians like W. E. B. Du Bois and Aimé Césaire proved during this period, and these were authors that Pool was well acquainted with.[75] But the specific case of Anne Frank did not provide enough concrete material to make meaningful comparisons.

Media Circus

The media circus around Anne Frank might have overwhelmed other people, but not Pool: she was flattered by the momentary attention, and she presented herself as a loveable educator who was never too tired for a photograph. Although she found it highly emotional to talk about Anne Frank as well as to see Jim Crow signs, she believed that her own personal "heartbreak" had "a good purpose" and ought to be an inspiration to African Americans.[76]

Although her heart was in the right place, one problematic issue was that she had made quite a profit with this tour, especially in the North, and barely had to pay for anything herself in the South. None of that money was going to charities—for instance, the Anne Frank Foundation. Although Pool liked to claim she was still in touch with Otto Frank (which there is no evidence of in their archives), he never uttered a word about this tour, and it is likely he was not amused that a former teacher of his daughter acted as an unauthorized spokesperson. Pool was the only former teacher of Anne Frank who did such a thing, even though her connection with the young girl was not that strong. And because Pool downplayed and even ignored her own Jewish background, she was also charged with cultural appropriation. On at least one occasion she was accused of making money on the back of a dead girl. "You trade a lot on Anne Frank's name," one poet wrote to her in a furious letter. "I hope you have something of her soul and all my suspicions are invalid."[77]

Pool's intentions were good, however. She went to the South to emphasize that Anne Frank had been an actual person and to relate not only the suffering of European Jews but of that of fellow citizens of the world. By the 1960s Anne Frank had become a heroine, almost a saint-like figure, beyond human, and Pool could not alter this image. She would rarely ever speak again about her former pupil in public. Later in life she even described Anne Frank's fame as the result of "a morbid interest" and "sensationalism" that had little to do with sincere human sympathy.[78] On her next visits to the Deep South she decided to do things differently, starting in Mississippi.

CHAPTER 8

Mississippi, 1960–1963

Pool returned to the Deep South in 1963, where she visited Tougaloo College near Jackson, Mississippi. She had been at this college before for one week in early 1960. German Jewish refugee scholar Ernst Borinski, her point of contact at Tougaloo, arranged for her to return for an entire month in February 1963. Soon word got around among conservative prosegregationists that a Dutch scholar had arrived on campus. Almost daily Pool received angry phone calls and letters filled with "abusive and filthy words."[1] More than once white people spat at her feet when she went out for a stroll outside the campus. Seeing segregation in practice during her first time in the South had been a "nightmare only comparable to about the same time I spent in nazi prisons and concentration camps"; the second time around was not much better.[2] Nevertheless, Tougaloo was her "favourite Southern College," and she was thrilled to be back.[3]

Mississippi had historically been a rich cotton-producing area that relied on enslaved Black laborers, and throughout the twentieth century the majority of the population remained African American. During the Jim Crow era every aspect of society was rigidly segregated, which seriously compromised the civil rights of Black people, who were systematically subordinated and also terrorized by the Ku Klux Klan, the White Citizens' Council, and the Mississippi State Sovereignty Commission. Perhaps the worst place was the Mississippi Delta. This region was widely known as the "most Southern place on earth," which is probably why it became the center of civil rights activism in the 1960s.

In late January 1963 Pool again found herself just outside the Mississippi Delta, in what she called "one of the many ghettos of the South."[4] This time Pool was not sponsored but mostly there under her "own steam."[5] All

Figure 19. Pool with students at Tougaloo College, near Jackson, Mississippi, February 1963. There were twelve students in this class (not all are pictured): Johnny Earl Chattman, Rubastine M. Clark, Lela Garner, Joyce Gatlin, Naomi Golf, Mary Ann Hall, Etta M. Jackson, Oteria Kincaid, Memphis Norman, Jutha Pinkston, Audrey Prentiss, William Francis Route, Evelyn Sadberry, Annie Belle Williams, Dianella Williams, and Melinda Lois Willis.

SOURCE: SxMs19/5/2/5, Rosey E. Pool Collection, University of Sussex.

she asked for was travel fares, daily expenses, and Tougaloo's hospitality. Since Tougaloo was in dire need of qualified personnel, it was happy to oblige this request. Pool romantically described the Tougaloo campus, which was situated in a quiet rural area, as featuring "sad spanish moss" dangling from the trees and red cardinal birds flying all around.[6] Tougaloo College was also an enclave and not as stereotypically southern as its surroundings. Pool called the private college "that remarkable bit of free world in Mississippi."[7] With its liberal outlook and integrated faculty (and a handful of white students as well) this Black college became a refuge for human rights activists from all over the United States.[8] Pool called it the "only 'terra franca' in Mississippi," where black and white were able to "eat, drink, study, discuss, walk and sing together."[9]

To liberals, Tougaloo College was an "oasis of freedom," but prosegregationists thought it was "alien and unwanted," a "cancer college" that they sought to get rid of.[10] By the mid-1960s Tougaloo College had become so (in)famous that a state official called it a "hangout for Communists and fellow travelers" and—with much drama and exaggeration—a "haven for queers, quacks and quirks."[11] The white college president Adam Daniel Beittel (in office 1960–64) did little to counter this image. On the contrary, he allowed and occasionally encouraged student activism, even though he surely was "no wild-eyed radical" as one historian put it.[12] When a group of Tougaloo students were arrested in 1961 after a sit-in at the local library—the "Tougaloo Nine" as they became known—he visited them in prison. Beittel even joined the famous 1963 sit-in at a local Woolworth. Tougaloo students could even earn college credits for their work in the movement.[13] So this was clearly not an everyday Black southern college.

Ernst Borinski's "Stigma Management"

Wherever Pool went in the South, she familiarized herself with the local rules, regulations, and "maze of local by-laws" that were meant to keep Black people "in their place."[14] In Mississippi she quickly found someone who could explain the local laws of "race madness," Ernst Borinski (figure 20).[15] He was born in 1901 in Katowice, Silesia, then still part of the German Empire. Raised in a secular Jewish family, he had been active in Social Democrat groups and labor unions. Borinski obtained his PhD in law in Berlin—around the same time Pool's ex-husband had studied law there, although they probably never met. He fled to the United States in 1938, serving in the U.S. Army before finally ending up in Tougaloo in

Figure 20. Ernst Borinski (third from the right) with unidentified students and possibly staff members, early 1963.
SOURCE: SxMs19/10/1/8, Rosey E. Pool Collection, University of Sussex.

1947, where he specialized in the sociology of law. The signs saying "whites only" looked uncomfortably familiar to him, although he now found himself on the other side. "I had no difficulties understanding oppression," he remarked in an interview, and he saw many similarities between the White Citizens' Council and the Nazis.[16] "When I see the kinds of laws you have here," Borinski told his students, "I assure you it cannot last very long."[17] Borinski was convinced that in Nazi Germany the problem had been that "good people" were "not getting involved."[18] He made it his life goal to awaken the white "neutrals" in the Deep South by exposing the injustices of Jim Crow and by showing the students that segregation was not inevitable in society. Since it was impossible to take all of his students outside of Mississippi, Borinski vicariously brought a freer world to his students with his Social Science Laboratory—"the lab," or, as he pronounced it with his thick German accent: *ze Lab*.[19]

Under the auspices of the lab, a wide variety of cutting-edge speakers came to Tougaloo; some were famous, some were not, but all had an unorthodox perspective on current affairs. Famous speakers included diplomat and Nobel Peace Prize winner Ralph Bunche, writer James Baldwin, Student Nonviolent Coordinating Committee activist Kwame Ture (aka Stokely Carmichael), and folk singer Joan Baez. "Meeting people at Tougaloo College who are now historical figures was commonplace," one student nostalgically recalled.[20] Pool herself delivered three talks here, two in 1960, one of which was titled "Anne Frank, One of My Children" and the other of which was titled "My Five Years of Underground Work in Nazi-Occupied Holland." During her second visit, in 1963, Pool was finally able to talk about what she loved most: the poetry of African Americans.[21] These meetings, unlike those held elsewhere in Mississippi, were interracial. Borinski would ask his Black Tougaloo students to come in early and occupy every other chair around the table. As a result white guests, who came in on time, had no other option than to sit among Black people at one table. For many whites this was the first time they interacted with a Black person who was not their cleaner.[22]

When Pool and Borinski met for the first time in 1960, they immediately hit it off. Both had lived in Berlin in the 1930s, both had been Social Democrats, and both opposed segregation. According to Borinski, however, it was also their shared "Jewishness" that brought them together: he admired Pool's "subtle humor" which he found profoundly Jewish.[23] In return Pool was inspired by how Borinski made practical use of his own background through what he called "positive marginality" or "stigma management."[24] We might now describe this as using intersectionality to achieve social change. Local newspapers denounced Borinski as a "foreigner" and a "communist"; he was simply unable to get rid of his thick German accent, no matter how hard he tried. He thus decided to turn the tables and utilize this foreignness to "momentarily disarm . . . Mississippi's system of racial apartheid," as he called it.[25] "I played their game very carefully," he said, trying to "sort of blunder through" segregation etiquette.[26] With his disarming approach, he could ask thought-provoking questions that liberal Americans would not even dare to ask. "We went in a downtown drugstore and sat down," Borinski remembered, "and I said, 'I want ice cream.' They looked at the black students and said, 'I cannot serve them.' I said, 'Why do you not serve them?' and they said, 'You know.' I said, 'I don't know anything.'"[27] Playing the naïve outsider, he critically questioned segregation, one diner at a time.

Pool, perhaps inspired by him, also decided to use humor to fight segregation and prejudice. She remembered how one time she passed by a launderette in North Carolina, probably near Greensboro, where she saw a sign on the window that read MONDAY: WHITE ONLY. "It was ludicrous," she said. "Idiotic. Maddening. Filthy. The South hit me good and hard." So she decided to enter. Faking a heavy Dutch accent (that she had worked on so hard to conceal), she said, "Please, I am from Europe, from Holland. There are many things I cannot understand in America."

She continued: "We have washing machines too at home and we always hear that American machinery is better than ours." Then she delivered the punchline: "Then why can you not wash coloured things on Mondays?" The woman behind the counter was unaware that she was being mocked, and Pool quoted her in the "vernacular," as if she was a rare species: "O, honey—child, you don't understand... This don't mean that you cain't wash coloureds, it means that coloured cain't wash." In an attempt to further explain local customs, the clerk remarked that some white families simply could not afford a maid and had to do their washing themselves. "So... naturally they don't want to [do] that when there's coloured around," she said. "Naturally?" Pool asked. "Why should that be so natural?" The woman responded: "Look honey, that is our way of life... perhaps it isn't quite right. I've never thought about these things before."[28]

Pool wrote short stories about such experiences, which she perhaps hoped to publish as a book of essays. These stories were peppered with anecdotes like these: funny, short tales about random encounters with ordinary people that revealed how discrimination structured everyday practices. During such personal encounters, Pool tried to fight segregation by using jokes to open the eyes of white people or, at the very least, to cause a small lifting of an eyelid. This humoristic approach, which Pool shared with Borinski, "didn't solve anything" according to one skeptical eyewitness.[29] Yet perhaps they did contribute to laying the groundwork for the desegregation of people's minds. Although it is impossible to say whether this particular encounter happened or had any effect at all, Pool's description of it certainly reflects her character: a witty, big-mouthed person who fought prejudice against all odds. These encounters (fake or not) made for great stories that Pool would repeat tirelessly wherever she went, often, one friend remembered, with a "mischievous twinkle in her eye."[30]

Creative Writing as "Group Therapy"

Pool came to Mississippi to teach creative writing. Although she was formally merely trained as an elementary school teacher, she had spiced up her CV by the late 1950s, claiming to have both a PhD, which was very unlikely as we have seen, and the even higher D.Litt., even more unlikely, from the University of Berlin. To circumvent questions about discrepancies, she turned her CV into a nonchronological hodgepodge that referenced friendships with famous Black intellectuals, her escape from a Nazi transit camp, and her personal contacts with Anne Frank. However, this could not fully hide the fact that formally she had zero experience teaching creative writing, except for "teaching literature (American, Negro) by radio and... public readings."[31] Teaching was secondary to her goal of fighting injustices, but that goal did not materialize into a well-defined plan. Perhaps this was why she kept the curriculum for her creative writing class as broad as possible. "I must make a confession," she stated. "When I arrived at Tougaloo my ideas about the course were as vague as everybody else's."[32]

The class had six meetings of two hours per week over four weeks, during which students were encouraged to do one thing: write. What Pool liked best about her teaching was how these students still allowed "free insight into their vulnerable souls, their anxieties, their dreams."[33] She fondly remembered her student William Route, an African American teenager from a poor family of cotton laborers. He "appeared for the first discussion with an armful of copybooks full of stammered stories and page-long poems," Pool remembered. "He didn't say a word all afternoon [and] left all his copybooks on my table."[34] Pool had great trouble understanding his writing. Sentences like "granpop was not a polittion nor could he read or rite but time had eddicate him in wisdom" were written largely phonetically in a southern dialect.[35] Pool called it "negro language" or "Black American."[36] But by the end of the course the student was allegedly able to write a full paper in perfect English—not because of her but, she said, as a "result of the workshop's 'group therapy.'"[37]

By "group therapy" Pool referred to one of the underlying goals of this course, which was to work with " young people who want to express and perhaps *liberate* themselves while writing."[38] Although these students did not literally liberate themselves from segregation through writing, they were certainly able to (temporarily) step outside the framework of Jim Crow, a system that not only controlled their bodies but, as the Supreme Court had concluded some years before, also invaded their minds and created a deep sense of inferiority and self-hatred.[39] Pool therefore envisioned her classes as deeply therapeutic: "Writing is difficult and [a] wonderfully rewarding job, a healing job too."[40] Students were challenged to define themselves through writing and to share their reflections with the group. "After a while a situation develops which can best be compared to psychiatric group therapy," Pool wrote.[41]

In the twenty-first century, the idea of writing one's life narrative is firmly embedded in a wide range of therapeutic practices, but in the early 1960s this approach was unorthodox. It was connected to "bibliotherapy," in which the reading of (specific) books was used to explore and heal trauma, albeit never with students.[42] Perhaps Pool had been in therapy herself or had learned about such methods through her partner, radiologist Isa Isenburg, who worked at a London hospital. Or perhaps Pool based her methods on participatory European education models that were practiced in socialist youth groups, like the collective Links Richten in which her friend Jef Last had played a central role. They declared in the early 1930s that art should be "used as a weapon in the class struggle," serving the proletariat, and that self-expression of laborers was essential to create awareness.[43] Or perhaps she learned such methods during her time at the Karl Marx Schule in Berlin. It can be assumed that her teaching methods were influenced by the old left and were utterly subversive and radical, meant to instigate the oppressed.

Her students were not immediately convinced of the value of self-discovery. Most of them were initially very shy, but after a few sessions "the creativity" could "hardly be dammed," Pool proudly remarked.[44] "Traumatic experiences just poured out of them."[45] That was ironic, since she did not deal with her own trauma nor was she trained as a psychotherapist. Yet she envisioned her own job as simply listening. For many of these African American students she might have been one of the few whites that actually listened to what they had to say. By the late 1960s Pool had come to believe that it was not just being Black under Jim Crow but being Black in America that could create severe psychological damage.[46] She therefore saw herself more as a therapist than a teacher: "My creative writing class . . . was something like an analyst's couch to the Kids."[47]

The exercises she gave lacked a clear focus, although it seems that the students were encouraged to write about their experiences with discrimination. Most vented their frustration with segregation and racism. Dianella Williams, a nineteen-year-old sociology student, was "well acquainted with the vocabulary of discrimination," Pool wrote, and with all kinds of abusive terms for different types of minorities associated with it. Pool was amazed by how her poem "Racist" challenged the "melting pot" ideal of American society:[48]

> What is he?
> How does he look?
> Is he a cracker,
> A dago, a spook?
> What is his I.Q.?
> What shade is his hue?
> And could a Paddy
> be a racist too?
> I really don't know;

and it's strictly taboo
to say that a racist
could even be you.⁴⁹

Pool reprinted the poem in her 1968 book *Lachen om niet te huilen*, a remarkable acknowledgment of the student's eloquent articulation of her experiences with racism. By sharing these students' work in her many publications, she seriously boosted their self-esteem. In her archives countless thank-you notes can be found, like one written by a student named Rhoda M. Voth: "Thank you for all you've done here on campus," she wrote, "not only for widening our horizons and stimulating our imaginations, but especially for bolstering our morales."⁵⁰

Mississippi or Nazi-Occupied Europe?

Pool's struggle against what she called American "apartheid," together with her use of socialist-inspired methods, was perhaps only possible in Tougaloo and nowhere else in Mississippi.⁵¹ This was a private and elitist UNCF college that enjoyed relative autonomy, and the college administration was in favor of movement activism. Students were far more eager to speak out here than elsewhere in the state and were more accustomed to interacting with whites on campus.⁵² Pool herself also admitted that this college was atypical and was "more militant in respect of the Civil Rights struggle."⁵³

Despite these students' relatively privileged position, the Black population of Mississippi was far from liberated. Black people were subject to intimidation, and Black activists who opposed this system were harassed or even disappeared. Pool felt that she took "a giant step back" to the years 1940–45 and again began to think about the implications of every single step in a paranoid manner.⁵⁴ This paranoia was not completely unfounded. After all, African Americans faced serious dangers, including police brutality, in Mississippi. Whites who went to the Tougaloo campus were often tapped, followed, or threatened. In 1964, for example, a burning cross was placed on the lawn of Ed King, Tougaloo's young white campus minister.⁵⁵ By the mid-1960s the campus entrance was flocked with cars from the prosegregationist Sovereignty Commission who meticulously wrote down license plate numbers of those who entered the campus in an attempt to intimidate and terrorize them.⁵⁶ Rosey Pool was especially affected by this menacing atmosphere, as it immediately reminded her of Nazi Berlin and occupied Amsterdam.

While at Tougaloo, Pool found "a daily ration" of letters in her mailbox, "typed, hand-written, or composed of cut-outs from newspapers," filled with "abusive and filthy words." And "when my telephone rang, I could hardly identify myself to the caller before being interrupted by a wave of similar idiomax [*sic*] as expressed in the notes." Occasionally the intimidation turned into actual violence. "Once or twice a few pebbles happened to fly through my window"; one time "even a small bullet" reached her room, "which most fortunately got stuck high up in the wall."[57] It is not hard to see how the Mississippian atmosphere would have brought her mentally back to World War II, reigniting her trauma: "A car stopped outside my 'dorm,' just when I had dozed off into much-needed sleep. The sound of those brakes must have touched exactly that spot of my sleep-conscious mind which has stored memories of fear caused by cars stopping outside our house in Holland during the years 1940–45. I half-awoke. I was at home in my room on [the Nieuwe] Prinsengracht in Amsterdam. I thought: 'Here they are,' sat up in bed and listened for approaching jackboots."[58]

Pool and her parents were arrested on the Nieuwe Prinsengracht during a razzia in May 1943, the last place where she and her family had lived more or less peacefully. Shortly afterward both her parents, her brother, and her sister-in-law were deported to Sobibór and murdered. Given that Pool's first visit to Tougaloo had brought back war memories ("1940–45 haunts me," she then wrote on arrival), Pool perhaps used her return visit to Mississippi as a form of therapy for herself as well, a kind of regression therapy, in which she relived old experiences of persecution in the hope of giving them a new meaning and bringing about a different, less horrific outcome.[59] Her story about the car stopping outside her door shows how traumatic thoughts could invade her brain at any time, even twenty years later. Many people she had known had simply vanished during the war, making it hard for her to recover the past or to pen an ending to unfinished narratives.[60] Her self-imposed regression therapy was perhaps a result of a (conscious or unconscious) compulsion to repeat her past.[61] Mississippi became the place where she could expose herself to situations that bore resemblances to situations she had encountered in her past.

"She cannot stop now"

It is impossible to say how open Pool was with others about her own trauma and the Holocaust in general. Had traumatic experiences "poured out" of her as they did with her students in their creative writing? In general, the handful of German Jewish refugee scholars who worked at HBCUs did not tend to talk about their pasts, with Borinski being a notable exception.[62] There are also no other known cases of Dutch refugees teaching at HBCUs. Pool's outspokenness with journalists certainly set her apart, although the way she acted in public appearances could have been utterly different from how she acted in the classroom. We can only retrace her steps as a therapist-teacher through her own words, the memories of students, and contemporary accounts that she kept in her scrapbooks. One of the most intimate recollections comes from a student named Audrey Prentiss, who carefully observed Pool:

> When I first met her she was in a classroom trying to arrange a schedule for a class in which I had enrolled. During this time I really observed [her], noticing her little movements and the dignified air that seemed to hover around her.... Her eyes to me was the most impressive thing about her. No, not because of their shape, size or color but because of what I could see in their depths and because of what they seemed to tell me. I don't really know what started me to notice her eyes but after I started it became a regular habit for me. Nor did I know the experiences and trying things through which those eyes had traveled and the sights they had seen.[63]

Prentiss wrote that she was deeply impressed by Pool's story of her work in the Dutch underground movement "that transferred Jews to other parts of the country and particularly Holland . . . during the annihilation of the Jews in the twentieth century." But what impressed her the most was Pool's embodiment of resilience: "As she told the story to the class, a little sadness would slip into her voice but her eyes would twinkle and convey their message to her mouth which would eventually smile."[64] With Pool's presence it seems that the shadow of the past, especially that of the Holocaust, was cast over Tougaloo. Although the plain horror of that past was perhaps a burden to some students, other students saw Pool's memories of the Holocaust as providing a historical precedent of social exclusion that furthered the cause of civil rights.[65] Pool certainly saw her recounting of the past this way as well. By telling her story here, she situated the oppression of African Americans in the wider historical context of race oppression in the Western world.

In her 1968 book *Lachen om niet te huilen*, Pool described racism as "one of the most fatal diseases of mankind." She believed racism was "not caused by the existence of various races and cultures" but "by our failure to accept their realities," an idea that aligned with her "anti-otherisms" theory—the thesis that weaved together systematic exclusion, whether this was anti-Black racism or antisemitism.⁶⁶ Her work in the socialist movement convinced her that races—like classes or nations—were artificially constructed divisions designed to keep the working class divided. These divisions kept revolution at bay. Her personal library shows that her beliefs were influenced by different streams of thought. W. E. B. Du Bois's theory of double consciousness showed her that being Black entailed a double-edged identity as well as a heightened sensitivity, while works by Léopold Senghor and Aimé Césaire taught her about negritude, the idea of a global Black consciousness. All these ideas led her to believe that people were not born different but were made different through their own experiences as individuals or as a group. And from this framework she saw remarkable similarities between Jews and Black people, as they were "both groups that had to endure many hardships over the centuries."⁶⁷

On a more personal level, Pool's attempt to consciously use her own trauma to inspire others was certainly a sign of posttraumatic growth that might have been impossible for her just a few years before.⁶⁸ What certainly helped was that here her experiences were acknowledged far more than they were in Europe. Yes, the South was a "nightmare," but her students were everything she wished for. Here she encountered compassion and respect, and the students found her resilience inspiring. In this respect her "therapy sessions" were not only healing to others but to herself as well. "The students began to sympathize with her," her former student Audrey Prentiss recalled, as Pool "told of her experiences in the concentration camps, prisons and as a leader in the underground movement."⁶⁹ She also remembered how Pool showed the continuity between anti-Nazi resistance and the ongoing civil rights movement and how she imagined her own role in this narrative: "She has hope, faith and a will that says she must carry on," because "she cannot stop now."⁷⁰

The goodwill Pool encountered perhaps encouraged her to continue her former resistance work against fascism. After she arrived in Tougaloo for the second time in January 1963, activists started a boycott against white shop owners who welcomed Black customers but refused to hire Black people. Pool soon became involved with the boycott, albeit behind the scenes, by helping with the distribution of boycott leaflets in the Jackson area.⁷¹ She also spent many of her evenings in classes sponsored by the Congress of Racial Equality for passive resistance, although it is unclear if she took an active role in any of them.⁷² It is possible that her personal friendship with NAACP president Arthur Spingarn facilitated her participation in direct action. Only a few days after she returned, President Beittel invited her to a private meeting at his home with students and a NAACP representative. Pool found such meetings deeply inspiring: "Black and White together . . . we shall overcome one day my students used to sing on those evenings," Pool wrote, echoing the famous spiritual gospel song that became an anthem of the civil rights movement.[73]

The most famous direct protest action in the Jackson area, however, took place after Pool had left. The sit-in at Woolworth in May 1963 garnered nationwide attention because of the shamelessly brutal and violent way the protesters were treated. A group of viciously jeering white men smeared peaceful protesters with mustard and ketchup before burning them with cigarettes. These protesters were students and professors from Tougaloo College. One of Pool's former students, Memphis Norman, was a participant. Norman came from a poor family of rural sharecroppers, but the promising student soon became Ernst Borinski's assistant. Borinski "had a very profound influence on my life in terms of race relations," Norman later recalled.[74] Borinski's impact and the unfolding civil rights movement drove the initially reluctant Norman into the movement and eventually into this particular sit-in as well. Unfortunately he was also the one who was most severely beaten. Pool defiantly reprinted the report of this former student of hers in her 1965 anthology *Ik ben de Nieuwe Neger*: "Someone struck me from my back with a blow that caused me to fall from my stool. I fell to the floor half-conscious. And then as to never have an end, I was kicked and stomped again in the face, on my head, in my stomach and on my back. . . . The kicking and stomping and beating continued until blood streamed from my mouth, from my nose, and from my ears."[75]

Pool had already left Mississippi when this sit-in took place, and it is unlikely that she was the prime agitator for it (it was probably recent events in Birmingham, Alabama, that motivated it).[76] Yet she did have influence in an indirect way. In her classes and lectures she offered—just like Borinski—a wider philosophical framework in which students could historically place civil rights activism. For example, when Pool discussed Black protest poetry, she consciously linked it to anti-Nazi resistance poetry. It is important to realize that at this point in time it was not clear the civil rights movement would succeed: the segregationist pushback was significant, and many activists felt they were skating on thin ice. The confidence that Pool had in that fight and the steadfastness with which she demonstrated it was an inspiration, if one of many.

Norman's training in Pool's creative writing class no doubt came in handy when he decided to write about his experiences. The ability to write compellingly was crucial to persuading a wider audience of the justice of the movement. Pool's class certainly gave him and others opportunity to develop such skills. Most of the participants of that sit-in also participated in the same passive resistance classes that the Congress of Racial Equality organized that Pool attended.

Pool's influence was also noticeable in her close collaboration with Lois Chaffee, a white teacher from Idaho who had taught remedial writing and reading at Tougaloo before becoming a full-time activist with the Congress of Racial Equality. In 1964, she served as a curriculum coordinator for the Freedom Schools, and in the curriculum she devised, she included a study on Nazi Germany and a discussion of "parallel conditions of persecution."[77] Although the case study focused on Denmark, echoes of Borinski's as well as Pool's main arguments were evident. Some of Pool's publications were even included in later Congress of Racial Equality education programs in Mississippi.[78] The Holocaust was slowly becoming a moral benchmark throughout the Western world that was used by "outside agitators" like Pool and local activists alike to dismantle racial segregation.

Confronting Her Own Past

Pool had always felt a deep connection with the global Black cause, but after this time in the Deep South she identified even more deeply with the ongoing African American struggle. Curiously, she felt like she belonged there. These feelings were stronger, ironically, after she was back home in London. When in 1964 peaceful marchers in Mississippi were beaten, arrested, and tear gassed, while other activists were kidnapped and never to be heard of again, Pool became outright desperate. She read about all this in British news outlets, and she wrote that the "madness" severely "depressed" her for weeks: "It wakes me up in the night, gives me nightmares of frustration and helplessness."[79] Being on the ground in Mississippi might have been painful, but at least it gave her the ability to act.

Although Pool wanted to fight segregation, her ideas as to how to achieve this were as vague as her plans for her creative writing class. Hinting at Pool's unrealistic expectations, one friend wrote: "Now don't go on any Freedom Rides or try to integrate the entire South by yourself."[80] Still, she succeeded in some of her ambitious goals, however small these might have been. She practiced integration by attending Borinski's interracial meetings. She confronted white people like the launderette worker in an effort to make them conscious of their own prejudices. Her "group therapy" creative writing sessions encouraged Black people to break the silence on discrimination. To achieve her goals she fully exploited her outsider status, which became her badge of honor: "The excellent relationship between myself and the students," she noted, could be explained to an extent by "the fact that, although I am not black, I am not an American either."[81] However, this did not mean that she automatically stood outside of American race relations, or at least not as much as she hoped she did. Her work did foster students' sense of empowerment and self-discovery, but it did not and could not dismantle white power structures at this school: she was still a white person in front of a (predominantly) Black class, and there is no evidence that Pool collaborated with Black faculty members in her classes.

The students in Pool's class found her inspiring, however, and also noticed connections she made between her World War II activism and current American affairs. From where Pool sat, these connections were obvious. Many of the peaceful sit-ins and boycotts reminded her of the interwar socialist movement and her own World War II resistance group, which had also been confrontational and yet nonviolent. But these connections also yielded surprising insights. After Tougaloo, Pool retrospectively used the movement's phrase of "passive resistance" to describe the inner resistance that she believed many Jews had practiced during the Holocaust.[82] She also learned to be less critical of her former self, whom she had still blamed for having been too passive during the war. Here she saw that passivity was an ambivalent state of being and less accommodating than it might first appear. Her time in Mississippi significantly changed how Pool perceived her own past, allowing her to take the first steps toward forgiving herself.

CHAPTER 9
Alabama, 1965–1966

The mid-1960s were the high point of Pool's career as well as when she was most active in her fight against racism. By now, the civil rights movement had achieved successes. Within a few years the tide would turn, especially after the assassination of Martin Luther King Jr. in 1968. Although that was still in the future, cracks in the Black-Jewish alliance would soon become apparent, both generally and personally in Pool's own life.

Pool returned to the Deep South for extended periods of time in 1965 and 1966 after being hired as a lecturer-in-residence at Alabama A&M College, a predominantly Black institution in the outskirts of Huntsville, Alabama, in Normal. This town near the Tennessee border had until a century ago been the seat of Alabama's highest cotton-producing county, thanks to a large population of enslaved Africans.[1] It was this dubious historical background—the town was symbolically situated between Scottsboro, where the infamous Scottsboro case of 1931 started, and Pulaski, Tennessee, where the KKK was founded a century before—that attracted Pool to Normal. Pool's deep sense of justice led her to this "hamlet," one of the "most conservative apartheid areas," in the middle of nowhere that was not so "normal" as its name suggested.[2]

And yet also this was an atypical southern town. Huntsville had grown to prominence through the NASA space center that had opened there in 1960. This center had greatly benefited from a group of German rocket scientists that had secretly entered the country in 1945, a group that included the well-known Wernher von Braun. With their emigration, a Third Reich legacy was brought to American soil: von Braun and other members of the group had worked in Nazi Germany's rocket development program during World War II, and even though some of them were "ar-

Figure 21. Pool (seen from the back) surrounded by unidentified students, at Alabama A&M College, 1967.
SOURCE: SxMs19/5/2/5, Rosey E. Pool Collection, University of Sussex.

dent Nazis" according to U.S. government standards, they were brought in because their expertise was now in high demand in the postwar space race.[3] Their controversial pasts were eagerly swept under the carpet by various parties.[4]

The NASA space center transformed Huntsville into "Rocket City, U.S.A." As a key player in the American-Soviet space race, Huntsville was unlike any other city in the South. The NASA space center attracted engineers from all over the world, making the city rather cosmopolitan. Local administrators made efforts to meet African American demands for civil rights so as not to embarrass NASA. As a result, Huntsville was quietly desegregated.[5] This did not mean, however, that Jim Crow was abolished altogether. The Rocket City consisted of two separate societies, one white, one "colored." Racial segregation was enforced in every societal institution. Throughout Alabama, signs that read "white only" and "colored" hung over water fountains, restrooms, restaurants, hotels, and bus stations.

While Jim Crow laws affected all people's private and public lives, they naturally had the most effect on those of African Americans. Huntsville's Black neighborhoods were poverty stricken, overcrowded, and often even lacked clean water.[6] Although notable prosegregationist administrators such as Governor George Wallace and Birmingham commissioner Eugene "Bull" Connor claimed that segregation was founded on a principle of "separate but equal," in reality the services provided were not equal. Alabama was one of the most racist states in the South and the country, along with Mississippi.

The civil rights movement reached its peak in the mid-1960s. During Pool's stay peaceful protests were violently repressed by state troopers, and assassinations of activists created a climate of fear. Being in Alabama, Pool witnessed up close the random violence that Black people were subjected to on a daily basis:

> In 1966 I was a guest lecturer in Alabama. Some few miles outside Huntsville, the space-research centre which is in some ways a federal enclave in southern territory, Alabama's toughest segregation area can be found. It still lives in anti-bellum [sic] days. Between the villages of Arab and Boas [Boaz] e.g. negroes cannot even buy petrol. Negroes who have to cross those forty-odd miles of hot road pray very hard that they will not have to stop before they're past the worst, especially if they carry white passengers like myself![7]

Rural Alabama was a dangerous place for African Americans. Pool recalled the story of a youngster called Charles Dorsey, "one of my students in those days," who was driving back home through the Boaz area when his car broke down. Knowing he was in a dangerous situation, he risked his life to walk to the office of a nearby gas station, where he called his parents. "His father advised him to go back to his car, sit inside and wait for him," Pool remembered, because it would take him thirty minutes to get there. "When he arrived he found his son crumpled up on the road, bleeding heavily from three bullet wounds in his head." He was the victim of a random "nigger shooting," a form of entertainment for white racists during the weekend. Although the teenager survived the incident, he lost his eyesight. His shooter was never convicted. "It may sound unbelievable," Pool wrote, "but such things happen more frequently than one dares to think, down there."[8]

"Bootsie"

Pool's affiliation with Alabama A&M College was the result of a chance encounter. A&M librarian Binford Conley happened to be in the audience when she delivered a guest lecture at Tuskegee College in 1960 and subsequently invited her to give a talk during A&M's Library Week. She wasn't able to immediately accept, but a few years later she finally made it to Huntsville; by that time, A&M had decided to turn the one-time guest lecture into a four-month lecturer-in-residence position. A&M at that time was a small college and in desperate need of staff members. The school offered Pool a salary that was far above that of her future colleagues, yet it was still a major step back, even for a freelancer like Pool.[9] Because she was in high demand, she was able to negotiate an arrangement whereby she only had to be on campus on Tuesdays, Wednesdays, and Thursdays, which left her the rest of the week to engage in other activities ("outside lectures, visits etc.").[10] Every other weekend she taught courses at Tuskegee on protest literature.[11] A&M was just the kind of challenge she was looking for, though. The HBCUs were perfect, as they offered her a way to help African Americans achieve long-term, structural positive changes in their lives.

Even a decade after the Supreme Court declared segregation in schools unconstitutional, more than 75 percent of all schools in the South were still segregated.[12] The integration of Black people on white schools was usually met with great protest, such as by Governor George Wallace himself, who opposed integration at the University of Alabama in Tuscaloosa in 1963 by simply standing in the doorway to the college. Pool regarded her own affiliation as "inverted integration," and as A&M was a public, state-run "land-lease" college, it fell under the jurisdiction of the state board of education, which made Pool "virtually gov. Wallace's employee!," she exclaimed mockingly.[13] The mere presence of whites at Black colleges could arouse fierce resistance among local white citizens. When Pool arrived at A&M, President Morrison said, "I hope you don't mind that we don't give much publicity to your presence here. . . . We are not so fond of journalists on our campus."[14]

Upon arrival Pool found that A&M students were practically almost cut off from society. There were shops, medical services, and a hairdresser on site, and so students almost had no need to go off campus. But if they wanted to leave at night, it was difficult because they were restricted by a curfew, and there also was no public transport to the city center.[15] A "ghetto in the desert" was how Pool aptly described A&M.[16] Poverty in the local Black community only exacerbated the students' isolation. One former A&M student, for example, who recalled that she rarely went to downtown Huntsville, was actually unaware that Black people were unable to eat at lunch counters. "My ruralness gave me no exposure to all these things," she said.[17] In a strictly segregated society, contacts across the color line were "rare and freighted with significance," as one historian put it.[18]

But one of the primary reasons Pool had wanted to come to A&M was so she could challenge the color line. Unlike the students, she frequently went outside the borders of the campus, occasionally together with Black colleagues. One colleague remembered that they went to a diner. The owner of the restaurant told them that while they were allowed to eat together the legislature could not force him to smile as he served them. Another time Pool went to a coffee bar together with two Black colleagues. Pool remembered how the two-hundred-pound owner came to their table, steaming with rage. "There is a law that forces me to serve your kind," he snapped at the two Black men, "but I don't think there's a law that tells me to feed *her*," nodding his head at Pool.[19] Although her initial intentions might have been to live Black, it was immediately evident that her white skin did not allow that. Yet such incidents did teach her to think Black and to see everyday life from a Black perspective.[20] As an outsider who learned about race consciousness, she believed she was more attuned to the nuances of race relations than African Americans themselves.

On another notable occasion, Pool and her colleague Audrey Vinson went to a segregated burger joint downtown. The interracial duo received cold stares. Pool, clearly irritated, wanted to leave the "filthy" establishment, but her Black colleague laughed at Pool. "I'm supposed to do that," Vinson called out at Pool. "You're worse than Bootsie." Bootsie was a well-known cartoon character from the *Pittsburgh Courier* (1930s to 1970s), who blamed everything that happened to him on being Black. "Once a bear ran him up a tree, and he called down to the bear, 'You're just doing this because I'm colored,'" Vinson recalled. "From that day I always called Rosey 'Bootsie.'"[21] On occasion as she was in the middle of delivering a lecture, Pool would burst out laughing because she could see Vinson in the audience forming the word "Bootsie" with her lips. Such teasing was a sign of acceptance but also hinted at Pool's white privilege: she was able to *choose* whether she "acted" Black or not. Southern Black folks, obviously, did not have that choice.

Rembrandt and Claude McKay

Throughout her time at A&M, Pool was aware not only of that privilege but also her own whiteness. It was immediately apparent to her how different this school was from the other twenty-two HBCUs she had visited a few years before during her tour as a Fulbright and UNCF scholar. A&M College was state run and had a far smaller budget than the prestigious, private UNCF colleges. Many talked about the school as a "bricklayers college."[22] Just how financially underdeveloped the school was was evident in the fact that neither the school nor the students were able to afford textbooks. Luckily, Pool had designed her own course manuals during her appointments at Livingstone College in North Carolina (1962–63) and Tougaloo College in Mississippi (1963), which now came to serve as textbooks at A&M.

According to Pool, even A&M college president Richard D. Morrison condescendingly described his students as "boys and girls" who came from "the *rimboe*," meaning "jungle."[23] Such remarks infuriated Pool. African Americans had for centuries gone through a "thorough process of brainwashing," she believed.[24] "In several centuries of unrelenting efforts," she wrote, "white man succeeded in implanting a fateful sense of inferiority in black man."[25] Pool, who was well intentioned but nevertheless paternalistic, saw the students as "a fine bunch of young ones" who were above all victims of their education and of American society at large. So at A&M, she became determined to show this college president and others the potential of these students.[26]

Pool regarded Black literature and Black history as means of rehumanizing African Americans living under Jim Crow. One of her handouts that covered both African and Black American literature and history started off with a classic Eurocentric view of history, noting that "our modern world began in Athens" but also pointing out that ancient Egypt and

China had been "two powerful streams of literary influence" on Western culture as well.²⁷ She presented a surprisingly global perspective on Western history, especially for that day and age. In her handouts she also juxtaposed ancient Greek poets with those of the Harlem Renaissance. She set important figures in Western thought side by side with Black writers, intellectuals, and leaders. She not only discussed Rembrandt, for example, but also Claude McKay; she mentioned Karl Marx but also Frederick Douglass; she spoke about Michelangelo and Harriet Tubman. During her exams students were asked to name "who painted the Mona Lisa" as well as to "mention the title of ONE poem by the following authors: Countee Cullen, Langston Hughes, James Weldon Johnson."²⁸ Countering dominant racism and whitewashed Western history, her classes were essentially subversive acts of education. Pool showed that works by Black writers surely matched European classics, presenting a Black past to these students that they could be proud of. This was revolutionary in a time when Black history was rarely seen as a legitimate topic.²⁹

After four months, she flew back to London, only to return to A&M College one year later, in September 1966, this time for two semesters. Her approach remained largely the same, but now she opted for even looser, liberal-arts-type classes, offering the students everything from "simple reading ability to music, visual arts, poetry and whatnot," she said, while also organizing a "workshop" with no fixed teaching hours during which she made books and records available to students.³⁰ She practiced a student-centered approach, a method that was unquestionably based on a tradition of European reform education. She relied heavily on student input, allowing them to find their "OWN voice."³¹ Pool also hoped to find budding authors who spoke with their own voice, possibly for a new poetry anthology.

One A&M student who made a particular impression was the twenty-year-old Catherine Leslie. Raised in a family of cotton laborers, she had picked cotton herself to make money for her family. The expectations were high when she went to college as a first-generation student. Although she did not participate in Pool's classes, her material was passed on to Pool just before her final departure. Pool immediately recognized an "unusual writing talent" and called her "one of the most talented" of her generation. She especially admired her honesty. "We've had plenty of 'mocking bird poets' in the past," Pool wrote to her, adding, "I rather hear an honest seagull screech or the tweet tweet of a sparrow than the best bird imitator in vaudeville do a nightingale! But you, you are a nightingale all by yourself. Listen to your own voice and perfect it as you hear it."³² She reprinted one of Leslie's poems called "Soliloqui" in her 1968 book *Lachen om niet te huilen*:

> Who are you?
> I am a black boy
> Mister, are you colorblind?
> I MEAN WHAT'S YOUR NAME?
> Why do you want to know my name, Mister?
> You look white to me.[33]

Pool later wrote that she could "fully identify" with the boy in Leslie's poem: "If one of the guards of the camp where I was a prisoner in 1943 had asked me 'What is your name?' I would not have asked him: 'Are you colour blind?' but rather 'Don't you see I am wearing a star?'"[34]

Leslie deeply appreciated Pool's encouragement and called her an inspiration. Pool introduced Leslie's work to Langston Hughes and wrote her letters of recommendation when she applied for graduate school. Although a pregnancy limited her career, she was very touched by Pool's personal interest. "Dr. Pool was also concerned about me as an individual," she said.[35] Such contacts were invaluable and meaningful to many students in the context of the civil rights movement and an environment in which race relations were tense.

Segregation and Isolation

Interacting with African American students was Pool's top priority. In an attempt to be as close to Black America as possible she also took a room in the women's dorm on campus, which was quite unusual for staff members to do, but it worked out very well. Vinson remembered that her spontaneity and gregariousness made her "known campus-wide in a very short time."[36] Pool wrote proudly to a friend that both her private room and her office became "clubrooms" where students would meet.[37] One of her fondest memories was of serving Dutch snacks to a group of female students. The fact that these students let this foreign woman enter their private lives shows how by emphasizing her own otherness Pool was able to carry out what she called "inverted integration."[38] "[The] students... accept me," she proudly concluded.[39]

Other staff members might have thought that it was not appropriate to engage with students in this way, but not Pool. She was able to penetrate the student population and have discussions with students that staff members typically were not able to have, owing to the Deep South, which frightened students and staff members alike. To the outside world, A&M

College was a conservative college that had to take orders from Governor Wallace. Those with dissident voices were marked as "troublemakers," and more than once they were silenced by being fired, often under political pressure.[40] It was also generally believed that racial segregation and poor education had made many students at southern Black colleges apathetic and passive.[41] The history of Huntsville's civil rights movement has barely been explored, and the few sources that exist rarely mention A&M College.[42] Yet Pool received pamphlets from student activists in which they demanded that their education accommodations be improved. These were never meant to be given to teachers: "Do not show this to anyone," the pamphlet said. "Do not talk to anyone about it except students."[43] Pool likely was given these pamphlets because she was an intermediary on campus; she hovered somewhere between being a teacher and a student herself and was regarded as neither Black nor white.

Pool's major achievement at A&M was the two Black writers' conferences she organized, which she extensively documented in her scrapbooks. The April 1965 conference, "The Negro Writer in Our Time," featured Mari Evans, Hoyt Fuller, Owen Dodson, John O. Killens, and Robert Hayden. At the second conference, which was held in December 1966, Samuel Allen (aka Paul Vesey), Mari Evans, Dudley Randall, and Margaret Burroughs came to speak, and Margaret Danner made a guest appearance (figure 22). It was rare that so many distinguished artists gathered in the South, let alone at A&M College. Attesting to her involvement with the college, Pool was depicted in a 1967 mural at the school.

"Nazi Scientists" in Alabama

Although Huntsville remained largely segregated, certain parts of the city had symbolically desegregated in an effort to satisfy the Black community and outside journalists alike. Pool was surprised to find that most warehouses, dime stores, and hotels had quietly been desegregated in the years before. "White and brown can eat together at one table. Nowhere else in Alabama," she wrote. "Only here in Huntsville, because ... you can never know, those negroes could perhaps be connected to the space program."[44] The village of Normal, to the north of Huntsville, was a Black enclave. It was part of "the geography of Huntsville, the rocket city," Pool wrote, yet it remained a separate municipality.[45] Pool believed that this separation was the result of the fact that "the many federal officers who populate[d] Huntsville's space research centre" consciously wanted to keep "black folk off the electoral roll" in Huntsville.[46]

Figure 22. Second Writer's Conference, Alabama A&M College, December 1966. From left to right, standing: A&M president Richard D. Morrison, Samuel Allen (aka Paul Vesey), Mari Evans, and Dudley Randall. Seated: Margaret Burroughs, Pool, and Margaret Danner.
SOURCE: F010641, Jewish Museum, Amsterdam.

NASA had helped this city on the wane grow miraculously, and this growth was largely attributed to Wernher von Braun. He had become a national celebrity in the mid-1950s when he made three educational films about space engineering with Disney. Although his Nazi past was questioned, in the minds of white citizens the rebirth of the city owed to the German rocket scientists: they lovingly and ironically called them the "saviors" of Huntsville.[47] Von Braun and his team were welcomed with open arms, and most whites were eager to forgive von Braun for his Nazi past—and his SS membership—by claiming he was a "good German" and, more importantly, "our German."[48] When in 1970 von Braun left to work at NASA's headquarters in another city, Huntsville honored him by celebrating "Wernher von Braun Day."

Across the color line von Braun and his team were perceived quite differently or not at all. Some African Americans did not even know the German scientists were there because of the separate worlds that segregation created.[49] Others, including students at A&M College, were vocally critical of how von Braun had pushed to found the white University of Alabama in Huntsville in 1961 rather than exploring the options of opening an aerospace engineering department at the already existing Black A&M College. "It was nothing out of the ordinary for him to . . . advocate the opening of a Jim Crow school," one former A&M student remarked.[50] Still, such remarks were mostly made in hindsight. White and Black people had thoroughly different experiences owing to segregation and also very different views about the past.[51]

We might expect Pool, who prided herself on "acting Black" and was never afraid to criticize segregation, to have made similar remarks. She easily expressed her disgust of "whites only" signs, calling them a form of "insanity" in front of American journalists.[52] Yet there is not a shred of evidence that Pool ever said anything about von Braun, either in her public writings or in her private letters. Perhaps this was because while Pool was there, in the spring of 1965, von Braun quite unexpectedly declared that segregation was a threat to Alabama's economic and industrial growth.[53] Although this peace offering might have given her an opportunity to write about him, she did not take it, possibly because he did not fit in her perfect black-and-white stories of good against evil. Yet in a context of the Cold War, her silence also might have been a way to avoid being confronted with difficult questions about her own past.

Pool did, however, heavily criticize people within the African American community. Whether this was because she operated within that milieu and therefore felt more comfortable expressing her views in it or because she needed an outlet for venting frustrations is unclear, but her anger toward, for instance, A&M president Richard D. Morrison seemed disproportionate. She described his administration as the "very image of Black Bourgeoisie and the worst conformists on earth."[54] His willful cooperation with the prosegregationist governor George Wallace—who in his efforts to keep the races separate ironically greatly contributed to the financial growth of Black colleges—as well as his friendly contacts with Wernher von Braun were signs that he was one of A&M's notorious "self-hating black teachers."[55] Pool was sad to see how many activists were "forced to restrain their militancy under the pressure of school administrators who are the employees of racist state governors," obviously referring to public HBCU presidents like Morrison.[56] She even called him a "dictator" after he required male staff members with beards to shave them off owing to the connection between beards and Black Power.[57] Pool thus shifted her focus from wrongs committed by whites to the wrongs of what she regarded as collaborating Black people. As the South often reminded her of Nazi Germany, she no doubt saw Morrison as collaborating in a similar way that she herself had done during the late war when she worked for the Jewish Council in Amsterdam. Collaboration and accommodation would not change the minds of racists, she believed; rather, only opposition would.

Silences and Gaps

The way Nazi scientists were embraced in Alabama indicated how painfully little Americans knew or wanted to know about the recent genocide in Europe and also showed how similar southern prosegregationists were to antisemites in Nazi Germany. So, what did Pool think about these scientists and why did she not mention them? In his seminal book *Multidirectional Memory*, Michael Rothberg argues that debates on the Holocaust have made possible the articulation of other histories of victimization, often at unexpected moments.[58] But how can and should historians deal with multidirectional *silences*? Individuals may keep silent about things because they are painful, embarrassing, or, of course, because they are self-evident or simply irrelevant to them. Moreover, silence can also be a sign of trauma.[59] Recently, scholars have suggested that silence can also be a form of resistance or a sign of subjugation.[60] In addition, that which remains unsaid can be what defines us most *because* it is unbearable or unsayable.[61] Silence can be a coping mechanism. There are, in other words, many possible explanations for Pool's silence.

Perhaps it was simply too painful for Pool to address this issue, as her parents, brother, and sister-in-law had been murdered in Nazi extermination camps. Perhaps she consciously wanted to focus her attention on marginalized people, choosing a positive approach to dealing with her past. Pool's impact on Alabama A&M College is clearly traceable in the memories of people she met and in material objects, such as that peculiar mural. Many found her stubbornness inspirational. Pool "could smell discrimination miles away," her colleague Vinson recalled, who said that she "intended to brook nothing that resembled racism."[62] At the height of her career and influence and at the height of the civil rights movement, Pool chose to go to a college that was not particularly noteworthy or prestigious. She consistently supported the underdog and went wherever her help was needed most. At A&M she organized conferences and encouraged young people to make the most of their lives. But her life was about to change. The mural with her depiction was demolished only a few years later, a sort of foreshadowing of the demise of her own career.

CHAPTER 10

Befriending Langston Hughes, 1945–1967

Pool had many famous and powerful acquaintances, including the scholar W. E. B. Du Bois, the singer Nina Simone, the opera singer Paul Robeson, and the poet and playwright Owen Dodson. And then there were many celebrities that she occasionally saw, such as the Dutch writer Annie M. G. Schmidt, lyricist Ira Gershwin, and the composer Benjamin Britten. She had many "instrumental friendships" that she relied on to achieve her own goals.[1] Strategic alliances, especially with powerful men, were crucial for women to access the public sphere, and Pool understood this.[2]

However, although these friendships might seem merely opportunistic, especially given that Pool often liked to brag to others about her famous "friends" and even included their names on her resumé, there was more to them than that. Interracial friendships were also a way for her to put her humanistic ideals into practice, and so Pool also no doubt formed "friendships out of conviction" to make the world a better place.[3] On a more personal level, Pool also looked for new friends, a new family, simply because many of her old friends and family members had been killed during the war. The Black freedom struggle enabled her to start all over. The connections she made were often very personal, and as time passed by she even came to see many of these new friends as surrogate family members.[4]

This family bond was particularly strong with Langston Hughes, who emotionally became a substitute for her brother, Jopie. Langston and Jopie shared the same birthday: February 1. Pool had never felt a deep connection with her brother, as he did not have her intellectual capacity nor her political zest. Hughes filled the void of Pool's longing for sibling love. Not only did Hughes acknowledge her suffering but each year he

Figure 23. The Anglophone Grand Jury at the festival in Dakar, April 1966. From left to right: dancer-anthropologist Katherine Dunham (USA), chairman Langston Hughes (USA), Pool (England), author and college president Davidson Nicol (Sierra Leone) holding Christopher Okigbo's book *Limits*, and on the far right Clifford Simmons (England).

SOURCE: F010642, Jewish Historical Museum, Amsterdam.

sent a message to Pool to commemorate her brother.[5] Perhaps that is why Pool called him the "gentlest, kindest, most considerate, thoughtful friend I ever had."[6]

Hughes was an African American poet, playwright, novelist, and activist. Perhaps best known for poems like "The Negro Speaks of Rivers" (1921) and "I, Too, Sing America" (1926), the handsome and likeable man became a spokesperson for Black America. Early in his life he was a "fellow traveler," intrigued by the promise and idealism of communism as an alternative to American segregationism. He explored the world as a sailor, doing all types of jobs, including working in a Paris nightclub and traveling the Soviet Union with a group of African American filmmakers.[7] In 1937 he set off to war-torn Spain, where he worked as a correspondent for several newspapers, including the *Baltimore Afro-American*. He immediately understood the problem with fascism. "Negroes do not have to be told what fascism is in action," he said at a writer's conference in Paris. "We know. Its theories of Nordic supremacy and economic suppression have long been realities to us."[8]

In the Netherlands his work was translated by the Jewish socialist writer Manuel van Loggem, whom he had met in Paris, and also by the socialist writer Jef Last, who was a volunteer in the International Brigades during the Spanish Civil War.[9] Last was also a friend of Pool's, and likely she was familiar with Last's translations of Hughes's work that were published in leftist journals such as *Links richten* (Aim left), but it would be another two decades before Pool actually got to know Hughes himself. Although by the 1960s she would brag about their "forty years" of friendship, her first letter to him was dated 1945 and showed no signs of familiarity whatsoever.[10] On the contrary, Pool introduced herself, suggesting they did not yet know each other. Hughes was touched by her story of being "one of the millions that were put into concentration camps by the Germans,"[11] and he started sending materials and books as well as names and addresses of other poets, including those of Gwendolyn Brooks, Ralph Ellison, Jessie Fauset, Chester Himes, Melvin Tolson, Julian Bond, Audre Lorde, and Derek Walcott.

Hughes became Pool's gateway to Black America. "Les amis de mes amis sont mes amis" ("friends of my friends are my friends"), she wrote to him.[12] Having Langston Hughes as a pen pal was a boon. She started using his name when she met new people with a convincing "easy assurance and familiarity" that opened many doors.[13] The over 250 letters, postcards, clippings, and notes they exchanged over the course of twenty-two years certainly gave Pool the impression that he valued their relationship as much as she did, yet in reality this was only a fraction of his total correspondence: in his archives he left behind over 250 boxes (121 linear feet) of letters. Despite how many letters a day he must have written, he had a talent for making people feel special. "He was the kind of man," one biographer notes, "who could even nurture an enduring friendship through the mails with someone he never saw."[14] And even more importantly, he remained conscious of his own celebrity status, which he exploited to enable others to fulfill their dreams as well.

The first phase of their friendship, from 1945 to 1959, was perhaps more of a pen pal correspondence than true relationship. Pool made an effort to keep the correspondence going, eagerly trying to get closer to this famous poet, while Hughes consistently addressed her as "Dear Miss Pool." Their relationship deepened in 1952 when Pool introduced him to the Guyanese poet Jan Carew, an anticolonialist activist and novelist from British Guiana. Around this time, Pool also mentioned that she had gotten to know Hughes's old Harlem friend Hermie Dumont Huiswoud, who by then was living in Amsterdam. It was likely no coincidence that she described her as "the wife of one of my very best Surinam friends," not mentioning the name of her husband Otto Huiswoud, the Suriname activist and Communist Party USA cofounder who was followed by various secret services.[15] Hughes certainly knew Huiswoud. They had even traveled the Soviet Union together in the 1920s, where they had been allowed to visit Vladimir Lenin on his deathbed.[16] Presumably, Hughes appreciated this old left type of confidentiality.

With the advance of the Cold War, Hughes had quietly disassociated himself from left-wing politics, but his past as a "fellow traveler" continued to haunt him, especially during the red scare of the 1950s. He was even questioned by a McCarthy committee in 1953. "You'll be hearing from me soon, especially about my TV show with McCarthy," he wrote to Pool in amusement in 1953.[17] But soon Hughes was no longer "laughing to keep from crying" (to use one of his famous quotes), as the hearing affected him more than he initially had anticipated, both personally and professionally. The 1953 McCarthy trial was a turning point: in future publications he removed most of his old "red" work. He also stopped publicly discussing his controversial past.[18] He also never wrote about the hearing to Pool, and she was wise never to ask him about it.

A breakthrough in their friendship came in 1959, when Pool visited the United States, at which time Hughes was introduced to what was perhaps Pool's greatest quality: her "talent for friendship."[19] His career had gotten rusty in recent years. Young Black writers like Richard Wright and James

Baldwin made Hughes, who was by then over fifty, look outdated.[20] Perhaps this is why the usually cool Hughes was unable to resist Pool's charm and opened up to her, offering her insight into his private life. He seemed to take particular pleasure in name-dropping. "Wole Soyinka was just here," he wrote. "Senghor, too—with whom I had luncheon at the White House (with our President, too)" (Léopold Senghor was president of Senegal at the time).[21] "Rosey," another postcard said, this time from Hollywood, "Loved hearing from you. I'm out with Harry Belafonte doing a TV script for his autumn show. Working by the swimming pool. Hello to Isa."[22] Pool's influence expanded significantly as a result of her relationship with Hughes, who consciously lent a hand to help a friend to advance her career as well.

Lagos, Nigeria

While similarities among individuals such as age, education, gender, religion, and social context can foster friendships, there is no blueprint for them, although most are characterized by trust, openness, honesty, acceptance, reciprocity, solidarity, and loyalty.[23] Hughes and Pool likely immediately clicked owing to their shared interest in Africa, a continent that was freeing itself from colonialism at this time.[24] Pool had just finished a series of articles on what she called the "African Renaissance," discussing modern art and writing from Nigeria, Kenya, and other places. This interest was most certainly politically motivated. As she explained in one of those articles, although she was not a politician, she knew that "the ignorance about the arts of Africa and the political position of that continent" were "closely connected."[25] This brought her surprisingly close to Hughes's position at a propitious moment, as he was just working on an anthology called *African Treasury* and was on the brink of a series of momentous trips to Africa.

Hughes was also an honorary member of the American Society of African Culture, an organization of African American writers, artists, and scholars founded in 1957 as a subdivision of the French Société Africaine de Culture. This organization embraced the ideals of negritude and pan-Africanism and believed that people from the Black diaspora, whether they lived in Africa, the Caribbean, or the Americas, shared a "natural bond." The year 1960—also known as the "Year of Africa"—was a watershed in the decolonization of Africa, and the continent also became a source of inspiration to activists of the American civil rights movement.[26] As a result, a public debate arose in the United States regarding the relationship between African Americans and Africans, and the American Society of African Culture organizers sadly concluded that Black Americans and Africans were quite alienated from each other. They decided to organize a massive event in Lagos, Nigeria, to bring Africans and Black Americans closer together.[27]

The organization started looking for celebrities and experts to participate in the event. Hughes suggested Pool as "really a stimulating personality" who ought to be included in it.[28] And so Pool went on a fully paid trip across Nigeria for nine days in December 1961. In press releases her photo appeared next to those of Nina Simone, Odetta, Randy Weston, Michael Olatunji, Lionel Hampton, and of course Langston Hughes.[29] Needless to say, Pool was an outsider among these "leading personalities" of Black America. Although she was "thrilled" about taking her first visit to Africa, she felt rather uncomfortable being one of the few white people of the delegation. "I feel all at once: deeply grateful, honoured, unworthy, humble and . . . very white," she noted in a letter to Hughes before the trip.[30] This feeling only intensified once she was there. The group went to receptions, went on sightseeing tours, had meetings with Nigerian officials, and—the grand finale—performed at a massive festival in front of five thousand people. Her initial excitement slowly gave way to deep discomfort: "Never before had I felt so pale, so colourless as during those first days of that humid-hot December in Nigeria. My voice appeared lifeless to me, my laughter unreal and thin, my face ridiculously drained of colour. I felt caught in a vacuum."[31]

Sitting in front of her typewriter, Pool could easily say that she belonged "more to the American Negro community than to teadrinking England."[32] But here, with an almost all-Black group in a Black country, she felt painfully out of place, a feeling that she had been trying to escape since childhood. "Suddenly I knew how coloured people must feel when pale faces look at them," she wrote.[33] And she experienced something she had never experienced before: stage fright. "Nothing could relieve it," she later recalled. "Not Langston Hughes's laughter, not Randy Weston's soothing piano, not the helpfulness and cordiality of every single one in our group, not the generous hospitality, the warm welcome of our african hosts."[34]

Her feeling of estrangement was not just subjective. At a festival centered around Blackness, it only seemed logical that white people should be serving, not shining. In photographs, the American Society of African Culture consistently put the biggest stars up front. Langston Hughes was often the center of attention, along with the newly appointed Nigerian governor general Nnamdi Azikiwe: he and Hughes had been classmates at Lincoln University back in the 1920s and therefore were the epitome of pan-African brotherhood.[35] The less prominent members of the group were featured further in the back. In one photograph, Pool's face is half visible on the far right of the frame; she is more behind than with the group. She was far removed from the center of power, an outsider almost, because of her skin color but also because of her gender. Pool had no place in this fraternity.

Yet she still had a voice when she read her paper at a panel on drama and literature two days later. There she told her own life story, presenting herself as an atypical white person. "During World War II, I was a member of the Dutch Underground Resistance against Fascism and eventually a prisoner of the Nazis," she said, once again oddly failing to mention her Jewish background. She also chose not to mention the Netherlands' colonial past. Instead, she referenced a much more distant past: "Believe me," she said, "the freedom struggle of Holland against Spain, a struggle that took place three hundred years ago, inspired us to fight oppression in the years 1940–1945."[36] She likely hoped to give a boost to anticolonial activists by pointing out what the Dutch underground had accomplished, but by mentioning Spain she was possibly also hinting at the struggles of the far left during the Spanish Civil War in the late 1930s as well, especially as her dear friend Langston Hughes sat in the crowd.

As friendships have the potential to level hierarchies and enable outsiders to blend in, Pool tried to get as close to Hughes as possible in an attempt to overcome the problem that she was not a person that mattered.[37] It certainly seemed to work because here she made some new powerful friends, including Horace Mann Bond, dean of Atlanta University, and the singer Nina Simone. Pool remembered how one morning Simone burst into her hotel room. "Rosey," she shouted, "come out to the lobby. They've put up these presspictures of yesterday's party. You look one hell of a lot of funny!" Pool rushed downstairs to see them and saw her white face, heavily overexposed on film. Pool exclaimed that she looked "like a spook," by which she meant a ghost, and everyone burst out in laughter, since this was also a derogative term for African Americans. With the laughter she finally felt welcomed and accepted. She was forever grateful to Simone "for showing me that I was not an intruder but just a friend who looked one hell of a lot of funny."[38] Pool used this encounter in her later writings to exemplify not only the peculiarities of transracial belongings but also the unconditional acceptance she encountered in Black circles, although the experience was also melancholy because it underscored her perennial fear of being left out. And as often in her stories, the celebrity names made it all sound very glamorous.

Between the A List and the Blacklist

After her first trip to Africa, Pool and Hughes continued their whirlwind correspondence. Hughes was especially fond of Pool's partner, Isa Isenburg, the stoic and usually reserved figure in the background. When Pool was working in Alabama in the mid-1960s, Hughes would occasionally call her to see how she was doing so that he could then send a note to Isenburg to let her know that she was managing. "That sort of kindness is so rare among human beings," Pool remarked.[39] Pool and Isenburg were in a same-sex relationship, but to outsiders Pool often said that she lived with her "best friend."[40] Hughes, for his part, lingered somewhere between being asexual and homosexual, remaining forever ambiguous and elusive about his sexuality.[41] Pool, however, assumed that Hughes was homosexual. In 1962 she translated his work for *Vriendschap* (Friendship), a journal published by a Dutch organization for gays and lesbians. She did not ask him for permission; she wrote to him to say that she had told the editor, Benno Premsela, that she "could not get hold of you because you were wandering about Africa." Although she told Hughes in excitement that "homo-sexuality . . . is not a criminal offense in Holland!," he responded by simply ignoring what she said.[42] Their friendship seemed to be partly based on sweeping secrets under the proverbial carpet and never mentioning painful moments again. One notable exception was when Hughes was in Europe in 1965, during which time he briefly visited Holland. He wrote exultantly to Pool: "I *absolutely adored* Amsterdam. I could live there." He added ambiguously that "the acceptance of one's private life is just fabulous: I hated to leave."[43]

This covert admittance of his sexual orientation is an example of what James Smethurst refers to as the "small, unveiling gestures" that Hughes's letters make, offering "a sort of rhetorical and ideological striptease." Like most radicals at this time, he generally assumed that his correspondence was read by intelligence agencies, at least occasionally, and so he used muted language to affirm his "political identity while maintaining plausible deniability."[44] The Cold War was a minefield for people with an old left past, and thus it should not come as a surprise that the correspondence between Pool and Hughes leaves considerable room for interpretation. She did not write, for example, that after the festival in Lagos she traveled on to Ghana to meet several African American radicals living in exile, including W. E. B. Du Bois and his wife, Shirley Graham, as well as the writer Julian Mayfield. All of these luminary figures were closely followed by the FBI.[45]

The caution Pool demonstrated suggests that she was far more left on the political spectrum than her other materials suggest. Her correspondence is likely therefore not the best way to assess her friendship with Hughes, as McCarthyism limited what they could say. "In his letters I do not find any speeches or . . . references to world events," Pool proudly wrote. "Only warmth and human contact."[46] Pool also remembered when she and Hughes met at an international festival in Spoleto, Italy, in July 1962. While they were having dinner a white American man loudly started to yell at Hughes about how he was a "communist" and an "atheist."[47] Despite these confrontations, face-to-face meetings were still far less dangerous than the writing of letters, and when they met at different international festivals, they spoke more openly.

Dakar, Senegal

After Lagos, Pool and Hughes were closer than ever, and he even visited her a couple of times. On a trip in 1964 to London he informed Pool about another gigantic festival that would take place in Senegal. The "First World Festival of Negro Arts," as the 1966 event became known, promised to be the event of a lifetime. According to Pool, Hughes told her that she was "the world's authority on American Negro Poetry" and that she should therefore be there. "See that you get there," he said.[48] How was irrelevant. "Maybe Radio Haversum [sic] in Holland," he suggested.[49] After a long struggle, Pool was only able to become a member of the British preselection jury. She was about to give up trying to go until one week before the festival an invitation arrived out of the blue from the British committee to join the festival as a member of Dakar's grand jury, no less. Undoubtedly, this was due to the influence of the head of that same grand jury, Hughes himself.

Dakar was flooded with more than twenty-five hundred artists and twenty thousand visitors from forty-five countries. The festival attracted visitors as diverse as the Nigerian playwright and writer Wole Soyinka, the African American dancer Alvin Ailey, and the Martinican writer Aimé Césaire. It presented a challenge to all the senses. Pool saw a dance group from Mali and was impressed by the Benin treasures that had been sent from museums all over the world. She was also invited for a meeting at the house of American ambassador Mercer Cook, where Duke Ellington gave a private performance and posh African officials, waiters, and taxi drivers all danced together.[50] If there was such a thing as the ultimate meeting place of the Black Atlantic, it was Dakar in 1966.

Although Pool was now officially part of the establishment owing to her position on the grand jury, she was not at all pleased with it. She actually felt clobbered by all the formalities and rules. "I am not at all an 'organization' lover," she confided to a friend. "I believe in priorities and the waving of inessential rules in favour of more important points."[51] For most of her time in Dakar she was "stuck," compelled to sit and listen to presentations, attend jury meetings, and participate in discussions with other committee members. "And outside the sun shines," she noted. She briefly considered "skipping class" to look at the "stunningly beautiful" people on the street, perhaps betraying a hint of what Edward Said calls orientalism.[52]

Pool felt that a desire to waive "inessential rules" was an inherently "feminine" quality that was clearly not fully appreciated at this event.[53] Idealism notwithstanding, Black Atlantic networks often mirrored white power structures: they were male dominated and centered around ideals of fraternity and brotherhood, which often led to sexist hierarchies and masculinist rhetoric.[54] Pool was not immune to sexism and no doubt felt she had to bend to the power hierarchy. Yet she was also transfixed on important men who attended the event. In a Dutch article she described how she met African drummer Philip Gbeho and how she was hugged in the middle of the Place de l'Indépendance by Nigerian artists Ben Enwonwu and Akinola Lasekan. "Look, there is Jan-Heinz Jahn, the German Africanist and [Paul] Lebeer from Paris (of the journal *Afrique*)," she bragged, "and there comes Duke Ellington with the American ambassador Mercer Cook."[55]

Despite these heartwarming encounters, she remained practically invisible to these important men. President Senghor addressed her as "monsieur" in his letters, even after the festival.[56] Even more disappointing was that she could not rely too much on Hughes this time. He was also consumed by all-male networks. Reportedly he spent many nights on a Russian cruise ship that was used as a floating hotel, mostly drinking vodka with the Russian poet Yevgeny Yevtushenko. Pool did not have access to that man's world.

Here, her white skin was a serious obstacle, much more than it had been in Lagos. Pool tried to address her feelings of alienation by emphasizing that she firmly believed in negritude, which was a central theme of the festival. Both a concept and a movement, negritude embraced the cultural and artistic richness of African society and Black pride, highlighting the ways African heritage had been degraded through the slave trade and subsequently by colonialism.[57] Pool interpreted the concept as the "unconditional acceptance of one's own individual self" and concluded that "I, in my *blanchitude* can fully accept my Negritude."[58]

Unlike in Lagos, Pool was not assigned a lecture to deliver in Dakar, which was probably for the best. White was increasingly seen as the color of the oppressor and the colonizer, and the presence of whites at the festival was openly criticized.[59] Antiwhite sentiment had not increased; rather, it was just now more openly voiced by Black activists, most notably James Baldwin, Harry Belafonte, Ralph Ellison, Ossie Davis, and Sidney Poitier, all of whom boycotted the festival because they thought negritude was hopelessly outdated. They also lambasted Senghor's uncritical stance toward the West. Pool's status as a Jewish woman made her place within these discussions on whiteness ambiguous. She was white, but she believed that she did not "act white."[60] In the second half of the sixties, however, she was increasingly confronted with the Black/white dichotomy that dominated U.S. society and later also global Black communities, and ultimately her place was determined by it. Although Baldwin acknowledged that Jews indeed had suffered abroad, he also claimed that in the United States it was only relevant that Jews were white.[61] Whiteness was no longer a source of authority, a status Pool had relied on without fully realizing it.

One notable writer who was excluded from Dakar was Amiri Baraka, who was still using the name LeRoi Jones at the time. Pool had included his work in her poetry anthologies a few years before, but shortly after that he had embraced Black nationalism and had written a play ironically called *The Dutchman* (1964), which called for the destruction of the white Western aesthetic and "THE DESTRUCTION OF AMERICA."[62] Hughes, a moderate, especially after his 1953 trial, firmly disassociated himself from Baraka in Dakar by saying that his own generation of writers "never dreamed of revealing the Negro people to themselves in terms of mother-fuckers."[63] In his defense, however, Hughes had always been a fierce supporter of a Black consciousness. At a time when dreams of interracial harmony were being replaced by Black pride, Hughes was suddenly surprisingly contemporary: "The very fact that all the major publishers of African writers are in Paris or London or New York, and the ultimate editors are white, is not unlike a similar problem that has long faced American Negro writers. Until the recent formation of the Johnson Publishing Company in Chicago, all the major publishers in the United States where

Negro writers might get published were white. All the major literary magazines are white."[64]

By mentioning London, he was possibly hinting at his friend Pool sitting in the crowd. After all, she was one of those white editors he mentioned who published with white publishers. Pool was part of the problem of white editors and publishers that were forcing Black writers to also write "white."

Meanwhile, Pool shifted her attention from trying to fit in to charting her own course. She made it her mission to give the literary prize to the relatively unknown poet Robert Hayden, a fifty-three-year-old professor whom she had met at Fisk University in 1960.[65] She convinced the rest of the grand jury that Hayden deserved the prize for his book *A Ballad of Remembrance* (published by Pool's former protégé Paul Breman in 1962, one of those white publishers from London). In the jury report, Pool justified her choice in her own peculiar way: "Hayden sees the suffering of the men and women who died at Dachau and Buchenwald for their specific *Négritude*," she wrote.[66] This could not fully hide that giving the award to the clearly moderate Hayden was at the expense of relatively young and radical writers, such as Christopher Okigbo and the future Nobel Laureate Derek Walcott. The 1966 Dakar festival was an important barometer of shifting power relations, both globally as well as in Black Atlantic networks. But despite her success in persuading the committee to award Hayden the prize, the winds were not blowing in Pool's favor.

The Curtain Falls

In hindsight, Dakar was the beginning of the end of Pool's career and her influence in transnational networks. A cultural revolution was now sweeping the United States, and Pool was suddenly out of touch with the times. "I am enjoying reading your anthology," Jean Blackwell Hutson, curator of the prestigious Schomburg Center in New York, wrote to her in 1965, regarding her 1962 *Beyond the Blues*, "but I am somewhat distracted by a review copy of the *Autobiography of Malcolm X*."[67] It was symbolic for the years to come. Most regard 1968 as the symbolic end of the sixties: hope, promise, and Martin Luther King's "dream." His dream was shattered that year, only to be replaced by hostility, resentment, and further polarization.[68] This turning point came particularly early for Pool, when Langston Hughes unexpectedly died in May 1967, at the age of sixty-five. Pool was heartbroken when she heard the news. Never again would she receive letters or postcards from him. It created "a big gap" in her life.[69]

Both Hughes's death as well as 1968 kickstarted the deterioration of Pool's network. Many of her transnational friendships did not survive this cultural revolution. "Old friendships have lost their lustre," Pool wrote. "Reservedness and careful wording crop up in letters from friends of decades."[70] She went on to say that "people whom I thought were my real friends, don't reply to letters; turn their backs on me."[71] Loyal writers, such as Julia Fields and Samuel Allen, suddenly stopped sending letters to her. Pool now had to learn about their publications via *Negro Digest*, a magazine that she found "more and more unreadable" with each passing month.[72]

This exclusion not only affected her personally but also professionally. Poet after poet, including Waring Cuney, Betty Lattimer-McKinney, Jessie Collins, and Ted Joans, sent her abrupt notes stating that they no longer wanted to be included in her anthologies. For a freelancer, this disintegrating network was disastrous, for it had been her social capital. She was rapidly estranged from her American contacts now that her "best friend" and "substitute brother" was gone: "Since Langston was called away from this world, I feel much further away from the U.S.," she confided in Margaret Danner, one of those few friends that kept writing.[73] Out of sight across the Atlantic Ocean, Pool became more and more isolated. What was worse was that she merely became what others thought she was: white. But perhaps even more painful was that her newly acquired family abruptly disappeared from her life, bringing back the desolate times of the late war.

Dakar should have been the highlight of Pool's life. Instead, it set her off on the road to oblivion. While the Black Atlantic was celebrating independence, Pool maintained an anticolonial focus, failing to make the transition to a postcolonial rhetoric. By 1971 little remained of Rosey Pool's life work and transatlantic Black Atlantic networks. For the last three years of her life, she largely withdrew from the public sphere. Her income had run dry, and she was in and out of the hospital. Still, she refused to be victimized and convinced friends she was fine, while in reality she was struggling with leukemia.

Yet even from her hospital bed she continued to work, although she could now only type with two fingers of each hand, as the rest of her fingers had gone numb. Her partner, Isa, was a great support to her in her new project, a book on Chester Himes. Pool had a warm correspondence with this Harlem Renaissance detective author, who by then had moved to Spain. Perhaps it was his recent stroke, but out of the blue Himes coldbloodedly wrote her: "This is to state that you do not have the permission or authority to quote from any of my written work under any circumstances."[74] Luckily, Pool never got to see that heartbreaking note, as it was sent one month after she passed away. Her death on 29 September 1971 came unexpectedly for many, as she was only sixty-six years old. Only a handful of people showed up at the cremation in north London. As her ashes were scattered afterward, it now seemed final: she no longer had a place in this world.

EPILOGUE

Pursuing Ghosts

In Virginia Woolf's *Orlando*, the eponymous character notes that "a person may ... have as many thousand [selves]," but a "biography is considered complete if it merely accounts for six or seven."[1] I tried to define about one of Rosey Pool's multiple personalities in each chapter. Still, I do not really think I "know" her. I like to think I "got" her, or saw through her, once or twice. Those moments in which I thought I understood her often happened when I had real-life encounters with people that seemed "just like" Pool, appeared to be the "same type of person," one might say. However, these "eureka moments" were often followed by mild disappointment when these individuals turned out to be nothing like Pool. Real life does not bow to labels or categories.

The elusiveness of my research topic made me desperate at times, but it also allowed me to experience the world. Tormented by a sense of unfulfillment (and egged on by an appetite for a holiday), I traced Pool's life in not only her archives but also around the globe. I visited places she had been to including Harlem, New York, where she met Langston Hughes during her first American visit; Acre in Israel, where she experienced a religious conversion, and Vierhouten, the Netherlands, where she held her first poetry recitals as a participant in the socialist movement. By visiting these places, Pool's life became more real, more tangible, to me but also more malleable, and it allowed me to reflect on Pool's own constructions of herself. I discovered that the campus of Tougaloo College, Mississippi, was much bigger than she liked to depict in her stories.

I also learned to go beyond my own constructions and preconceptions. I had one of the most revelatory and yet humbling experiences when I went to her former home at 23a Highpoint in North London. I had seen that address so many times in her archives that I just felt I had to go there, perhaps in an attempt to find something of her soul there. I went to the apartment and rang the doorbell, all excited. Unexpectedly, an American woman opened the door. I explained her the story, which she listened to halfheartedly, as she was just in the middle of moving. "We're not really history buffs," she said, apologized for not having time, and closed the door. A potential magical moment was ruined. I looked around the corridor—which had apparently not changed that much since the 1950s and touched the banisters. Better than nothing at all. Perhaps the woman could smell my desperation through the door, because after a moment she opened her door again and let me in anyway, in a moment of temporary sanity or insanity perhaps. It was a revelation to me to be able to walk around the house that had been Pool's home for over twenty years. I could literally see how small the apartment truly was and where she had cooked her food. However, this visit also confronted me with my own voyeurism. While I was standing on the exact same spot where her bed had been I suddenly felt I was betraying Pool's privacy. Did I have the right to be here? Did I even have the right to be "her biographer"?

Over the years, I came to realize that writing a biography is a curious undertaking. My biographical subject influenced me, while I in turn created an image of Rosey Pool. It is often said that dogs look like their owners, and the same can be said about biographers (although it is unclear who is the dog in this case. Probably the biographer?). When I started this research, Rosey E. Pool was almost a blank page that almost no one had tried to write on. There was no significant public memory, no popular preconceptions, and no consensus among historians. In addition, since there was no one who had truly, critically reflected on Pool, I was able to project my own ideas, perceptions, and fantasies onto her. This biography thus inadvertently reveals quite a lot about myself as well. It reflects my own values, dreams, and insights from my own life. After all, any long-term research requires self-reflection, but perhaps a biography most of all.

Some chapters wrote themselves because of the amazing material. Others needed a more thorough orchestrating. A story needed to be created by paragraphing words, picking out sentences, and framing certain sources. The choices I made to make these connections were both conscious and unconscious, although I tried to convince myself they were only the former.

It has been tempting to create an illusion of reality in this book, and occasionally I broke the spell of the immersing narrative structure by reflecting, questioning, and disproving some "facts." The distinction between fiction and academic writing is a thin one, as many authors before me have argued.[2] But in this case the book does not tell a fictional story—it all really happened. This biography highlights particular characteristics of Rosey Pool, but it does not claim to provide the "final" account of her. Rosey Pool's life was incomplete and inconsistent, revealing that she often forged ahead without having a sense of where she was going—much like us in our own lives.

SOURCES AND METHODOLOGY

About the Sources

The research for this biography was done in archives, through interviews, with audiovisual materials, digitized sources, contemporary sources like periodicals, and of course secondary literature. One of the most important sources was the Rosey Pool Papers at the Moorland Spingarn Center at Howard University in Washington, D.C., which have been microfilmed and are available at the Royal Library in the Hague. When Pool turned fifty-five years old, in 1960, she started sending parts of her correspondence to Howard University, which wanted to set up an African American history collection.[1] Containing 883 letters, this archive is absolutely essential to anyone researching Rosey Pool, her work, and the people she corresponded with.

The Rosey Pool Collection based at the University of Sussex in Brighton, United Kingdom, is also crucial. An enormous archive, it is certainly not "badly kept," as Pool's former protégé Paul Breman stated in an interview published after Pool died.[2] This archive is a mine of information on Pool, especially on her life and contacts during the 1950s. This archive consists of all the materials that Pool kept to herself. Housing another 715 letters, the Pool Collection is the second largest archive on her and also, significantly, the most personal one. It includes photographs, scrapbooks, and even her own library, which offers a fascinating insight into how she lived her life.

One source deserves special attention: the memorial pieces on Rosey Pool in the Pool Collection at Sussex (SxMs 19/13/1), which were unfortunately never published. Contra Breman, the fact that they were not published did not owe to a "complete lack of anybody's interest."[3] With almost sixty contributors, including Otto Sterman, Owen Dodson, Shirley Graham Du Bois, Wim Ibo, Gordon Heath, Earle Hyman, Nola Hatterman, Albert Mol, Robert Hayden, and many, many others, the contributions to the unpublished memorial volume were a crucial and rich source for me as I wrote this book. Unfortunately for Pool's legacy, Breman decided to not publish the volume, although he could have easily done so.

Another significant source was the private archive of Anneke Buys, author of an unpublished 1986 biography on Pool. Her comprehensive correspondence and interviews with eyewitnesses were not just incredibly helpful but necessary to the success of this project. Most of these eyewitnesses had passed away by the time I started my research in 2014, which was forty-three years after Pool's death. Throughout my research I did maintain contact with Rudi Wesselius, a distant cousin of Pool's. Additional help came from my supervisor, Susan Legêne, who had researched Pool back in 2009 and offered me her materials and unpublished paper on Pool.[4]

I also found material in the archives of organizations that Pool was affiliated with, including the Workers Youth Center, the American Society of African Culture, and Fulbright. Additionally, I explored the archives of people Pool collaborated with or merely corresponded with, including those of Langston Hughes, Melvin Tolson, and Margaret Burroughs. The Dutch Institute for Sound and Vision deserves special attention, as this archive holds audiovisual material of Rosey Pool, enabling me to see her physically move. My research came to life with that. Also, the Anne Frank House in Amsterdam holds an audio tape of Rosey Pool talking about Anne Frank in the 1960s, which confirmed the existence of speeches on the diary that I only knew about from newspaper reviews. This was important, because although the University of Sussex holds various audio recordings of Pool, most of them were not accessible due to outdated recording equipment. Perhaps these recordings will be digitized in the future, but they might also be lost forever due to age and deterioration. Certain archives were restricted, including that of the FBI, the CIA, and the Dutch AIVD, which will perhaps be made public in the future.

Other published sources were a significant portion of the source material. Pool published nearly 150 books and articles, mostly in Dutch but also in English and German. Pool's own poetry is scarce. She published one poem in 1926 and then the largely autobiographical book of poems titled *Beperkt zicht* immediately after the war. But after that Pool switched back to promoting the work of others, like she had done before the war as well. In addition, Pool gave many interviews to newspapers, magazines, and radio and television stations, most of which are preserved in the collection at Sussex. Moreover, there is a lot of secondary literature about the different epochs and events Pool lived through, including the socialist movement, the Dutch resistance, and of course the civil rights movement. Despite the copious source material and literature, there are still notable gaps and gray areas. To address those, I had to undertake extensive archival research as well. Occasionally I found very little or even nothing, such as in archives in Berlin, where I spent over two months scrutinizing various collections. This is a part of historical research that remains invisible in the end product, although I have reflected on gaps and silences throughout the book.

Although my research was extensive and exhaustive, it is safe to say that the last word on Rosey Pool has not yet been spoken. Hopefully this book is the start of a return of Rosey Pool to many fields of research.

Privacy and Bias in Archives

Pool was a diligent curator of her own archives in many ways. Her "official" archive in the United States only contains what Pool considered "valuable material" that she wanted to be "preserved for future generations."[5] But attempts to shape her own legacy are visible in her British archive as well; for example, on one folder she wrote "Librarian please note. This section contains very important documents."[6] Both collections were largely created in her own self-image. In other words, she created them at her liberty after she had destroyed all of her correspondence from before 1940, producing a great inequality in the archives, with the fifties and sixties being highly overrepresented (see figure 24).

Her wiping out of this period from her archives raises another issue: that of privacy. My truth searching was not unproblematic, and I was confronted with a moral dilemma. Does a biographical subject have a right to privacy?[7] Should I write about all of my findings? Do—or should—we know anything about Rosey Pool? To be clear, Pool herself would absolutely have hated certain chapters of my book, especially the one about Berlin. When in 1968 one journalist described her as "homophile" she was deeply shocked to find such information about her "most private life" related in a public forum. She wrote a letter to the editor, but decided not to post it at the very last minute in which she notes that "my whole life and all my work are directed at not putting people in boxes and not putting labels on them."[8] After thoughtful consideration, however, I did decide to

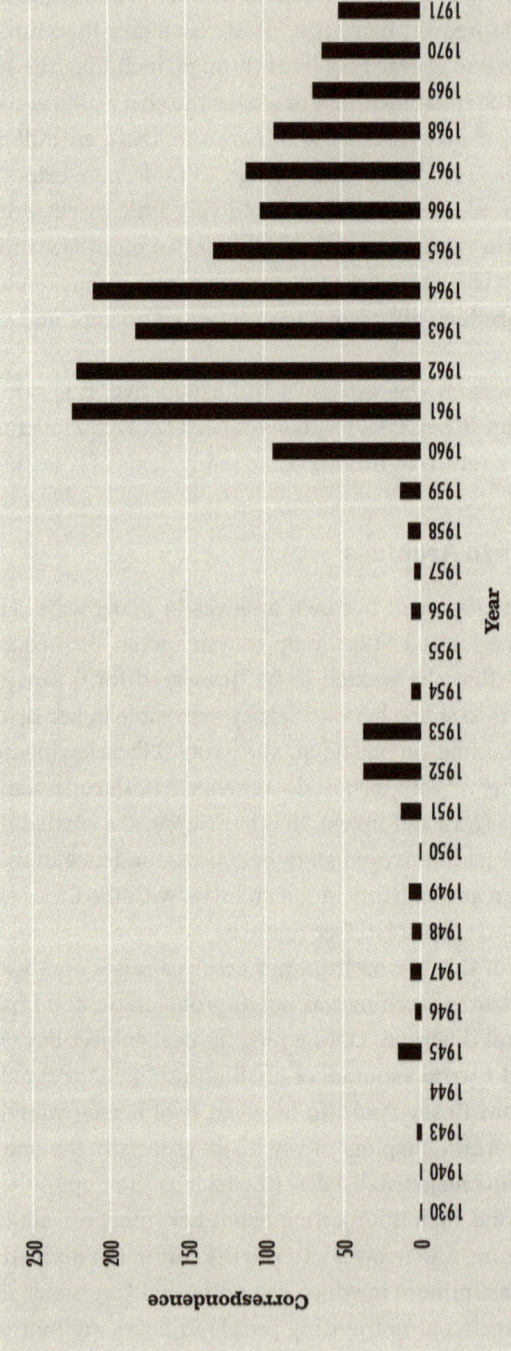

Figure 24. Graph depicting total amount of archived correspondence sent and received by Pool, from 1930 to 1971 (n=1730). The statistical data is based on correspondence housed at the Rosey E. Pool Collection at University of Sussex, the Rosey E. Pool Papers at Howard University, NIOD Institute for War, Holocaust and Genocide Studies in Amsterdam, the International Institute of Social History in Amsterdam, and the Langston Hughes Papers at Yale University.

describe many parts of Pool's private life, because they explain so much about her life and work and also offered a way to tell the story of Nazi Germany's oppressed people, stories that are rarely told and thereby easily forgotten.

Her postwar archives were not merely treasure troves waiting to be discovered but also a "repository of absence," leaving as much out as in.[9] Needless to say, her deliberate obfuscation of even the simplest details of her life makes researching her very time consuming. However much I have been able to uncover, many aspects of her life remain unclear. The gaps and silences in her papers forced me to read "against the grain" and search for subtle or hidden messages.[10]

Additionally, many of these materials were created in hazardous times, including World War II and the Cold War. The historian James Smethurst has called Pool's postwar correspondence "fascinating documents of Cold War political circumspection," as "the correspondents cautiously come out of their political closets," often by mentioning names that reveal their sympathies while still maintaining a plausible deniability.[11] Many of the people she corresponded with assumed their letters were read by intelligence agencies, at least occasionally. The things that were thus not said in these letters were often just as telling as what was being said.

The same is true of the numerous scrapbooks she left behind. Filled with photographs, newspaper clippings, interviews, and receipts from restaurants, they shed light on Pool's international travels. The seemingly random selections create an illusion of reality and offer us a sense of being near the biographical subject.[12] But despite the apparent transparency of the scrapbooks, Pool's personal life is largely absent from them. Her life partner Ursel "Isa" Isenburg is carefully left out, as are some of the threatening letters and hate mail she received when she was in the Deep South. These scrapbooks were thus not entirely private and casually put together after all but were rather likely created to impress visitors at her home or for her own pleasure, so she could look back at the highlights of her own career. Her papers likewise feature sources that convey a similar authenticity or transparency, including photographs, audio recordings, and video tapes. Yet much like the written sources, these were recorded within a certain frame, with a particular topic in mind, and also have a limited scope.[13]

The line between secondary sources and primary, autobiographical sources—which some historians have called "the most dangerous sources of all"—is thus shown to be porous.[14] On top of the 1,700-plus letters in these archives, Pool also left behind nearly 150 articles, poems, books, edited poetry collections, popular biographies, introductions, book and theater reviews, and translations. Many of these were a means to an end: "to end the curse of a segregated society," as she once wrote.[15] The personal was political, which becomes especially apparent in her 1968 essay collection *Lachen om niet te huilen* (Laughing to keep from crying). Although Pool pitched it to the publisher as a book about the African American struggle for civil rights, it can be seen as her memoir with its stories about her early youth in the Jewish Quarter as well as its explications of her views on life. Practically all of her writings contain autobiographical elements (including anecdotes or personal recollections). I have used some of them while also reflecting on them as constructions and as products of their time.

NOTES

Introduction

1. Sterling A. Brown, "Liedje voor kinderen," 16.
2. Rosey E. Pool, "As Waves of One Sea," 244, SxMs 19/11/3/18, Rosey E. Pool Collection, University of Sussex.
3. Sterling Brown and Rosey E. Pool, recording of poetry reading, Howard University, 1963, SxMs 19/9/1/10, Rosey E. Pool Collection, University of Sussex.
4. Ibid.
5. Barbara Johnson to Anneke Buys, 22 November 1986, in Buys's possession.
6. Buys, "The Marvellous Gift for Friendship."

Chapter 1. Amsterdam, 1905–1927

1. Rosey E. Pool, "As Waves of One Sea," 29, SxMs 19/11/3/18, Rosey E. Pool Collection, University of Sussex.
2. Michman, Beem, and Michman, *Pinkas*, 284; Leydesdorff, *Wij hebben als mens geleefd*, 62; Bregstein, Bloemgarten, and Bloemgarten-Barends, *Herinnering aan Joods Amsterdam*, 11.
3. Louis Pool to Frank van der Goes, 1903, 1486/1, Frank van der Goes Collection, International Institute of Social History, Amsterdam.
4. "Vriendelijk verzoek," *Het Volk*, 21 July 1901, 4.
5. "Comité tot ondersteuning der werklooze Diamantbewerkers: Opgave van tot en met 30 December 1899 ontvangen gelden," *Het nieuws van den dag*, 10 January 1900, 11; "Attentie uitgesloten en werklooze arbeiders van alle vakken," *Het Volk*, 2 March 1902, 4; "Attentie werkeloozen," *Het Volk*, 10 August 1902, 4; "Attentie!!! Stakers en uitgeslotenen!," *Het Volk*, 8 April 1903, 4; "Ingezonden: Nogmaals oproep Jordaanbuurt," *Het Volk*, 24 April 1903, 3.
6. M. W. Ferrée-Beugeling, memories of Rosey E. Pool, December 1972, SxMs 19/13/1, Rosey E. Pool Collection, University of Sussex.
7. Pool, *Lachen om niet te huilen*, 22–23.
8. Blom and Cahen, "Joodse Nederlanders, Nederlandse joden en joden in Nederland," 273.

9. Interview with unidentified person by Anneke Buys, ca. 1985, in Buy's possession.

10. Joy Lee Taylor, "Anne Frank's Teacher Discusses Dangerous Wartime Experiences," *Spectator* (Highland Park High School, Highland Park, Mich.), ca. November 1959, SxMs 19/10/1/5, Rosey E. Pool Collection, University of Sussex; Pool, "As Waves of One Sea," 28.

11. Pool, *Lachen om niet te huilen*, 24.

12. Ibid., 23.

13. Ibid., 24.

14. Pool, "As Waves of One Sea," 29.

15. Stutje, "Antisemitisme onder Nederlandse socialisten in het 'fin de siècle,'" 9.

16. Michman, Beem, and Michman, *Pinkas*, 108.

17. Pool, "As Waves of One Sea," 28.

18. "Aantekeningen omtrent leerlingen, in alfabetische volgorde van 1910–1914, daarna elk jaar afzonderlijk," 298, 9, Gerrit van der Veen Collection, 708, Amsterdam City Archives.

19. Ferrée-Beugeling, memories of Rosey E. Pool.

20. Interview with Hilda Verwey-Jonker by Anneke Buys, n.d., and interview with Jaap Reens by Anneke Buys, 22 January 1985, in Buys's possession.

21. The name of this brother was Arie den Hollander.

22. Pool, "As Waves of One Sea," 29–30.

23. Ibid., 30. Child obesity indeed became increasingly unacceptable in the 1920s. See Dawes, *Childhood Obesity in America*, 2, 7.

24. Olweus, "Bullying at School," 100.

25. Anonymous, reminiscences printed on Barlaeus Gymnasium paper, ca. 1971, SxMs 19/13/1, Rosey E. Pool Collection, University of Sussex.

26. Ferrée-Beugeling, memories of Rosey E. Pool.

27. Talwar, Gordon, and Lee, "Lying in the Elementary School Years," 804–10.

28. Ferrée-Beugeling, memories of Rosey E. Pool. Ferrée-Beugeling notes that her own family was half Jewish.

29. Rosey E. Pool, resumé and biography, 2, SxMs 19/13/1, Rosey E. Pool Collection, University of Sussex.

30. "Uitgaan: Intieme oorspronkelijke kunst," *Nieuw Israelitisch weekblad*, 12 January 1923, 3.

31. Santen, *Dapper zijn omdat het goed is*, 81.

32. Van der Steen, "Met de Roode Auto op reis," 8.

33. Harmsen, *Blauwe en rode jeugd*, 298.

34. "Instituut voor Arbeidersontwikkeling," *Het Volk*, 10 January 1927, 12; Michielse, *Socialistiese vorming*, 111–15.

35. "Van de Jeugdgroepen: Afd. Amsterdam," *Onze strijd*, 1 July 1932, 8.

36. Pool, resumé and biography, 1.

37. Rosey E. Pool, "Mijn zwarte ziel," 2, *Zielen vol soul*, SxMs 19/11/1/2 Rosey E. Pool Collection, University of Sussex.

38. Interview with Jaap Reens by Anneke Buys.

39. Interview with Henk Weggelaar by Anneke Buys, 25 September 1985, in Buys's possession.

40. Interview with Jaap Reens by Anneke Buys.
41. Gans, *De kleine verschillen die het leven uitmaken*, 415.
42. Bregstein, Bloemgarten, and Bloemgarten-Barends, *Herinnering aan Joods Amsterdam*, 162.
43. Hofmeester, *Jewish Workers and the Labour Movement*, 95.
44. "Aantekeningen omtrent leerlingen, in alfabetische volgorde van 1910–1914, daarna elk jaar afzonderlijk."
45. Buys, "The Marvellous Gift for Friendship."
46. Rosey E. Pool to Mari Evans, 9 February 1966, folder 48, box 82-1, Rosey E. Pool Papers, Howard University. Howard Pool's elopement was also confirmed by Rudi Wesselius in an interview with the author.
47. "Examens: Akte-examen L.O.," *Het Volk*, 4 July 1924, 10.
48. Interview with Jaap Reens by Anneke Buys, 22 January 1985.
49. Bertus W. Schaper to Anneke Buys, 28 July 1985, in Buys's possession. See also Knegtmans, "Voor wetenschap en maatschappij," 45, 48.
50. Interview with Hilda Verwey-Jonker by Anneke Buys.
51. Van der Steen, *Drift en koers*, 60.
52. Santen, *Dapper zijn omdat het goed is*, 81.
53. Interview with Jaap Reens by Anneke Buys.
54. Pool, "Ça Ira."
55. Pool, "Clubnieuws."
56. Pool, "De Diets-Akademiese Leergang te Amsterdam."
57. Pool, "Feest."
58. On 24 July 1926, Pool accompanied a man named de Broer who was speaking about socialism and theosophy on VARA radio. On 19 July 1926 she accompanied a Roel Stenhuis who was addressing the class struggle at the Instituut voor Arbeidersontwikkeling, in the Haarlemschen Kegelbond building in Haarlem. On 4 April 1927 she accompanied another man named Schuhmacher who was delivering a lecture about alcohol and civilization at Het Tolhuis in Amsterdam. See "Radioprogramma: Zaterdag 24 Juli," *Amersfoortsch dagblad/De Eemlander*, 23 July 1926, 1, "Instituut voor Arbeidersontwikkeling: Filmavond," *Haarlem's dagblad*, 21 November 1927, 3, and "Instituut voor Arbeidersontwikkeling," *Het Volk*, 2 April 1927, 14.
59. Santen, *Dapper zijn omdat het goed is*, 81.
60. "Instituut voor Arbeidersontwikkeling: R. Stenhuis te Haarlem," *Haarlem's dagblad*, 26 November 1927, 14.
61. Wijfjes, *VARA*, 41, 50, 56; Verwey-Jonker, "De ideologie van de SDAP (1930–1940)," 21.
62. Wijfjes, *VARA*, 44–45.
63. De Jong, "Kunst en Cultuur," 246.
64. "Radio-Agenda: Zaterdag 1 October, Hilversum (1060 M.)," *De Telegraaf*, 30 September 1927): 7.
65. Veldmeijer, "Considering Art," 41.
66. H. van der Velde to Anneke Buys, 5 November 1985, in Buys's possession.
67. Ibid. This eyewitness compared Pool to Dutch politician Charles Schwietert, who was forced to resign in 1982 after lying about studying at a university on his resumé.

68. "Ex. Hoogduitsch L.O.," *Algemeen handelsblad*, 12 August 1927, 2.
69. Pool, resumé and biography, 2.
70. Hofmeester, *Jewish Workers and the Labour Movement*, 38.

Chapter 2. Berlin, 1927–1939

1. Interview with Bernhard van Tijn by Anneke Buys, n.d., in Buys's possession; Sommer-Semester 1926, Friedrich-Wilhelms-Universität, 1 von 2, 57, martikelnummer 3078/114, Gerhard Kramer, Verzeichnisse der Studierenden, Universitätsarchiv Berlin.
2. Untitled newspaper article, *Die Welt*, 13 December 1961, Gerhard Kramer Collection, 731-8, A760, Staatsarchiv Hamburg. This article mentions Kramer's past as a *Vorsitzender* (president) of the Berlin branch of the Association of Social Democratic Students.
3. Interview with Abraham S. (Wim) Rijxman by Anneke Buys, 14 December 1984, in Buys's possession; interview with Bernhard van Tijn by Anneke Buys.
4. Maria Helena Verhoeven, quoted in Van Kooten Niekerk and Wijmer, *Verkeerde vriendschap*, 153.
5. Gay, *Weimar Culture*, 128.
6. Den Boef and Van Faassen, "*Verrek, waar is Berlijn gebleven?*," 6.
7. During the war Kramer became a Dutch-German interpreter. In his "fictional" 1952 antimilitaristic novel *Wir werden weiter marschieren* (translated as *We Shall March Again* in 1955), he displays a thorough knowledge of the Amsterdam Jewish Quarter and also uses some Dutch Jewish expressions. See Kramer, *We Shall March Again*, 82, and "Bei dem Kammergericht und für den Landgerichtsbezirf Berlin beedigte Dolmetscher," Niederländische Sprache, 1640, *Berliner Adreßbuch für d. Jahr 1941*, Digitale Landesbibliothek Berlin.
8. Heath, *Deep Are the Roots*, 90.
9. Gijsbertus M. van Wees, "Rosey E. Pool," 6, 1976, 29750, Stichting 1940–1945, Diemen; "Onze gast vandaag, Rosey E. Pool: Negerliteratuur," *Het Parool*, 2 September 1954, SxMs 19/10/1/3, Rosey E. Pool Collection, University of Sussex. It is possible that the journalist accidentally used the word "antiquariaat" ("bookstore") instead of "kunsthandel" ("gallery" or "antique shop"), a common mistake in Dutch.
10. Interview with Albert Mol by Anneke Buys, 18 February 1985, in Buys's possession.
11. Interview with Rudi Wesselius by Anneke Buys, 27 September 1984, in Buys's possession.
12. Rosey E. Pool to Henk Sneevliet, 4 February 1930, 437, Henk Sneevliet Collection, International Institute of Social History, Amsterdam.
13. This bookstore was located at the same address from where she once sent a letter: Potsdamer Straße 123.
14. Although Pool's name does not show up in the archives of this school, multiple eyewitnesses remember Pool mentioning that she was affiliated with it. It is therefore possible that she was at least a substitute teacher here. See Archiv der Bibliothek für Bildungsgeschichtliche Forschung, Berlin, Karl-Marx-Schule, microfilm 1929–32, and Radde, "Fritz Karsens Reformwerk in Berlin-Neukölln," 175–87.
15. Rosey E. Pool to Langston Hughes, 4 January 1946, folder 2429, box 130, JWJ, mss 26, Langston Hughes Papers, Yale University. Marion Palfi (1907–78) was a German

photographer who moved to the United States and often focused on racial discrimination in her work.

16. Interview with Henk Vermeyden by Anneke Buys, n.d., in Buys's possession.
17. Pool, "Arbeiderstooneel en film te Berlijn," 125.
18. Ibid., 125.
19. Ibid., 125.
20. Christie, "Eastern Avatars," 153; Kolker, *Film, Form, and Culture*, 102.
21. Pool, "Arbeiderstooneel en film te Berlijn," 126.
22. Ibid., 125.
23. Van der Steen and Blom, *Wij gingen onze eigen weg*, 11; Van der Steen, "'Kiest Sneevliet uit de cel!,'" 82–83.
24. Rosey E. Pool to Henk Sneevliet, 4 February 1930, 437, Henk Sneevliet Collection, International Institute of Social History, Amsterdam. In this letter, Pool mentioned the communist riots of 1–2 February 1930, which were actually part of a failed revolution that was violently repressed. The first of May—Labor Day—was traditionally widely celebrated. Attached to the letter was a manuscript of Henk Sneevliet's article "Die jüngste Explosion kolonialen Machtsübergriffes in Indonesien," which Pool translated in 1930.
25. Tichelman, "Hendricus Josephus Franciscus Marie (Henk) Sneevliet," 111–19.
26. By the mid-1930s revolutionary and radical socialists were describing social democrats as pat and cowardly. See De Jong, "Kunst en Cultuur," 228.
27. "Nieuw Socialistische Concentratie," *De Tribune*, 19 January 1928, 6.
28. Eekman and Pieterson, *Linkssocialisme tussen de wereldoorlogen*, 137.
29. Koos Vorrink, quoted in Hartveld, De Jong Edz, and Kuperus, *De Arbeiders Jeugd Centrale AJC*, 149.
30. Interview with Nico Gorlee by Anneke Buys, 19 September 1985, in Buys's possession.
31. Smaldone, *Confronting Hitler*, 12–15.
32. "Parteinachrichten für Groß-Berlin," *Vorwärts*, 8 June 1930, morning edition, 14; "Parteinachrichten für Groß-Berlin," 24 June 1930, morning edition, 8.
33. "Van de Jeugdgroepen: Afd. Amsterdam," *Onze strijd*, 2 January 1931, 12. On 2 January 1931 Pool gave a talk titled "Het Fascisme in Duitschland" at the offices of the Algemeenen Nederlandschen Bond van Handels- en Kantoorbedienden in Amsterdam.
34. "'Jonge Strijders' tegen den oorlog," *Het Volk*, 1 September 1932, evening edition, 9; "Agenda," *Het Volk*, 3 September 1932, morning edition, 3. This event was held on 3 September 1932 at 8 p.m. at the Handels- en Kantoorbediendenbond, a union for office personnel, in Amsterdam.
35. "Kramer over oorlog en fascisme: In een bijeenkomst van de 'Jonge Strijders,'" *Het Volk*, 5 September 1932, evening edition, 9.
36. Ibid.
37. Smaldone, *Confronting Hitler*, 15.
38. "Senator Kramer wird sechzig: Ein Berliner repräsentiert die Freie und Hansestadt in Bonn," *Die Welt*, 8 October 1964, Gerhard Kramer Collection, 731-8, A760, Staatsarchiv Hamburg.
39. Kramer became a translator for the Nazi army. He later claimed that he had had no other choice. His postwar work suggests he was not a Nazi. After the war, he again became active in the German Social Democrat Party. As a Hamburg minister of law

he fought to arrest Nazi judges ("Duitse Bondsraad is voor ontslag nazi-rechters: Oorlogsmisdadiger ontmaskerd door katholiek tijdschrift," *Leeuwarder courant*, 13 March 1965, 3), and in 1964 he published a book decrying Portuguese colonialism titled *Portugal am Pranger*.

40. "Van de Jeugdgroepen: Afd. Amsterdam," *Onze strijd*, 2 September 1932, 320.

41. Interview with Ina van der Hogen by Anneke Buys, 18 July 1985, in Buys's possession.

42. Figer, "Vragen aan een arbeidersvrouw," 1.

43. Interview with Bea Polak by Anneke Buys, 24 September 1985, in Buys's possession.

44. Interview with Henk Vermeyden by Anneke Buys; interview with Herman Rabbie by Anneke Buys, 8 May 1985, in Buys's possession.

45. Pool, *Beperkt zicht*, 19.

46. Schuyf, *Een stilzwijgende samenzwering*, 263–67.

47. Pool, *Beperkt zicht*, 9.

48. Spurlin, *Lost Intimacies*, 58; Schoppmann, *Days of Masquerade*, 17.

49. Pool, *Beperkt zicht*, 19, 11.

50. Interview with Bea Polak by Anneke Buys.

51. Espinaco-Virseda, "'I feel that I belong to you,'" 87; Schuyf, *Een stilzwijgende samenzwering*, 254.

52. Rosey E. Pool to Querido, ca. 1953, 18-2 QUE, Literatuurmuseum, the Hague.

53. Heddon, "Performing Lesbians," 217–38; Ponse, "The Social Construction of Identity and Its Meanings within the Lesbian Subculture," 246–60.

54. Schuyf, *Een stilzwijgende samenzwering*, 258.

55. Rosey E. Pool, "Sapphische Ode voor Emily Dickinson," 1943, D013703, 19, Jewish Historical Museum, Amsterdam.

56. Rosey E. Pool, "Vriendinnen, VI: Bobby N.," 1943, 17 D013703, Jewish Historical Museum, Amsterdam. Sadly, the poem concludes that this woman ended in a "sanatorium hall" and so did not survive.

57. Beachy, *Gay Berlin*, 170.

58. Breman, *The Heritage Series of Black Poetry*, n.p.

59. The information regarding Pool's divorce is found on her identification card (NL-SAA-3924223) in the Amsterdam City Archives. The Landesarchiv Berlin provided a document that states that barely a year after the divorce was final, in April 1936, Gerhard Kramer married a woman named Maria Schulz (1905–?).

60. Interview with Abraham S. (Wim) Rijxman by Anneke Buys.

61. Interview with Jaap Reens by Anneke Buys, 22 January 1985, in Buys's possession.

62. Schuyf, *Een stilzwijgende samenzwering*, 266.

63. Rich, "Compulsory Heterosexuality and Lesbian Existence," 631–60; Rich, "When We Dead Awaken," 18–30.

64. Walker, "In Search of Our Mothers' Gardens," 50.

65. D. R. D., "Hohes Amt für Kramer: Leitender Oberstaatsanwalt wurde Generalstaatsanwalt," *Hamburger Abendblatt*, 26 November 1956, Gerhard Kramer Collection, 731-8, A760, Staatsarchiv Hamburg. Kramer is quoted here: "I love to cook. But I'm only allowed to do so occasionally by my wife, who is afraid for the mess in the kitchen!" Although the statement is clearly not serious, there is also no evidence that Kramer saw a role for women outside of the home.

66. Pool, "Arbeiderstooneel en film te Berlijn," 126. Pool condemned not only tsarist Russia's stance on divorce but also that of Austria, the Catholic Church, and the Eastern European Jewish community.

67. Ibid., 126.

68. Interview with Jaap Reens by Anneke Buys.

69. Pool, *Ik ben de Nieuwe Neger*, 20. "Their songs show who they are," Pool notes of "supporters of Hitler."

70. Pool, "Anne Frank," 53.

71. Hyman, "Keeping Calm and Weathering the Storm," 41.

72. Van Kooten Niekerk and Wijmer, *Verkeerde vriendschap*, 151.

73. William A. Fowlkes, "Author Pool Notes Similarity of Nazi Oppression, Segregation," *Atlanta Daily World*, 12 February 1960, 1.

74. Joy Lee Taylor, "Anne Frank's Teacher Discusses Dangerous Wartime Experiences," *Spectator* (Highland Park High School, Highland Park, Mich.), ca. November 1959, SxMs 19/10/1/5, Rosey E. Pool Collection, University of Sussex.

75. In the April 1936 edition of *Amtliches Fernsprechbuch für Berlin* (898) and the 1937 *Berliner Adreßbuch* (2096), both accessible from the Digitale Landesbibliothek, Pool is listed as living at Helmstedter Strasse 6, Wilmersdorf, Berlin.

76. Taylor, "Anne Frank's Teacher Discusses Dangerous Wartime Experiences."

77. Bart de Cort to author, 3 February 2016.

78. This information comes from Pool's identification card (NL-SAA-3924223) in the Amsterdam City Archives.

79. Gordon Heath, memories of Rosey E. Pool, 1972, SxMs 19/13/1, Rosey E. Pool Collection, University of Sussex.

80. Heath, *Deep Are the Roots*, 90.

81. Friedländer, *Nazi Germany and the Jews*, 112.

82. Pool, "Anne Frank," 53.

83. Fowlkes, "Author Pool Notes Similarity of Nazi Oppression, Segregation," 1.

84. "Youth Allowed to Forget Nazi Horror, Dr. Pool Says: Anne Frank Teacher Speaks Here," *Knoxville News-Sentinel*, 17 February 1960, 25.

85. Rosey E. Pool, "As Waves of One Sea," 148, SxMs 19/11/3/18, Rosey E. Pool Collection, University of Sussex.

86. Pool, "The Negro Actor in Europe," 265.

87. "Nederlandse vrouw expert van de neger-literatuur," *Algemeen dagblad*, 19 April 1966, SxMs 19/14/1/8, Rosey E. Pool Collection, University of Sussex; "Dutch Visitor: Strengthening Ties," *Otherlander*, SxMs 19/14/1/4, Rosey E. Pool Collection, University of Sussex; Rosey E. Pool UNCF grant application, 16 March 1959, UNCF microfiche 1924, box 5, folder 69, Atlanta University Center. The German title of her dissertation, "Die Dichtung des nordamerikanischen Negers," is also mentioned occasionally; see "Schrijfster Rosey Pool in Londen overleden," *Het Parool*, 2 October 1971, 9.

88. After 1936, Schönemann held the only chair for North American literature and art history in Nazi Germany and was associated with the Amerika-Abteilung des Englischen Seminars of the Friedrich-Wilhelms-Universität (Hausmann, "English and Romance Studies in Germany's Third Reich," 345; Frank-Rutger Hausmann to author, 2 January 2018).

89. Pool's name does not appear in the university archives. It is possible that Pool wrote a PhD thesis and perhaps even a *Habilitation* off the record, maybe with an ex-

pelled professor. The University of Berlin had become a dangerous place for Jews, and after 1935 Jews were no longer even allowed to take doctoral exams. This did not stop Pool from adding "PhD" or an occasional "D.Litt." to her name after the war.

90. Interview with Harry Hagedorn by Anneke Buys, ca. 1985, in Buys's possession.

Chapter 3. Westerbork, 1939–1945

1. "Anne Frank's Diary Genuine, Says Teacher," *New Orleans States and Item*, 14 March 1960, SxMs 19/14/1/4, Rosey E. Pool Collection, University of Sussex.

2. Robert Cromie, "Cromie Looks at Authors and Books," *Chicago Tribune*, 20 May 1965, sec. 2, 6, SxMs 19/13/5, Rosey E. Pool Collection, University of Sussex.

3. "Anne Frank's Diary Genuine, Says Teacher."

4. Joy Lee Taylor, "Anne Frank's Teacher Discusses Dangerous Wartime Experiences," *Spectator* (Highland Park High School, Highland Park, Mich.), ca. November 1959, SxMs 19/10/1/5, Rosey E. Pool Collection, University of Sussex.

5. Rosey E. Pool to Benjamin Britten, 8 December 1963, folder 20, box 82-1, Rosey E. Pool Papers, Howard University; Pool, "Anne Frank," 53.

6. "Nieuwe stoomcursussen in de Engelsche taal voor vluchtelingen," *Nieuw Israelitisch weekblad*, 26 April 1940, 14; "Engelsche avond voor Joodsche vluchtelingen," *Nieuw Israelitisch weekblad*, 8 March 1940, 6.

7. Lotte Medak-de Wolff, memories of Rosey E. Pool, ca. 1971, SxMs s19/13/1, Rosey E. Pool Collection, University of Sussex.

8. Pool, "Vijfentwintig minuten 'Damnyankee.'"

9. Max Gruber, memories of Rosey E. Pool, 1972, SxMs 19/13/1, Rosey E. Pool Collection, University of Sussex.

10. Grünberg-Klein, *Zolang er nog tranen zijn*, 61–62; Lubbers, *Lloydhotel*, 78, 81.

11. Pool, "Anne Frank," 53.

12. Gans, *De kleine verschillen die het leven uitmaken*, 493; Herlemann, "Het Exil als operatiebasis," 129.

13. Moore, *Refugees from Nazi Germany in the Netherlands*, 11, 29.

14. Max Gruber, memories of Rosey E. Pool, 1972, SxMs 19/13/1, Rosey E. Pool Collection, University of Sussex.

15. Monroe, "Cracking the Code of Genocide," 703; Staub, "The Psychology of Bystanders, Perpetrators, and Heroic Helpers," 315–41; Block and Drucker, *Rescuers*, 6.

16. Pool, *Lachen om niet te huilen*, 29.

17. Chronological register of donated archival and library materials, 1935–40, 131, entry 16 June 1939, 295, ARCH00619, International Institute of Social History, Amsterdam. I want to thank Myriam Everard for directing my attention to this entry.

18. Pool, "Wat is 'normal' in Alabama?," 15.

19. Rosey E. Pool, "Carry Me," 1, 1960, SxMs 19/11/3/18, Rosey E. Pool Collection, University of Sussex.

20. Dave Tarr, "Anne Frank's Teacher Says Diary a Surprise," *Ann Arbor News*, November/December 1959, SxMs 19/10/1/5, Rosey E. Pool Collection, University of Sussex.

21. Rosey E. Pool to Shirley Graham, 25 June 1966, 19.4, Shirley Graham Papers, Sch00211, Schlesinger Library, Harvard University.

22. Sterling Brown and Rosey E. Pool, recording of poetry reading, Howard University, 1963, SxMs 19/9/1/10, Rosey E. Pool Collection, University of Sussex.

23. Tarr, "Anne Frank's Teacher Says Diary a Surprise."
24. Van der Boom, *"Wij weten niets van hun lot,"* 163.
25. Rosey E. Pool to Richard Wright, 3 March 1946, folder 1553, box 104, JWJ, mss 3, Richard Wright Papers, Yale University.
26. Pool, *Beperkt zicht*, 26.
27. Rosey E. Pool to Melvin Tolson, 2 June 1946, P-Q, box 1, Melvin Tolson Papers, Library of Congress.
28. Pool, "Anne Frank," 53.
29. Ruth Klemers Wiener, quoted in Hondius and Gompes-Lobatto, *Absent*, 123.
30. Willem Elte to Louis Wijsenbeek, 17 February 1943, 364, folder 5, 181e, NIOD Institute for War, Holocaust and Genocide Studies.
31. Melkman, "David Cohen," 223.
32. Tarr, "Anne Frank's Teacher Says Diary a Surprise."
33. Rosey E. Pool to Willem Elte, 14 May 1943, 41, folder 3, 181e, NIOD Institute for War, Holocaust and Genocide Studies.
34. Presser, *Ondergang*, 254–55. Presser's account is based on testimony from Jakob Hemelrijk, principal at the Jewish Lyceum in Amsterdam.
35. Interview with Hajo Meyer, 9 November 1995, 5715, USC Shoah Foundation. Meyer later concluded that this man was associated with the Westerweel resistance group, but since there was contact between Westerweel and the Van Dien group (Kurt Hirschfeld, b. 1922, is one example) it is possible that the hiding of the boy was a joint effort. Meyer was discovered and sent to Auschwitz, but he survived the war.
36. Rosey E. Pool, sound recording on Anne Frank, BgetuigenV007B, Anne Frank House, Amsterdam.
37. Pool, "Anne Frank," 53.
38. Pool, sound recording on Anne Frank.
39. Rosey E. Pool to Catherine Leslie, 20 June 1967, folder 92, box 82-2, Rosey E. Pool Papers, Howard University.
40. Pool, "Anne Frank," 54.
41. Pool to Leslie.
42. Alice Heymann-David, quoted in Braber, "Passage naar vrijheid," 68.
43. Kay Pittman, "Anne Frank's Teacher Relates Sad Memories: Visits Mississippi," undated and unnamed newspaper, SxMs 19/10/1/5, Rosey E. Pool Collection, University of Sussex.
44. Seidman, *Transatlantic Antifascisms*, 1–8; Cornelissen, "Tegen het fascisme," 148–73.
45. Anstadt, *Kruis of Munt*, 195, 200.
46. "Manifest bij de invoering der slavernij," *De Waarheid*, 3 August 1942, 1.
47. Galesloot and Legêne, *Partij in het verzet*, 127–31.
48. Pittman, "Anne Frank's Teacher Relates Sad Memories."
49. Brown and Pool, recording of poetry reading.
50. Martin Löwenberg, "Überprüfungs-Protokoll von 16.12.37," 3486, fiche 2, Emigration Holland, Kommunistische Partei Deutschlands, RY1/I 2/3/364, Bundesarchiv, Berlin; Braber, *Passage naar vrijheid*, 40.
51. Cilly Hansmann-Knopp, report, 30, SgY 30/1567, Bundesarchiv, Berlin.
52. Hilberg, *Perpetrators, Victims, Bystanders*, 116.

53. Taylor, "Anne Frank's Teacher Discusses Dangerous Wartime Experiences." Pool told this reporter that she worked at a "Nazi school for Jewish children," by which she meant the Jewish Lyceum in Amsterdam.

54. Blom, "Verzet als norm," 24.

55. Braber, *Passage naar vrijheid*, 40.

56. Pool, "Een reuze-baan!!!," 16–17.

57. Langer, *Versions of Survival*, 72.

58. Guido Abuys to author, 7 November 2018. See also Van Ginneken, *Kurt Baschwitz*, 220–23, and Braber, "Passage naar vrijheid," 109.

59. Tehuis Oosteinde to Rosey E. Pool, 8 August 1942, and Manfred Grünberg to Rosey E. Pool, 9 August 1942, N-R, Verzoekschriften van kampingezetenen aan commandant J. Schol en Lagerkommandant A. K. Gemmeker, 41, 250i, NIOD Institute for War, Holocaust and Genocide Studies. This correspondence included requests from the Oosteinde/Van Dien group for exemptions for Kurt Baschowitz (Baschwitz) (survived), Bruno Ast (survived), Albert Heppner and his wife (survived), Cilia Jacobs and her mother (died in Auschwitz the next month), Meyer Vorst (died in Auschwitz the next month), and the Mijrtiel Michel family (fate unknown). I want to thank Carlijn Keijzer for bringing these documents to my attention.

60. Gross, "Jewish Rescue in Holland and France during the Second World War," 470; Brown, "Beyond 'Good' and 'Evil.'"

61. Lysbeth Bledsoe Tirrell, "Anne Frank Was 'Very Ordinary' Girl," *Washington (N.C.) Daily News*, 4 April 1960, SxMs 19/10/1/4, Rosey E. Pool Collection, University of Sussex.

62. Brown and Pool, recording of poetry reading.

63. So far I have not been able to find evidence that Pool was arrested. However, she does consistently speak of "an underground struggle against Nazism, partly in prison, partly in slavery, partly in hiding," on multiple occasions. Anneke Buys states that her wrist was also broken during this questioning, a claim that also has not yet been proven.

64. Pool, "Kleurbekentenissen," 25 September 1965, n.p.

65. Pool, *Beperkt zicht*, 13.

66. Ibid.

67. Rosey E. Pool to Samuel W. Allen, 25 June 1961, folder 6, box 82-1, Rosey E. Pool Papers, Howard University.

68. Moraal, *Als ik morgen niet op transport ga . . .*, 17.

69. "Youth Allowed to Forget Nazi Horror, Dr. Pool Says: Anne Frank Teacher Speaks Here," *Knoxville News-Sentinel*, 17 February 1960, 25.

70. Rosey E. Pool, "Stacheldraht VI," ca. 1943, D013703, 6, Jewish Historical Museum, Amsterdam.

71. "Youth Allowed to Forget Nazi Horror, Dr. Pool Says," 25.

72. Moraal, *Als ik morgen niet op transport ga . . .*, 269.

73. Herman van Praag, quoted in Kramer, *De keuken van kamp Westerbork*.

74. Werner Stertzenbach, "Verzet in het 'Polizeiliche Durchgangslager [W]esterbork,'" 3, RA 2635, Werner Stertzenbach Collection, Memorial Center Camp Westerbork.

75. Werner Stertzenbach to Stella Pach, 14 June 1943, 10985-126, RA 1507, Werner Stertzenbach Collection, Memorial Center Camp Westerbork.

76. Max Gruber, memories of Rosey E. Pool.

77. Stertzenbach, "Verzet in het 'Polizeiliche Durchgangslager [W]esterbork,'" 3.

78. Van Riet, *De bewakers van Westerbork*, 65.

79. Identification card, Rosey Pool, 278364, Carthotheek Jewish Council, Memorial Center Camp Westerbork.

80. Braber, "Passage naar vrijheid," 112, 156fn48.

81. Rosey E. Pool, "As Waves of One Sea," 242–43, SxMs 19/11/3/18, Rosey E. Pool Collection, University of Sussex.

82. Cromie, "Cromie Looks at Authors and Books," 6.

83. Interview with Beth McKenty by Anneke Buys, 17 November 1984, in Buys's possession.

84. Westerbork, Popgids transporten 2.09.34.01, 24 August–16 November 1943, National Archives of the Netherlands; Westerbork, Popgids transporten 2.09.34.01, 31 August–7 September, National Archives of the Netherlands; Ministerie van Justitie, Commissie tot het doen van aangifte van Overlijden van Vermisten, inventory no. 20, National Archives of the Netherlands; "Transport from Westerbork Camp, the Netherlands to Auschwitz Birkenau, Extermination Camp, Poland on 07/09/1943," Yad Vashem, http://db.yadvashem.org/deportation/transportDetails.html?language=en&itemId=9446925 (accessed 18 December 2018).

85. One eyewitness noted that the Westerbork library was intended for Aryans who were being jailed and would serve their time at the camp. See Mechanicus, *In dépôt*, 168.

86. Alice Heymann-David to Anneke Buys, 5 February 1985, in Buys's possession.

87. Moraal, *Als ik morgen niet op transport ga . . .* , 196.

88. Pool told one journalist that she had been escorted out of Camp Westerbork by an SS officer that turned out to be a resistance fighter. However, this article is not necessarily reliable, as it contains a lot of incorrect information, including that Pool's head was shaved and that she wore striped clothes (these were not practices at Camp Westerbork). See Cromie, "Cromie Looks at Authors and Books," 6. Pool's absence from the camp did not go unnoticed. An interim barrack leader was designated once she disappeared and was called in for an interrogation, but there were no apparent repercussions (since by this point all remaining prisoners were being put on deportation trains). See Mechanicus, *In dépôt*, 168.

89. Gijsbertus M. van Wees, "Rosey E. Pool," 6, 1976, 29750, Stichting 1940–1945, Diemen.

90. Susanne Heynemann, memories of Rosey E. Pool, 1972, SxMs 19/13/1, Rosey E. Pool Collection, University of Sussex.

91. Wees, "Rosey E. Pool," 6.

92. M. J. van Wees, "Vervolgblad 3: Inlichtingen betr G. M. van Wees," 19 December 1975, dossier 29750, Stichting 1940–1945, Diemen.

93. Rosey E. Pool, "Stacheldraht VII," ca. 1943, 7, D013703, Jewish Historical Museum, Amsterdam.

94. Leys, *From Guilt to Shame*, 4–5; Griffioen, "Regaining the 'Lost Self,'" 43–57; Agamben, *Remnants of Auschwitz*, 87–136.

95. Rosey E. Pool to Melvin Tolson, 2 June 1946, P-Q, box 1, Melvin Tolson Papers, Library of Congress.

96. Düring, "The Dynamics of Helping Behavior for Jewish Refugees during the Second World War," 324.

97. Braber, *This Cannot Happen Here*, 131. By late 1943 the Van Dien group had

largely reorganized itself as the Association of German and Stateless Antifascists, a name it retained until after the war.

98. Susanne Heynemann to Stichting 1940–1945, 9 February 1976, SH0691, Susanne Heynemann Collection, Museum Meermanno, the Hague; Heynemann, memories of Rosey E. Pool.

99. Buys, "The Marvellous Gift for Friendship."

100. Interview with Rudi Wesselius by author, 9 October 2018.

101. Rosey E. Pool to John Lovell Jr., January 1970, SxMs 19/1/2, Rosey E. Pool Collection, University of Sussex; Pool, "As Waves of One Sea," 92.

102. Wees, "Rosey E. Pool," 6.

103. Ibid.

104. Rosey E. Pool to Querido, 5 December 1952, 7-2 QUE, Literatuurmuseum, the Hague.

105. Rosey E. Pool to Langston Hughes, 11 May 1947, folder 2429, box 130, Langston Hughes Papers, JWJ, mss 26, Yale University.

106. Even employees of the Five Pound Press refused to see their work as "resistance work," as they thought it did not require any "courage." See Lewin, *Het clandestiene boek*, 192, and Renders, *Gevaarlijk drukwerk*, 29, 31.

107. Dewulf, *Spirit of Resistance*, 162; Rozett, "Jewish Resistance," 359.

108. Pool, *Lachen om niet te huilen*, 63.

109. Rosey E. Pool, Women's Day speech, ca. 1962, 3, SxMs 19/11/3/18, Rosey E. Pool Collection, University of Sussex.

110. "How Should We Face Death?," *Perspective*, 10, episode no. 19, 06639A, TELI-D421-157, BBC Written Archives Centre.

111. Hillesum, *Etty*, 668. One eyewitness, Jopie Vleeschouwer, described the train departure of 7 September 1943: "Etty ended up in Wagon No. 12, after having gone to look for a friend in Wagon 14, who was pulled out again at the last moment." Since both knew Werner Stertzenbach, it is likely that this friend was Pool.

112. Sterztenbach, "Verzet in het Polizeiliche Durchgangslager [W]esterbork,'" 5.

113. Interview with Jaap Reens by Anneke Buys, 22 January 1985, in Buys's possession.

114. Rosey E. Pool to Querido, 9 July 1945, 1-2 QUE, Literatuurmuseum, the Hague.

115. Rosey E. Pool to Samuel Boyea, 13 June 1966, folder 17, box 82-1, Rosey E. Pool Papers, Howard University.

Chapter 4. Amsterdam, 1945–1949

1. Hondius, *Return*, 55.

2. Lipschits, *De kleine sjoa*, 191; Ibsch, "Writing against Silence," 389–402.

3. Rosey E. Pool to Querido, 17 November 1945, 64-2 QUE, Literatuurmuseum, the Hague.

4. Rosey E. Pool, "As Waves of One Sea," 233, SxMs 19/11/3/18, Rosey E. Pool Collection, University of Sussex.

5. Pool, *Beperkt zicht*, 27.

6. Pool, *Beperkt zicht*, 13.

7. Louis Pool and Jacoba Jessurun-Pool, European personal files, inventory no. EU 139.751 (S.O. A19 764/84), Dutch Red Cross, Information Bureau, 2.19.288, National Ar-

chives of the Netherlands. Their deaths were officially announced on 5 January 1950 in the *Staatscourant*.

8. In one autobiographical poem ("Aan mijn moeder"), Pool reveals that she often thought about her mother but that she simply did not know where to start looking for her. See Pool, *Beperkt zicht*, 9. See also Goldenberg, "'I had no family, but I made family,'" 22, and Greene and Graham, "Role of Resilience among Nazi Holocaust Survivors," s75–s82.

9. "Frik," aka Rosey E. Pool, "Zeg ik het nu goed?," *Vereniging van Duitse en Statenloze Antifascisten*, 28 October 1946, SxMs 19/13/5, Rosey E. Pool Collection, University of Sussex.

10. Van der Stroom, "The Diaries, *Het Achterhuis*, and the Translations," 64; Lee, *The Hidden Life of Otto Frank*, 228.

11. Rosey E. Pool, sound recording on Anne Frank, BgetuigenV007B, Anne Frank House, Amsterdam.

12. Otto Frank to Vallentine Mitchell and Company, 21 November 1950, reel 36, inventory no. 132, Great Britain, Translations, 2.2.4, Otto Frank Collection, Anne Frank House, Amsterdam.

13. I have not been able to find Pool's translation in the Otto Frank Collection in Amsterdam nor in the extensive Meyer Levin Collection in Boston, Massachusetts. I believe that it was either destroyed or has been lost. According to historian Ralph Melnick, Pool's translation was sent to Meyer Levin and then "retrieved" or stolen by Otto Frank in October 1951 from Levin's house in Paris. Pool's translation is largely forgotten in Levin's 1957 court case against Otto Frank and in Levin's subsequent accounts of the case (especially his 1974 book *The Obsession*), but not entirely. After Levin and Otto Frank fell out in 1954, Levin mentioned parallels he had noticed between Frank's treatment of him and his "cavalier treatment of the writer who undertook the first translation." See Melnick, *The Stolen Legacy of Anne Frank*, 13, 104.

14. Pool, sound recording on Anne Frank.

15. Pool, "Zeg ik het nu goed?"

16. Braber, "Passage naar vrijheid," 136.

17. Nola Hatterman, memories of Rosey E. Pool, ca. 1971, SxMs 19/13/1, Rosey E. Pool Collection, University of Sussex. During the war Hatterman and her partner Arie Jansma often hid in a small house on the Veluwe where Wilhelm Knöchel (an old friend from Jansma; they went to the International Lenin School in Moscow together in the 1920s) and Knöchel's partner Cilly Hansmann-Knopp often stayed. I believe that Pool and Hatterman met at the May 1945 celebrations that they attended with "other emigrant comrades" ("Erinnerungen Cilly Hansmann Knopp," 265, SGY30.1567, Bundesarchiv, Berlin; see also De Vries, *Nola*, 71–72).

18. Zichem, *Beeldspraak*.

19. Hatterman made illustrations for Pool's translation of James Weldon Johnson's poem "Noah Built the Ark," which appeared in *De Boekenmolen* in December 1948, a translation of Countee Cullen's "Incident in Baltimore" which also appeared in the December 1948 issue of *De Boekenmolen*.

20. "Vrouwen pleiten voor de negers: Dr Rosey E. Pool en Nola Hatterman in Mariënburg," *Gelders dagblad*, ca. 9 April 1948, SxMs 19/10/1/2, Rosey E. Pool Collection, University of Sussex.

21. Kaplan, *Miss Anne in Harlem*; Kellner, "'Refined Racism,'" 53–66. Other white women who acted as spokespersons for the Black race included the British "mother of Jamaican art" Edna Manley, the Austrian art collector Susanne Wenger, and the British writer and activist Nancy Cunard.

22. Pool, "As Waves of One Sea," 26.

23. Hermie Dumont Huiswoud, "Rosey Pool," Hermina Dumont Huiswoud Papers and Photographs, box 1, folder 35, Tamiment Library and Robert F. Wagner Labor Archives, New York University.

24. Geerlings and De Vries, "'Er is heel wat goed te maken,'" 199.

25. Rosey E. Pool to Langston Hughes, 3 February 1952, folder 2430, box 130, Langston Hughes Papers, JWJ, mss 26, Yale University.

26. Rosey E. Pool, "Mijn zwarte ziel," 3, *Zielen vol soul*, SxMs 19/11/1/2 Rosey E. Pool Collection, University of Sussex.

27. Meijer van der Sluis, "In Memoriam: Rosey E. Pool," by 5–6, in Anneke Buys's possession.

28. Van Rijsdijk, *Reünie op papier*, 59.

29. Enny van Alff-de Leeuwe, memories of Rosey E. Pool, ca. 1971, SxMs 19/13/1, Rosey E. Pool Collection, University of Sussex.

30. Sluis, "In Memoriam," 5–6.

31. Siertsema, *Uit de diepten*, 37.

32. Rosey E. Pool to Melvin Tolson, 2 June 1946, P-Q, box 1, Melvin Tolson Papers, Library of Congress.

33. Rosey E. Pool to Langston Hughes, 21 October 1945, folder 2429, box 130, Langston Hughes Papers, JWJ, mss 26, Yale University.

34. Sugrue, "Hillburn, Hattiesburg, and Hitler," 88.

35. Greenberg, *Troubling the Waters*, 114–68; Sugrue, "Hillburn, Hattiesburg, and Hitler," 88; Sundquist, *Strangers in the Land*, 221. Pool's arguments fit in perfectly with Langston Hughes's, see for example, "Nazi and Dixie Nordics," *Chicago Defender*, 10 March 1945, 1.

36. Melvin Tolson to Rosey E. Pool, 16 October 1946, folder 153, box 82-3, Rosey E. Pool Papers, Howard University.

37. Joe Willie Johnson, "Mood Negro," *Pittsburgh Courier*, 19 January 1946, SxMs 19/10/1/1, Rosey E. Pool Collection, University of Sussex.

38. "Why?," *Pittsburgh Courier*, 2 February 1946, SxMs 19/10/1/1, Rosey E. Pool Collection, University of Sussex.

39. Breman, *You Better Believe It*, 20.

40. Hondius, *Blackness in Western Europe*, 268.

41. Pool to Tolson.

42. Rosey E. Pool, "First Collection," unpublished anthology of African American poetry, 1939–40, SxMs 19/12/2/4, Rosey E. Pool Collection, University of Sussex; Querido to Rosey E. Pool, 14 November 1945, 66-2 QUE, Literatuurmuseum, the Hague. Querido's publisher, Alice von Eugen-Nahuys (1894–1967), was half Jewish through her parents.

43. Rosey E. Pool to Langston Hughes, 4 January 1946, folder 2429, box 130, Langston Hughes Papers, JWJ, mss 26, Yale University.

44. Rosey E. Pool to Richard Wright, 3 March 1946, folder 1553, box 104, Richard Wright Papers, JWJ, mss 3, Yale University.

45. Van Vree, *In de schaduw van Auschwitz*, 63.

46. Peter van Steen, "Rosey Pool draagt negergedichten voor," *De Waarheid*, Amsterdam edition, 15 October 1945, 3. Frank Mongo played the apinti drums, while Majo Oosie and Bill Olf (aka "Billy the Kid") of the Moengo Boys performed spirituals and preached.

47. "I, Too, Am America," *Het Parool*, Rotterdam edition, 14 December 1945, SxMs 19/10/1/2, Rosey E. Pool Collection, University of Sussex.

48. Galesloot and Legêne, *Partij in het verzet*, 266–67.

49. A. van der Steenhoven, "Politieke kunst: De Negerzangers in 'Kunstmin,'" *Dordtsch Dagblad*, 17 December 1945, SxMs 19/10/1/2, Rosey E. Pool Collection, University of Sussex.

50. Pool, "De kunst van den neger," 7.

51. Pool, "Schril licht op zwarte zijde der democratie in Amerika, het land van de zeven vrijheden. Dertien millioen negers vernederd door geschreven en ongeschreven wetten," 2.

52. Van Elteren, *Imagining America*, 29.

53. Pool, "As Waves of One Sea," 38.

54. Rosey E. Pool, "Devil's Food," 1960, SxMs 19/11/3/18, Rosey E. Pool Collection, University of Sussex.

55. Rosey E. Pool to Otto Frank, 9 September 1949, reel 25, inventory no. 100, Otto Frank Collection, Anne Frank House, Amsterdam.

56. Pool, "Devil's Food," 1.

57. Rosey E. Pool, quoted in Buys, "The Marvellous Gift for Friendship."

58. Pool, "As Waves of One Sea," 22.

59. Ibid., 29.

60. Ibid., 30.

61. Waldie van Eck, "Indrukken uit Zwart-Amerika," *De Groene Amsterdammer*, 19 April 1930, 16. This article mentions that the Amsterdam public reading room and the library owned books by authors like Countee Cullen, W. E. B. Du Bois, Langston Hughes, James Weldon Johnson, Nella Larsen, Claude McKay, and others.

62. Pool refers to "a bundle from Countee Cullen" in correspondence from September 1945. She is probably referring to the 1925 collection *Color*, a copy of which can also be found in her library at the University of Sussex (Rosey E. Pool to Miss Brugman, 9 September 1945, B00907 B1 Pool, R. E., 14.547, Literatuurmuseum, the Hague).

63. Pool, "As Waves of One Sea," 119; Rosey E. Pool, quoted in Buys, "The Marvellous Gift for Friendship." Pool thought that her appetite was partially racially determined: Jews had suffered throughout history, and so that is what had made her a "hearty eater."

64. Singh, "Mood, Food, and Obesity," 1; Zohar, Giladi, and Givati, "Holocaust Exposure and Disordered Eating," 50; Van der Kolk, *The Body Keeps the Score*, 144.

65. Hondius, *Return*, 91–112; Evelien Gans, "'Vandaag hebben ze niets,'" 313–53.

66. Herman, *Trauma and Recovery*, 162.

67. Pool, "As Waves of One Sea," 30.

68. Stearns, *Fat History*, 73; Gilman, *Fat*, 71–89; Bordo, *Unbearable Weight*, 5.

69. Interview with Hilda Verwey-Jonker by Anneke Buys, 19 February 1985, in Buys's possession.

70. Leydesdorff, "When All Is Lost," 27; Polletta, *It Was like a Fever*, 96.

71. Conway, *When Memory Speaks*, 3–18; Smith and Watson, *Reading Autobiography*, 266.

72. Pool quoted from letters written by Countee Cullen to "Dear R.," claiming it was her ("Mijn zwarte ziel," 5–7). The "R." actually referred to Ruth Walker (born Miller) from Columbus, Ohio. Pool possibly made photocopies (SxMS 19/1/1, Rosey E. Pool Collection, University of Sussex) of these letters from the Countee Cullen Papers (reel 3, box 6, folder 3) when she visited the Schomburg Center in New York in the 1960s.

73. Kuitenbrouwer, *De ontdekking van de derde wereld*.

74. Hermie Dumont Huiswoud, memories of Rosey E. Pool, ca. 1971, SxMs 19/13/1, Rosey E. Pool Collection, University of Sussex.

75. Rosen, "Sleep Disturbances in Survivors of the Nazi Holocaust," 62–66.

76. Rosey E. Pool, "White Monday," 1, 1962, SxMS 19/11/3/18, Rosey E. Pool Collection, University of Sussex.

77. Pool, *Beperkt zicht*, 9.

78. Interview with Albert Mol by Anneke Buys, 18 February 1985, in Buys's possession.

Chapter 5. London, 1949–1971

1. Rosey E. Pool to Langston Hughes, 12 August 1962, folder 69, Rosey E. Pool Papers, Howard University.

2. Rosey E. Pool, "As Waves of One Sea," 3, SxMS 19/11/3/18, Rosey E. Pool Collection, University of Sussex.

3. Heath, *Deep Are the Roots*, 88.

4. Rosey E. Pool to John Sherman Scott, 2 July 1963, folder 136, box 82-2, Rosey E. Pool Papers, Howard University; Pool, *'n Engelse sleutel*, 118.

5. Interview with Rudi Wesselius by author, 16 April 2018.

6. "Nederlandse vrouw expert van de neger-literatuur," *Algemeen dagblad*, 19 April 1966, SxMs 19/14/1/8, Rosey E. Pool Collection, University of Sussex.

7. Matera, *Black London*, 24; Procter, *Writing Black Britain*, 13; Carew, "Paul Robeson and W. E. B. Du Bois in London," 48.

8. Kynaston, *Modernity Britain*, 174.

9. Pool, "UNO in Croydon," 8. The current names of those countries are now Myanmar, British Guiana, and Ghana, respectively.

10. Pool compiled her first collection of African American poetry when she was in hiding during World War II. Because books were scarce, she wrote most of the poems down from heart. See "First Collection," ca. 1939–40, SxMS 19/12/2/4, Rosey E. Pool Collection, University of Sussex.

11. Gordon Heath, memories of Rosey E. Pool, 1972, SxMS 19/13/1, Rosey E. Pool Collection, University of Sussex.

12. Mozell Hill to Rosey E. Pool, 11 December 1960, folder 65, box 82-2, Rosey E. Pool Papers, Howard University; Earle Hyman to Rosey E. Pool, 10 October 1959, folder 72, box 82-2, Rosey E. Pool Papers, Howard University.

13. Graham and Walters, *Langston Hughes and the South African Drum Generation*, 145.

14. Heath, *Deep Are the Roots*, 88.

15. An and Wim Postema, memories of Rosey E. Pool, ca. 1971, SxMs 19/13/1, Rosey E. Pool Collection, University of Sussex.

16. Querido to Rosey E. Pool, 24 November 1945, 66-2 QUE, Letterkundig Museum, the Hague.

17. In the years following the appearance of such volumes as Beatrice Murphy's *Ebony Rhythm* (1948) and Langston Hughes and Arna Bontemps's *The Poetry of the Negro* (1949), little to no Black poetry was published. See Kinnamon, "Anthologies of African-American Literature from 1845 to 1994," 470.

18. John Carroll, "There Was a Publisher," audio recording, BBC Radio 3, 4 April 1981, T3921, Sound and Moving Image Catalogue, British Library, London; Newport, *A Hand and Flower Anthology*, 8.

19. Davis, *Eric Walrond*, 339–44.

20. The book *Tropic Death* can be found in the list Pool compiled of the books she owned. A copy of this list can be requested from the archivists of the Keep at the University of Sussex. Pool's former library is currently incorporated into the University of Sussex library.

21. Paul Vesey, aka Samuel Allen, memories of Rosey E. Pool, SxMs 19/13/1, Rosey E. Pool Collection, University of Sussex.

22. Rosey E. Pool, "Interviewer's Question to the Theme of How Did This Interest Come About," ca. 1960s, SxMs 19/12/2/6, Rosey E. Pool Collection, University of Sussex.

23. Buys, "The Marvellous Gift for Friendship."

24. Leslie M. Collins, "Creole Girl," in Pool, *Black and Unknown Bards*, 43.

25. Calvin Hernton, "The Distant Drum," in Pool and Breman, *Ik zag hoe zwart ik was*, 20.

26. Julian Bond, "Look at That Gal . . . ," in Pool, *Beyond the Blues*, 4. The first line comes from the Ray Charles hit single "What'd I Say" (1959).

27. This poem had also appeared in *Pegasus*, journal of Atlanta's Morehouse College, where Julian Bond was a student at the time.

28. Maria Lauret, presentation on Rosey E. Pool, "Treasures from the Rosey Pool Library" event, "Being Human: A Festival of the Humanities," University of Sussex, 21 November 2017.

29. Naomi Madgett, "Alabama Centennial," in Pool, *Ik ben de Nieuwe Neger*, 18.

30. Rosey E. Pool to Betty Ford, 11 October 1965, SxMs 19/1/1, Rosey E. Pool Collection, University of Sussex.

31. Sarah Webster Fabio to Rosey E. Pool, 29 October 1965, folder 50, box 82-1, Rosey E. Pool Papers, Howard University.

32. Dudley Randall to Rosey E. Pool, 30 October 1963, folder 130, box 82-2, Rosey E. Pool Papers, Howard University.

33. Thompson, *Dudley Randall, Broadside Press, and the Black Arts Movement in Detroit*, 43.

34. Rosey E. Pool to Catherine Leslie, 28 January 1969, SxMs 19/1/2, Rosey E. Pool Collection, University of Sussex.

35. Kellner, "Refined Racism," 53–66; Kaplan, *Miss Anne in Harlem*.

36. "POOL, Rosey," Moorland-Spingarn Research Center, Howard University, https://dh.howard.edu/finaid_manu/158 (accessed 7 December 2018).

37. Pool, "As Waves of One Sea," 205.
38. Babb, *Whiteness Visible*, 6; Foster, *Performing Whiteness*, 2; Dyer, *White*, 1–40; Morrison, *Playing in the Dark*, 1–28.
39. Pool, "As Waves of One Sea," 58–59.
40. Pattynama, "Etnocentrisme en waarheid," 213; Wekker, *White Innocence*.
41. Van Galen Last, *De zwarte schande*, 30–31; Hondius, *Blackness in Western Europe*, 45, 197.
42. Margaret Danner, "Sadie's Playhouse," in Pool, *Ik ben de Nieuwe Neger*, 117.
43. Paul Breman to Robert Hayden, 19 February 1960, 6-3.
44. Graham, "Black Atlantic Literature as Transnational Cultural Space," 508–18; Ramazani, *A Transnational Poetics*, 33.
45. Ed Simkins, quoted in Boyd, *Wrestling with the Muse*, 122.
46. Vinnette Carroll received a New York–area Emmy award for conceiving, adapting, and supervising the WCBS-TV production "Beyond the Blues" (Stage Two, 26 February 1964, produced by Merrill Brockway).
47. Boyd, *Wrestling with the Muse*, 109. Madgett here mentions the television series *Black and Unknown Bards*, broadcast by Wayne State University in 1963 (Boyd, *Wrestling with the Muse*, 109).
48. Madgett, *Exits and Entrances*, n.p.
49. Dudley Randall to Rosey E. Pool, 22 November 1962, folder 130, box 82-2, Rosey E. Pool Papers, Howard University. Snodgrass supposedly told Danner that he had borrowed the copy of *Beyond the Blues* from one of the university librarians. It is possible that this librarian was Dudley Randall. Wayne State University was also where Pool went on her Fulbright fellowship in 1959.
50. Oliver LaGrone to Rosey E. Pool, 10 July 1969, SxMs 19/1/2, Rosey E. Pool Collection, University of Sussex.
51. "Dr. Rosey Pool Speaks at Bowie," *Pacesetter* (Bowie High School, Bowie, Md.) February 1967, SxMs 19/10/1/9, Rosey E. Pool Collection, University of Sussex.
52. Julia Fields to Rosey E. Pool, n.d., folder 51, box 82-1, Rosey E. Pool Papers, Howard University.
53. Rive, *Writing Black*, 103–4.
54. Ibid., 104. See also Geerlings, "'23a Paradise,' a Dutch 'Salon' in North London," 127–28.
55. Rive, *Writing Black*, 103–4, emphasis added.
56. Rosey E. Pool to Langston Hughes, 23 May 1958, folder 2431, box 130, Langston Hughes Papers, JWJ, mss 26, Yale University.
57. Rosey E. Pool to Langston Hughes, 17 May 1962, folder 69, box 82-2, Rosey E. Pool Papers, Howard University.
58. "South African Tells of Brutality, Fear of War," *Atlanta Daily World*, 23 March 1963, 1; "S. African Writer Tours Dixie Schools," *Afro-American*, 2 March 1963, 18.
59. Pool, *Lachen om niet te huilen*, 24.
60. Gilroy, *The Black Atlantic*, 19.
61. Robert Hayden, memories of Rosey E. Pool, 1972, SxMs 19/13/1, Rosey E. Pool Collection, University of Sussex; see also Hayden, *How I Write*, 188–89. Pool read the poem "Runagate Runagate" during her visit to Fisk University in Nashville in 1960.
62. Ramey and Breman, *The Heritage Series of Black Poetry*, 3.

63. Rosey E. Pool to *Umbra* magazine, 3 February 1964, SxMs 19/1/2, Rosey E. Pool Collection, University of Sussex; Rosey E. Pool to Shirley Graham Du Bois, 17 January 1964, folder 46, box 82-1, Rosey E. Pool Papers, Howard University.

Chapter 6. Hilversum, 1958

1. Righart and De Rooij, "In Holland staat een huis," 17.
2. Rosey E. Pool to Langston Hughes, 31 October 1952, folder 2430, box 130, Langston Hughes Papers, JWJ, mss 26, Yale University.
3. For more information on the Dutch Service, see "The B.B.C. and Holland: Notes for D. G." and "Some Notes on the Dutch Service," file 1, 1940–57, E1.829 Countries, Holland, Dutch Service, BBC Archives, Reading, UK, and "Tien jaar B.B.C. in Nederlands: Vijf jaar oorlog, vijf jaar vrede," *Trouw*, 6 April 1950, 3.
4. "Pool, Dr. Rosey," Talks File 1, 1948, 1962, BBC Archives.
5. "Televisie-uitzending over Joodse gemeenschap: Een Radio-uitzending over 'Het Achterhuis,'" *Nieuw Israëlitisch weekblad*, 5 November 1954, 5.
6. Jack Dixon, "Wat anderen er van denken: Silberbauer en zijn Nederlandse helpers," *De Telegraaf*, 22 November 1963, 11.
7. "Jack Dixon: Televisie werd zijn levensdoel," *Het Parool*, 4 April 1959, 21.
8. Van Zoonen, "Pia, Maartje, Hennie en Joop," 471.
9. Interview with Joes Odufré by Anneke Buys, 6 May 1985, in Buys's possession; audiovisual recording of *God Bless Queen Victoria* presented by Rosey E. Pool, produced by Wim Ibo, and directed by Joes Odufré, 18 February 1962, 162306, Netherlands Institute for Sound and Vision; audiovisual recording of television show *Op bezoek bij Eric Bramall* presented by Rosey E. Pool and directed by Joes Odufré, 2 July 1962, 162621, Netherlands Institute for Sound and Vision.
10. "Hoofdrol van Nederlands TV-spel voor Amerikaanse neger," *De Telegraaf*, 13 August 1958, 7; R. M. S., "Losse notities van een weekeinde," *Het Parool*, 19 February 1962, 4.
11. Zijderveld, "Vrij zinnig eigenzinnig," 166.
12. Interview with Joes Odufré by Anneke Buys.
13. "Kijk naar," *De Telegraaf*, 1 April 1957, 5; "Radio-Televisie," *De Telegraaf*, 8 February 1958, 11; J. B. L., "Luchtpost: Stijlvolle avond met grove uitsmijter," *Trouw*, 10 February 1958, 5. "E Wa Jo" ("Let Us Dance") was broadcast by the VPRO on 1 April 1957.
14. "Morgenavond in Frascati: Een ton d'r op. Veiling ten bate slachtoffers apartheidspolitiek," *Friese koerier*, 11 May 1966, 2.
15. "The Thursday Play, *Radio Times*, broadcast 16 January 1958, https://genome.ch.bbc.co.uk/220064c8e2bc473eb9cb2072761b345f (accessed 8 February 2019).
16. Pool, "'Advocaat pro deo' pleit voor allen," 6.
17. Heath, *Deep Are the Roots*, 88.
18. Ibid., 87.
19. Ibid., 47.
20. Rosey E. Pool to Querido, 17 March 1953, 20-2 QUE, Literatuurmuseum, the Hague.
21. Crenshaw, "Mapping the Margins," 1299; Taylor and Whittier, "Collective Identity in Social Movement Communities," 104.
22. Heath, *Deep Are the Roots*, 90.

23. Pool, "The Negro Actor in Europe," 260.
24. Rosey E. Pool to Langston Hughes, 3 February 1952, folder 2430, box 130, Langston Hughes Papers, JWJ, mss 26, Yale University.
25. Heath, *Deep Are the Roots*, 91.
26. "Gordon Heath en Lee Payant in Nederland," *De Telegraaf*, 1 September 1956, 4; "Gordon Heath en Lee Payan [sic] voor VPRO-televisie: Precies als in Parijs," unidentified newspaper, 7 July 1956, SxMs 19/13/5, Rosey E. Pool Collection, University of Sussex.
27. Pool, "Ik zie, ik zie, wat jij niet ziet . . . namelijk," 36. Pool explains her vision here in a review of *Moon on a Rainbow Shawl* (1957), a play by the Trinidadian playwright Erroll John, which focuses on the social and economic circumstances of West Indian immigrants in London.
28. Pool, "'Advocaat pro deo' pleit voor allen," 6.
29. Pool, "Ik zie, ik zie, wat jij niet ziet . . . namelijk," 35; Pool, "The Negro Actor in Europe," 263. Pool here uses actor Otto Sterman as an example.
30. Pool translated some of Annie M. G. Schmidt's works into English.
31. *Algemeen Dagblad*, quoted in Kuipers, "1 oktober 1957," 302.
32. Rosey E. Pool to Gordon Heath, 14 January 1958, folder 324, box 27, Gordon Heath Papers, MS 372, University of Massachusetts.
33. Heath, *Deep Are the Roots*, 89.
34. "'Advocaat pro deo' by VPRO Television: American Gordon Heath acts in Dutch, Amsterdam, Wednesday," unidentified Dutch newspaper, folder 324, box 27, Gordon Heath Papers, MS 372, University of Massachusetts.
35. De Grazia, *Irresistible Empire*, 337.
36. "Gegolfde wereld: Durf," *Utrechts nieuwsblad*, 11 September 1958, 5.
37. "Amerikaan Gordon Heath speelt in Nederlands: 'Advocaat pro Deo' bij VPRO-televisie," *Het Parool*, 10 September 1958, 9.
38. "Hoofdrol van Nederlands TV-spel voor Amerikaanse neger," 7; "'Advocaat pro deo' by VPRO Television."
39. Jack Dixon to Gordon Heath, 16 June 1958, and Rosey E. Pool to Lee Payant, 4 March 1958, folder 324, box 27, Gordon Heath Papers, MS 372, University of Massachusetts. Pool changed all the words in the script that would have been too difficult for an American actor to pronounce.
40. Gordon Heath, memories of Rosey E. Pool.
41. "Avondprogramma: 10 september 1958," *Vrije seluiden: Radio- en televisieprogrammablad van de VPRO*, 6 September 1958, 27.
42. Ramey and Breman, *The Heritage Series of Black Poetry*, 128.
43. Breman, *The Heritage Series of Black Poetry*, n.p.
44. Hermie Dumont Huiswoud, "Rosey Pool," folder 35, box 1, Hermina Dumont Huiswoud Papers and Photographs, Tamiment Library and Robert F. Wagner Labor Archives, New York University.
45. W. E. B. Du Bois, speech note cards for "The United States and War," Amsterdam, 11 September 1958, 11, frame 1198, reel 81, W. E. B. Du Bois Papers, MS 312, University of Massachusetts. These are likely the notes of the speech Du Bois gave on 11 September 1958 in the Hague, not Amsterdam.
46. "Misplaatst politiek geluid op ere-avond voor DuBois: 'Ik zag hoe zwart ik was,'"

Haagsch dagblad, 12 September 1958. See also Geerlings, "W. E. B. Du Bois at Ons Suriname, Amsterdam," 81–97.

47. Baldwin, *Beyond the Color Line*, 35; Munro, "Imperial Anticommunism and the African American Freedom Movement in the Early Cold War," 52–75.

48. "Nationaal televisie-programma wekte verontwaardiging: Gekleurde behandeling van jongste geschiedenis van Nederland," *Het Vaderland*, 2 September 1957, 1.

49. "'Het concert': tv-spel van blind meisje en negerarts," *De Volkskrant*, 22 October 1959, 5.

50. "LD over Radio + TV: Kleurige T.V.," *Leidsch dagblad*, 11 September 1958, 2.

51. Video excerpt from *Advocaat pro deo*, document ID 44403, Netherlands Institute for Sound and Vision.

52. Heath, *Deep Are the Roots*, 89.

53. Stanley Mann, *Advocaat pro deo* script, SxMs 19/13/6, Rosey E. Pool Collection, University of Sussex.

54. Mann, *Advocaat pro deo* script, 37–38.

55. Some reviewers found Pool's acting merely "acceptable," but the majority of the reviewers praised her, saying she had "the best role of the evening." One even claimed that her acting was "the only acceptable aspect of the entire performance" ("'Advocaat pro deo': Amerikaan speelde hoofdrol in knap Canadees stuk," *Haagse Post*, 11 September 1958).

56. Pool, "'Advocaat pro deo' pleit voor allen," 6.

57. Mann, *Advocaat pro deo* script, 11.

58. Ibid., 69.

59. "'*Advocaat pro deo*': Goed seizoenbegin," *De Telegraaf*, 11 September 1958, 9.

60. "'TV-spel leverde stof voor gesprek': Kijkers voelden zich 'genomen' maar regisseur verklaart," *De Telegraaf*, 13 September 1958, 15.

61. "TV-kijkers wilden weten: Hoe liep het af met Donald?," *Het Parool*, 11 September 1958, 9.

62. "Advocaat pro deo," *Nieuwe Rotterdamse courant*, 11 September 1958.

63. "Amerikaan gast-acteur in boeiend TV-spel," *Rotterdams nieuwsblad*, ca. 11 September 1958.

64. "Gordon Heath," *Het Vizier*, 27 September 1958.

65. Hondius, *Blackness in Western Europe*, 272; Wekker, *White Innocence*, 12–13.

66. Kuipers, "1 oktober 1957," 293.

67. Ineke Horree to Gordon Heath, 11 September 1958, folder 324, box 27, Gordon Heath Papers, MS 372, University of Massachusetts.

68. Pool, "'Advocaat pro deo' pleit voor allen," 6.

69. Heath, *Deep Are the Roots*, 88. The French version was broadcast on 12 December 1958 by the Belgian Institut national de radiodiffusion.

Chapter 7. Up North / Down South, 1959–1960

1. "Covering Exchanges for the Academic Year September 1959–July 1960," 23, Fulbright Act, Program Year 1959, 79th Congress, PL 584, A.1, box 1, Fulbright Archives, Roosevelt Institute for American Studies, Middelburg, Netherlands. Pool was able to apply because of her affiliation with London's Holborn College of Languages, where she taught Dutch evening classes.

2. Johanna J. van Dullemen to Willem K. von Weiler, 14 January 1960, SxMs 19/10/1/5, Rosey E. Pool Collection, University of Sussex.

3. Doneson, "The American History of Anne Frank's Diary," 150.

4. Sundquist, *Strangers in the Land*, 233.

5. Rosey E. Pool to Mae Mallory, 5 July 1963, SxMs 19/1/2, Rosey E. Pool Collection, University of Sussex.

6. Barbara Williams, untitled newspaper clipping, Detroit area, ca. November 1959, SxMs 19/10/1/5, Rosey E. Pool Collection, University of Sussex.

7. Gordon Heath, memories of Rosey E. Pool, 1972, SxMs 19/13/1, Rosey E. Pool Collection, University of Sussex.

8. "Visiting Scholars in the United States Awarded U.S. Government Grants under the Fulbright and Smith-Mundt Acts, Academic Year 1959–60," SxMs 19/10/1/5, Rosey E. Pool Collection, University of Sussex.

9. "United States Government Grant: Terms of Award," 9 September 1959, SxMs 19/10/1/5, Rosey E. Pool Collection, University of Sussex.

10. Marion Edman to Anneke Buys, 11 April 1985, and Marion Edman to Anneke Buys, 30 April 1985, in Buys's possession; Marion Edman to friends, 18 March 1947 and 4 July 1947, Marion Edman Papers, New York Public Library.

11. "List of Talks and Fees," SxMs 19/10/1/5, Rosey E. Pool Collection, University of Sussex. Pool delivered these lectures on 12 and 13 October 1959 at Albion College in Michigan.

12. "Youth Allowed to Forget Nazi Horror, Dr. Pool Says: Anne Frank Teacher Speaks Here," *Knoxville News-Sentinel*, 17 February 1960, 25.

13. Charles Harmon, "Anne Frank's Friend Speaks at K-College: Urges: Don't Let Her Down Second Time," *Gazette* (Kalamazoo, Mich.), 16 October 1959, SxMs 19/10/1/5, Rosey E. Pool Collection, University of Sussex.

14. Unidentified pupil of Marcy School, Detroit, to Rosey E. Pool, 18 November 1959, SxMs 19/10/1/5, Rosey E. Pool Collection, University of Sussex.

15. Annette Harris, "My Report on the Diary of Ann Frank," 12 November 1959, SxMs 19/10/1/4, Rosey E. Pool Collection, University of Sussex.

16. Gregory Bynbrion to Rosey E. Pool, ca. 18 November 1959, SxMs 19/10/1/5, Rosey E. Pool Collection, University of Sussex.

17. Joanne Carley to Rosey E. Pool, 18 November 1959, SxMs 19/10/1/5, Rosey E. Pool Collection, University of Sussex.

18. Lysbeth Bledsoe Tirrell, "Anne Frank Was 'Very Ordinary' Girl," *Washington (N.C.) Daily News*, 4 April 1960, SxMs 19/10/1/4, Rosey E. Pool Collection, University of Sussex.

19. Lipstadt, "America and the Memory of the Holocaust," 195; Kushner, "Britain, the United States, and the Holocaust," 259.

20. Flanzbaum, *The Americanization of the Holocaust*, 4.

21. "Dr. Pool to Meet Another Anne," *Detroit News*, October 1959, SxMs 19/10/1/5, Rosey E. Pool Collection, University of Sussex.

22. Dave Tarr, "Anne Frank's Teacher Says Diary a Surprise," *Ann Arbor News*, November/December 1959, SxMs 19/10/1/5, Rosey E. Pool Collection, University of Sussex.

23. Rosey E. Pool, sound recording on Anne Frank, BgetuigenV007B, Anne Frank House, Amsterdam.

24. "Dr. Pool to Meet Another Anne."
25. Pool, sound recording on Anne Frank.
26. Priscilla Swiat to author, 28 November 2018.
27. Claudia O. Lucas to Rosey E. Pool, 5 November 1959, SxMs 19/10/1/5, Rosey E. Pool Collection, University of Sussex.
28. Harmon, "Anne Frank's Friend Speaks at K-College."
29. Pool, sound recording on Anne Frank.
30. Tarr, "Anne Frank's Teacher Says Diary a Surprise"; "Anne Frank's Diary Genuine, Says Teacher," *New Orleans States and Item*, 14 March 1960, SxMs 19/14/1/4, Rosey E. Pool Collection, University of Sussex.
31. Robert Churchwell, "Seeks Strong Anti-Semitism Controls," *Nashville Banner*, 14 January 1960, SxMs 19/10/1/5, Rosey E. Pool Collection, University of Sussex; "Anne Frank's Diary Defended," *Times-Picayune* (New Orleans), March 1960, SxMs 19/10/1/4, Rosey E. Pool Collection, University of Sussex.
32. Barbara Williams, untitled newspaper clipping.
33. Erll, *Memory in Culture*, 8.
34. Churchwell, "Seeks Strong Anti-Semitism Controls," 12.
35. Tarr, "Anne Frank's Teacher Says Diary a Surprise."
36. Barbara Williams, untitled newspaper clipping.
37. Breman, *The Heritage Series of Black Poetry*, n.p.
38. Joy Lee Taylor, "Anne Frank's Teacher Discusses Dangerous Wartime Experiences," *Spectator* (Highland Park High School, Highland Park, Mich.), ca. November 1959, SxMs 19/10/1/5, Rosey E. Pool Collection, University of Sussex.
39. Rosey Pool, talk about Anne Frank at Hadassah, notes, 6 December 1959, SxMs 19/10/1/5, Rosey E. Pool Collection, University of Sussex.
40. Adolph Markel Jr. to Rosey E. Pool, 5 May 1960, SxMs 19/14/1/4, Rosey E. Pool Collection, University of Sussex.
41. Roebuck and Murty, *Historically Black Colleges and Universities*, 37.
42. Rosey E. Pool to Frederick D. Patterson, 12 March 1959, microfilm 1925, UNCF Papers, Robert W. Woodruff Library, Atlanta University Center.
43. Pool had met Mozell Hill in 1952 when he was in England for a few months, and it was Hill who convinced BBC Radio to repeat Pool's earlier program on African American poetry.
44. Rosey E. Pool, CV 16 March 1959, microfilm 1924, UNCF Papers, Atlanta University Center.
45. There had been UNCF visiting scholars before, but their visits to the South were much shorter. Two who came near to Pool's twenty-two college tour were the South African writer Bloke Modisane, who visited ten colleges in four different states, and Lewis Nkosi, an exiled South African writer and professor at Harvard, who visited ten Black colleges in the 1960s. Others UNCF visiting scholars included Victor H. Wiseman, a British lecturer; the American psychiatrist Gloria Johnson; and psychologist Pandarinath Hari Prabhu from India.
46. Putnam, *Bowling Alone*, 116–33.
47. Gasman, *Envisioning Black Colleges*, 86–118.
48. January–March 1960 news releases, microfilm 2635, and April–May 1960 news releases, microfilm 2636, UNCF Papers, Atlanta University Center.

49. Calvin H. Raullerson to Rosey E. Pool, 11 May 1960, SxMs 19/14/1/4, Rosey E. Pool Collection, University of Sussex.

50. "Information Photos of Dr. Rosey Pool with Students," 21 January 1960, microfilm 2355, UNCF Papers, Atlanta University Center.

51. Rosey E. Pool, "Carry Me," 1,1960, SxMs 19/11/3/18, Rosey E. Pool Collection, University of Sussex.

52. Barbara Williams, untitled newspaper clipping.

53. William A. Fowlkes, "Author Pool Notes Similarity of Nazi Oppression, Segregation," *Atlanta Daily World*, 12 February 1960, 1.

54. Annual Report of the United States Educational Foundation in the Netherlands, program year 1959, 42, A.2, box 3, Fulbright Archives, Roosevelt Institute for American Studies, Middelburg, Netherlands. Anonymous quotation which clearly bears Pool's stamp.

55. Van der Pol, "Mazirel, Laura Carola."

56. Staub and Vollhardt, "Altruism Born of Suffering," 268.

57. McWilliams, "The Psychology of the Altruist," 193–213; De Vries, "Leadership Coaching and the Rescuer Syndrome."

58. The case was settled in 1958; Otto Frank was ordered to pay a financial compensation of $50,000 to the playwright (Van der Stroom, "The Diaries, *Het Achterhuis*, and the Translations," 59–77; Melnick, *The Stolen Legacy of Anne Frank*).

59. Lipstadt, *Denying the Holocaust*, 66, 229–35.

60. "Anne Frank's Diary Defended."

61. "Anne Frank's Diary Genuine, Says Teacher."

62. Tirrell, "Anne Frank Was 'Very Ordinary' Girl."

63. Kay Pittman, "Anne Frank's Teacher Relates Sad Memories: Visits Mississippi," undated and unnamed newspaper, SxMs 19/10/1/5, Rosey E. Pool Collection, University of Sussex. The revenues of the *Diary* were sent to the Anne Frank Foundation (founded in 1957), an organization ran by Otto Frank and others. Most of its activities focused on youth education.

64. Webb, *Fight against Fear*, 43–47, 49.

65. Fowlkes, "Author Pool Notes Similarity of Nazi Oppression, Segregation," 1.

66. For the full poem see Hayden, *Collected Poems*, 10. Pool later explained that the poem was not about Anne Frank but another student of hers named Shelly Visdrager who had survived Bergen-Belsen (Rosey E. Pool talks to P. Kenney, North Carolina, *Reader's Corner*, audio recording, 1963, SxMs 19/9/1/9, Rosey E. Pool Collection, University of Sussex).

67. Lillian W. Voorhees to Rosey E. Pool, 7 March 1960, SxMs 19/14/1/4, Rosey E. Pool Collection, University of Sussex. The stage performance of the *Diary* was scheduled to take place at Fisk University on 18 and 19 March 1960.

68. Rosey E. Pool, "As Waves of One Sea," 41 SxMs 19/11/3/18, Rosey E. Pool Collection, University of Sussex.

69. Rosey E. Pool to Herbert Woodward Martin, 26 June 1968, SxMs 19/1/2, Rosey E. Pool Collection, University of Sussex.

70. "Clark to Hear World War II Dutch Leader," *Atlanta Daily World*, 6 February 1960, SxMs 19/14/1/4, Rosey E. Pool Collection, University of Sussex.

71. Fowlkes, "Author Pool Notes Similarity of Nazi Oppression, Segregation," 1; Wil-

liam Fowlkes, "Seeing and Saying: A Visitor Winces," *Atlanta Daily World*, ca. mid-February 1960, SxMs 19/10/1/4, Rosey E. Pool Collection, University of Sussex. For more information on Fowlkes, see William Fowlkes, cassette 24, Oral History Collection, Auburn Avenue Research Library on African American Culture and History, Atlanta.

72. Sundquist, *Strangers in the Land*, 234.

73. Doneson, "The American History of Anne Frank's Diary," 149–60; Langer, "The Americanization of the Holocaust on Stage and Screen," 198–202.

74. Lester, *Lovesong*, 32–33.

75. Pool's list of books shows that she owned several books by Du Bois and Césaire. See also Cheyette, *Diasporas of the Mind*.

76. Rosey E. Pool to W. E. B. Du Bois, 19 February 1960, W. E. B. Du Bois Papers, MS 312, University of Massachusetts Amherst Libraries.

77. Samuel Boyea to Rosey E. Pool, 21 November 1968, SxMs 19/1/1, Rosey E. Pool Collection, University of Sussex.

78. Pool, "As Waves of One Sea," 24; Pool, *Lachen om niet te huilen*, 20.

Chapter 8. Mississippi, 1960–1963

1. Rosey E. Pool, "As Waves of One Sea," 196, SxMs 19/11/3/18, Rosey E. Pool Collection, University of Sussex.

2. Rosey E. Pool to Charles L. Anderson, 20 September 1961, folder 8, box 82-1, Rosey E. Pool Papers, Howard University.

3. Rosey E. Pool to American Society of African Culture, 19 May 1962, box 1, American Society of African Culture Collection, Howard University.

4. Rosey E. Pool, "Praise Him in Sound," SxMs 19/11/3/18, Rosey E. Pool Collection, University of Sussex.

5. Rosey E. Pool to Ernst Borinski, 12 June 1961, folder 16, box 82-1, Rosey E. Pool Papers, Howard University.

6. Rosey E. Pool to Dorothy H. Tilly, 17 December 1963, folder 118, box 82-2, Rosey E. Pool Papers, Howard University.

7. Rosey E. Pool to American Society of African Culture, 25 November 1963, box 1, American Society of African Culture Collection, Howard University.

8. Adam Daniel Beittel, biographical file, "Re: College Presidents," ca. 1963, microfilm 1536, UNCF Papers, Atlanta University Center. In 1963, half of the faculty members and 9 of the 503 students were white. See also "Hundreds of Whites Attending Negro Colleges in 'Reverse Integration,'" *New York Times*, 7 April 1963, 52.

9. Pool to Tilly.

10. Lowe, "An 'Oasis of Freedom' in a 'Closed Society,'" 486–520; Edgcomb, *From Swastika to Jim Crow*, 120.

11. Carroll Gartin, quoted in "Truth or Mud Slinging?," *Delta Democrat-Times* (Greenville, Miss.), 19 February 1964, 4.

12. Dittmer, *Local People*, 234.

13. Williamson, "Black Colleges and Civil Rights," 128.

14. Pool, "Praise Him in Sound," 3.

15. Pool, "White Monday," 3, 1962, SxMs 19/11/3/18, Rosey E. Pool Collection, University of Sussex.

16. Lowe, "An Unseen Hand," 33.

17. Ibid., 40.

18. Webb, *Fight against Fear*, 207.

19. Interview with Joan Trumpauer Mulholland by John Dittmer, 17 March 2013, 2015669178, Civil Rights History Project and Southern Oral History Program, Library of Congress.

20. Jerry Ward Jr. to author, 12 September 2017.

21. "Social Science Forums," *Tougaloo (Miss.) Southern News*, 70, no. 4 (1960), 6, microfilm 1254, UNCF Papers, Atlanta University Center; announcement of public lecture by Rosey E. Pool, 18 February 1963, SxMs 19/10/1/7, Rosey E. Pool Collection, University of Sussex; schedule, Humanities 21, second semester, 1962–63, SxMs 19/11/3/18, Rosey E. Pool Collection, University of Sussex.

22. Lowe, Morris, and Pizzo, "Academic Agitators in Mississippi," 8.

23. Ernst Borinski to Rosey E. Pool, 4 October 1960, folder 16, box 82-1, Rosey E. Pool Papers, Howard University.

24. Edgcomb, *From Swastika to Jim Crow*, 128.

25. Lowe, "An Unseen Hand," 41.

26. Edward King, quoted in Edgcomb, *From Swastika to Jim Crow*, 121.

27. Ernst Borinski, quoted in Lowe, "An Unseen Hand," 40.

28. Pool, "White Monday," 2.

29. Joyce Ladner, quoted in Edgcomb, *From Swastika to Jim Crow*, 121.

30. Hermie Dumont Huiswoud, memories of Rosey E. Pool, ca. 1971, SxMs 19/13/1, Rosey E. Pool Collection, University of Sussex.

31. Rosey E. Pool, biographical sketch, microfilm 1658, UNCF Papers, Atlanta University Center.

32. Rosey E. Pool, "Twelve Students in Search of Inspiration," SxMs 19/11/1/1, Rosey E. Pool Collection, University of Sussex.

33. Pool, "Creativity," in "As Waves of One Sea," 2 ("Creativity" is a separately paginated chapter in the "As Waves of One Sea" typescript).

34. Ibid., 9.

35. According to Pool the original sentence was "Grandpop was not a politician, nor could he read or write, but time had educated him in wisdom."

36. Pool, *Lachen om niet te huilen*, 153; Pool, "Creativity," in "As Waves of One Sea," 17.

37. Pool, "Creativity," in "As Waves of One Sea," 10; Pool, *Lachen om niet te huilen*, 148.

38. Pool, *Lachen om niet te huilen*, 144.

39. Gasman and Geiger, *Higher Education for African Americans before the Civil Rights Era*, 14.

40. Pool, "Twelve Students in Search of Inspiration," 3.

41. Pool, "Creativity," in "As Waves of One Sea," 2.

42. Rossouw, "Die bevrydingsstryd," 45.

43. "Beginselverklaring," *Links richten*, no. 1 (1932).

44. Pool, "Creativity," in "As Waves of One Sea," 2.

45. Pool to American Society of African Culture, 25 November 1963.

46. Rosey E. Pool to Margaret Burroughs, 25 November 1969, folder 270, box 31, Margaret Burroughs Papers, DuSable Museum of African American History.

47. Pool to American Society of African Culture, 25 November 1963.

48. Pool, "Creativity," in "As Waves of One Sea," 5; Pool, *Lachen om niet te huilen*, 144.

49. Dianella Williams, "Racist," SxMs 19/11/1/1, Rosey E. Pool Collection, University of Sussex.

50. Rhoda M. Voth to Rosey E. Pool, 30 January 1960, SxMs 19/10/1/4, Rosey E. Pool Collection, University of Sussex.

51. Pool, *Lachen om niet te huilen*, 33.

52. Turner, *Sitting in and Speaking Out*, 72.

53. Pool to Tilly.

54. Pool, "Wat is 'normal' in Alabama?," 15.

55. Keating, "'Keep up the agitation,'" 55.

56. Lowe, Morris, and Pizzo, "Academic Agitators in Mississippi," 12.

57. Pool, "As Waves of One Sea," 196.

58. Pool, "White Monday," 1.

59. Rosey E. Pool to Robert Hayden, 3 February 1960, box 16, Robert Hayden Papers, National Bahá'í Archives, Wilmette, Ill.

60. Caruth, *Trauma*, 152; Krystal, "Trauma and Aging," 97.

61. Van der Kolk, "The Compulsion to Repeat the Trauma," 389; Caruth, *Unclaimed Experience*, 1.

62. Edgcomb, *From Swastika to Jim Crow*, 78.

63. Audrey Prentiss, "A Glance at a Great Lady," 1, SxMs 19/11/1/1 Rosey E. Pool Collection, University of Sussex.

64. Ibid., 2.

65. Floyd-Thomas, "Between Jim Crow and the Swastika," 15; Sundquist, *Strangers in the Land*, 171, 221.

66. Pool, "Creativity," in "As Waves of One Sea," 7.

67. Pool, *Lachen om niet te huilen*, 85.

68. Lev-Wiesel and Amir, "Growing Out of Ashes," 257; Tedeschi and Calhoun, "The Posttraumatic Growth Inventory," 455–71.

69. Prentiss, "A Glance at a Great Lady," 2.

70. Ibid., 3.

71. Rosey E. Pool, "Suggestions for a Programme of Poetry by American Negroes," 3, SxMs 19/12/2/6, Rosey E. Pool Collection, University of Sussex.

72. Ibid., 3.

73. Dan Beittel to Rosey E. Pool, 28 January 1963, folder 12, box 82-1, Rosey E. Pool Papers, Howard University. It is possible that the NAACP representative Beittel here refers to was Medgar Evers.

74. O'Brien, *We Shall Not Be Moved*, 56.

75. "Statement by Mr. Memphis Norman, student at Tougaloo Southern Christian College, Tougaloo, Mississippi, at Broadway Congregational Church, New York City, Sunday, June 9, 1963," SxMs 19/4/36/3, Rosey E. Pool Collection, University of Sussex.

76. Dittmer, *Local People*, 160. Historian John Dittmer—a former Tougaloo College professor—states that after fire hoses and police dogs were used on Black demonstrators in Birmingham, Alabama (in early May 1963), the NAACP felt compelled to direct its full attention to another big city in the South, eventually choosing Jackson, Mississippi.

77. Lois Chaffee, 22 February 1963 assembly, Tougaloo Southern Christian College, SxMs 19/10/1/7, Rosey E. Pool Collection, University of Sussex; O'Brien, *We Shall Not Be Moved*, 63; "Nazi Germany: Curriculum Study for Mississippi Freedom Schools," FS-

RobinsonB1F9000, WIHVR1709-A, folder 9, box 1, Jo Ann Ooiman Robinson Papers, Mss 191, Freedom Summer Digital Collection, Wisconsin Historical Society. A large part of this case study was devoted to resistance in Denmark. See also Perlstein, "Teaching Freedom," 310.

78. *Beyond the Blues* is listed in the bibliography of "Correspondence and memoranda, 1964," fsCOREMS4thR2S21000, WIHVC239G-A, segment 21, reel 2, microfilm 793, Mississippi 4th Congressional District Records, 1961–66, Congress of Racial Equality, Freedom Summer Digital Collection, Wisconsin Historical Society.

79. Rosey E. Pool to Mari Evans, 31 August 1964, folder 48, box 82-1, Rosey E. Pool Papers, Howard University.

80. Vinnette Carroll to Rosey E. Pool, 21 September 1962, folder 26, box 82-1, Rosey E. Pool Papers, Howard University.

81. Pool, "Creativity," in "As Waves of One Sea," 3.

82. Pool, *Ik ben de Nieuwe Neger*, 14.

Chapter 9. Alabama, 1965–1966

1. Young, "Alabama's *Rocket City*," 8.
2. Pool, "Wat is 'normal' in Alabama?," 15; Pool, *Lachen om niet te huilen*, 33.
3. Laney, *German Rocketeers in the Heart of Dixie*, 32.
4. When in the early 1970s NASA diversity officer Ruth Bates Harris read in a newspaper that Wernher von Braun had used slave labor to build rockets for Hitler's regime, she went to his office. She asked him straight out whether the story was true. "The silence between us was deafening and awesome," she recalled. See McQuaid, "Race, Gender, and Space Exploration," 415.
5. "Ala. City Drops Bias to Keep from Embarrassing Space Work: Will U.S. Dollars Bring Integration to Ala.?," *Jet*, 14 March 1963, 51.
6. Hereford and Ellis, *Beside the Troubled Waters*, 6, 55.
7. Rosey E. Pool, "As Waves of One Sea," 155, SxMs 19/11/1/1, Rosey E. Pool Collection, University of Sussex.
8. Ibid., 155–56. Although the story is impossible to verify, Pool apparently thought it was representative, and she repeatedly wrote about such incidents in letters to friends and also in Dutch newspapers.
9. Official announcement of appointment of and contract for Rosey E. Pool, signed 18 July 1966, SxMs 9/1/1, Rosey E. Pool Collection, University of Sussex.
10. Rosey E. Pool to Langston Hughes, 13 November 1964, folder 2433, box 130, Langston Hughes Papers, JWJ, mss 26, Yale University.
11. Rosey E. Pool to Langston Hughes, 13 January 1965, folder 2433, box 130, Langston Hughes Papers, JWJ, mss 26, Yale University.
12. Roebuck and Murty, *Historically Black Colleges and Universities*, 25; Gasman, *Envisioning Black Colleges*, 22.
13. Rosey E. Pool, introduction to "I Am the New Negro," 18, SxMs 19/11/3/18, Rosey E. Pool Collection, University of Sussex; Rosey E. Pool to Jean Blackwell Hutson, 13 September 1965, folder 69, box 82-2, Rosey E. Pool Papers, Howard University. While Wallace was protesting the desegregation of the University of Alabama at Tuscaloosa (until a federal court order compelled him to desist), nobody seemed to notice that the Huntsville branch of the same university had admitted two African American students. It seems that these students were admitted as a compromise, and to this day Alabama

A&M University is an HBCU, while the University of Alabama in Huntsville is a historically white university. See Hella Pick, "More Trouble Feared in Alabama: President Considers Legislation," *Guardian*, 23 May 1963, 9.

14. Pool, "Wat is 'normal' in Alabama?," 15.

15. Rosey E. Pool to Langston Hughes, 1 October 1966, folder 2433, box 130, Langston Hughes Papers, JWJ, mss 26, Yale University.

16. Rosey E. Pool, quoted in Buys, "The Marvellous Gift for Friendship."

17. Mike Marshall, "Washiri Ajanaku, One of First Two People Arrested in Huntsville's Civil Rights Movement, Returns to Her Hometown," *Huntsville Times*, 17 September 2012. Washiri Ajanaku (formerly known as Frances Sims) was a student at A&M in 1962.

18. Turner, *Sitting in and Speaking Out*, 19.

19. Pool, "Kleurbekentenissen," 15 December 1965, n.p.

20. Pool, *Lachen om niet te huilen*, 31, 72.

21. Vinson, "Rosey Pool: A Reflection," 1984, in Anneke Buys's possession.

22. Rosey E. Pool to Mari Evans, 9 May 1965, folder 48, box 82-1, Rosey E. Pool Papers, Howard.

23. Pool, "Wat is 'normal' in Alabama?," 15.

24. Pool, introduction to "I Am the New Negro," 11.

25. Pool, "As Waves of One Sea," 65.

26. Pool to Hughes, 1 October 1966.

27. Rosey E. Pool, world literature handout, first semester, 1966, SxMs 19/11/3/18, Rosey E. Pool Collection, University of Sussex.

28. Rosey E. Pool, humanities handout, Livingstone College, end of first semester examination, 21 January 1963, SxMs 19/11/3/18, Rosey E. Pool Collection, University of Sussex. This is a handout Pool made when she worked at Livingstone College in North Carolina, but it is very likely that she reused it for her class at Alabama A&M College.

29. Wright, *Black History and Black Identity*, 46.

30. Rosey E. Pool to Barbara and John Beecher, 16 February 1966, folder 11, box 82-1, Rosey E. Pool Papers, Howard University.

31. Rosey E. Pool to Catherine Leslie, 15 May 1967, folder 92, box 82-2, Rosey E. Pool Papers, Howard University.

32. Ibid.

33. Pool, *Lachen om niet te huilen*, 53.

34. Ibid., 63.

35. Catherine Leslie to Anneke Buys, ca. 1985, in Buys's possession.

36. Vinson, "Rosey Pool."

37. Rosey E. Pool to Langston Hughes, 6 February 1965, folder 2434, box 130, Langston Hughes Papers, JWJ, mss 26, Yale University.

38. Pool, introduction to "I Am the New Negro," 18.

39. Pool to Hughes, 6 February 1965.

40. Professor Randolph T. Blackwell was one of those "troublemakers" who left the college in 1962 because he found it impossible to combine his teaching with his work to promote voter registration. Arts teacher Alando X. Jones (aka Willie Cook) was forced to leave A&M College in 1966 because he refused to shave off his beard (which was a sign of "militancy" according to the administration).

41. Turner, *Sitting in and Speaking Out*, 15.

42. The most important sources are two autobiographies and one unpublished thesis: Hereford and Ellis, *Beside the Troubled Waters*, Cashin, *The Agitator's Daughter*, and Curnel, "In the Shadows of Birmingham."

43. "Instructions: Office of the Student Council," Alabama A&M College, 30 May 1965, SxMs 19/4/36/3, Rosey E. Pool Collection, University of Sussex.

44. Pool, "Wat is 'normal' in Alabama?," 15.

45. Pool, "As Waves of One Sea," 197.

46. Ibid., 197.

47. Moss, "NASA and Racial Equality in the South, 1961–1968," 108.

48. Ibid., 2.

49. Hereford and Ellis, *Beside the Troubled Waters*, 88–89.

50. Michael Smith, quoted in Laney, *German Rocketeers in the Heart of Dixie*, 138.

51. Bindas, "Re-remembering a Segregated Past," 115.

52. Williams Fowlkes, "Author Pool Notes Similarity of Nazi Oppression, Segregation," *Atlanta Daily World*, 12 February 1960, 1.

53. Moss, "NASA and Racial Equality in the South," 108.

54. Rosey E. Pool to Virginia Callahan, 3 October 1966, SxMs 19/1/1, Rosey E. Pool Collection, University of Sussex.

55. Katsinas, "George C. Wallace and the Founding of Alabama's Public Two-Year Colleges," 449; Gill, "The Alabama A. and M. Thespians, 1944–1963," 50.

56. Pool, "As Waves of One Sea," 178.

57. Pool to Callahan.

58. Rothberg, *Multidirectional Memory*, 21.

59. Abrams, *Oral History Theory*, 123.

60. Halldórsdóttir, "The Narrative of Silence," 38.

61. Laanes, "Unsayable or Merely Unsaid?," 123–28.

62. Vinson, "Rosey Pool."

Chapter 10. Befriending Langston Hughes, 1945–1967

1. Granovetter, "The Strength of Weak Ties," 1360–80; Labun, Wittek, and Steglich, "The Co-Evolution of Power and Friendship Networks in an Organization," 364–84.

2. Byron, *Women, Revolution and Autobiographical Writing in the Twentieth Century*, 10.

3. Breines, *The Trouble between Us*, 10.

4. More than once Pool described herself as a "grandmother," and over time she came to see W. E. B. Du Bois as a "grandfather" (linearity clearly did not matter in this made-up family).

5. Rosey E. Pool to Owen Dodson, 29 January 1968, SxMs 19/2/1, Rosey E. Pool Collection, University of Sussex.

6. Rosey E. Pool to Hoyt Fuller, ca. July 1967, SxMs 19/1/1, Rosey E. Pool Collection, University of Sussex.

7. Moore, "Local Color, Global 'Color,'" 49–70; Carew, "Translating Whose Vision?," 1.

8. Rampersad, *I, Too, Sing America*, 344.

9. Emanuel van Loggem to Langston Hughes, 15 August 1938, folder 3715, box 224, Langston Hughes Papers, JWJ, mss 26, Yale University; Hughes, *The Collected Works of Langston Hughes*, 150.

10. Rosey E. Pool to Catherine Leslie, 20 June 1967, folder 92, box 82-2, Rosey E. Pool Papers, Howard University.

11. Rosey E. Pool to Langston Hughes, 21 October 1945, folder 2429, box 130, Langston Hughes Papers, JWJ, mss 26, Yale University.

12. Rosey E. Pool to Langston Hughes, 16 February 1953, folder 2430, box 130, Langston Hughes Papers, JWJ, mss 26, Yale University.

13. Heath, *Deep Are the Roots*, 87.

14. Meltzer, *Langston Hughes*, 265.

15. Rosey E. Pool to Langston Hughes, 30 January 1951, folder 2430, box 130, Langston Hughes Papers, JWJ, mss 26, Yale University.

16. Turner, *Caribbean Crusaders and the Harlem Renaissance*, 200–204; Van Enckevort, "The Life and Work of Otto Huiswoud," 108.

17. Langston Hughes to Rosey E. Pool, 1 April 1953, folder 2430, box 130, Langston Hughes Papers, JWJ, mss 26, Yale University.

18. Rampersad, *I Dream a World*, 259.

19. Boter and Geerlings, "Neerkijken en rondzien," 393–414; Gordon Heath, memories of Rosey E. Pool, 1972, SxMs 19/13/1, Rosey E. Pool Collection, University of Sussex.

20. Leach, *Langston Hughes*, 151; Rampersad, *I Dream a World*, 297.

21. Langston Hughes to Rosey E. Pool, 22 November 1961, SxMs 19/2/4, Rosey E. Pool Collection, University of Sussex.

22. Langston Hughes to Rosey E. Pool, 31 August 1965, SxMs 19/2/4, Rosey E. Pool Collection, University of Sussex.

23. Mollenhorst, Völker, and Flap, "Social Contexts and Personal Relationships," 60; Berenskoetter, "Friendship, Security, and Power," 51; Fehr, *Friendship Processes*, 1–20.

24. Won-gu Kim, "'We, Too, Rise with You,'" 422.

25. Pool, "Geven en Nemen: Afrikaanse Renaissance," n.p. See also Pool, "African Renaissance."

26. Meriwether, *Proudly We Can Be Africans*; Von Eschen, *Race against Empire*; Wilford, *The Mighty Wurlitzer*; Horne, "Who Lost the Cold War?," 613–26; Munro, "Imperial Anticommunism," 52–75; Parmar, *Foundations of the American Century*, 97–179.

27. "Opening of AMSAC's West African Cultural Center in Lagos to Be Marked by International 'Gifts of Art' Celebration," *American Society of African Culture Newsletter* 4, no. 2 (1961): 1.

28. Langston Hughes to John A. Davis, 22 November 1961, folder 5, box 35, American Society of African Culture Collection, Howard University.

29. Lagos Festival participants, transcript, folder 7, box 30, American Society of African Culture Collection, Howard University.

30. Rosey E. Pool to Langston Hughes, 3 November 1961, folder 2431, box 130, Langston Hughes Papers, JWJ, mss 26, Yale University.

31. Rosey E. Pool, "As Waves of One Sea," 67–68, SxMs 19/11/1/1, Rosey E. Pool Collection, University of Sussex.

32. Rosey E. Pool to Hank Raullerson, 25 November 1963, folder 55, box 1, American Society of African Culture Collection, Howard University.

33. Pool, "As Waves of One Sea," 67–68.

34. Ibid., 68.

35. Campbell, *Middle Passage*, 222–23; Geerlings, "Performances in the Theatre of the Cold War," 3.

36. Pool, "Beyond the Blues," 5.
37. Rawlins and Russell, "Friendship, Positive Being-with-Others, and the Edifying Practices of Storytelling and Dialogue," 39; Dewey and Rifkin, *Among Friends*, 5.
38. Pool, "As Waves of One Sea," 68.
39. Rosey E. Pool to Milton Meltzer, 27 September 1967, SxMs 19/1/2, Rosey E. Pool Collection, University of Sussex.
40. Ibid.
41. Vogel, "Closing Time," 425.
42. Rosey E. Pool to Langston Hughes, 12 August 1962, folder 2432, box 130, JWJ, mss 26, Langston Hughes Papers, Yale University.
43. Langston Hughes to Rosey E. Pool, 7 November 1965, folder 2433, box 130, JWJ, mss 26, Langston Hughes Papers, Yale University.
44. Smethurst, "'Don't Say Goodbye to the Porkpie Hat,'" 1226; Smethurst, "The Black Arts Movement and Historically Black Colleges and Universities," 90f13.
45. Gaines, *American Africans in Ghana*, 140.
46. Rosey E. Pool, "Langston Hughes," 1, ca. 1967, *Zielen vol soul*, SxMs 19/11/1/2, Rosey E. Pool Collection, University of Sussex.
47. Ibid., 4–5.
48. Rosey E. Pool to American Society of African Culture, October 1964, box 1, American Society of African Culture Collection, Howard University.
49. Langston Hughes to Rosey E. Pool, 22 October 1965, folder 2433, box 130, Langston Hughes Papers, JWJ, mss 26, Yale University. Hughes actually meant "Hilversum."
50. Pool, "Onbetwistbaar en luisterrijk zwart!," 13.
51. Rosey E. Pool to Arthur B. Spingarn, 22 February 1966, folder 144, box 82-3, Rosey E. Pool Papers, Howard University.
52. Pool, *Lachen om niet te huilen*, 47; Pool, "As Waves of One Sea," 63.
53. Pool to Spingarn, 22 February 1966.
54. Gaines, *American Africans in Ghana*, 16.
55. Pool, "Perspectieven van een artistiek Pan-Afrika," n.p.
56. Rosey E. Pool to Dorothy B. Porter, 6 January 1966, folder 128, box 82-2, Rosey E. Pool Papers, Howard University; Léopold Senghor to Rosey E. Pool, 12 July 1966, SxMs 19/4/36/8, Rosey E. Pool Collection, University of Sussex.
57. Harney, *In Senghor's Shadow*, 38.
58. Pool, "Robert Hayden," 43.
59. Fuller, *Journey to Africa*, 92. Many critics found it outrageous that a white woman was appointed as head of the American delegation. Fuller specifically referred to Virginia Inness-Brown, president and chairman of the American corporation for the Dakar Festival.
60. Pool, introduction to "I Am the New Negro," 19, SxMs 19/11/3/18, Rosey E. Pool Collection, University of Sussex. Quote from Elder Robinson (Hope Church, North Carolina).
61. Goldstein, *The Price of Whiteness*, 1.
62. Ratcliff, "When Négritude Was in Vogue," 178.
63. Hughes, "Black Writers in a Troubled World," 506.
64. Ibid., 508. The Johnson Publishing company was founded in 1942.

65. Hatcher, *From the Auroral Darkness*, 35.

66. Pool, "Robert Hayden," 43.

67. Jean Blackwell Hutson to Rosey E. Pool, 19 October 1965, folder 69, box 82-2, Rosey E. Pool Papers, Howard University.

68. Sundquist, *Strangers in the Land*, 226.

69. Rosey E. Pool to Robert Hayden, 28 July 1967, box 16, Robert Hayden Papers, National Baha'i Archives, Wilmette, Ill.

70. Rosey E. Pool to James C. Morris, 26 August 1968, SxMs 19/1/2, Rosey E. Pool Collection, University of Sussex.

71. Rosey E. Pool to Robert Hayden, 22 April 1969, SxMs 19/1/1, Rosey E. Pool Collection, University of Sussex.

72. Ibid.

73. Rosey E. Pool to Margaret Danner, 26 June 1968, SxMs 19/1/1, Rosey E. Pool Collection, University of Sussex.

74. Chester Himes to Rosey E. Pool, 26 October 1971, SxMs 19/2/3, Rosey E. Pool Collection, University of Sussex.

Epilogue

1. Woolf, quoted in Saunders, *Self Impression*, 445.

2. Kaplan, *Victoriana*, 65.

Sources and Methodology

1. Dorothy B. Porter to Rosey E. Pool, 29 December 1965, folder 128, box 82-2, Rosey E. Pool Papers, Howard University.

2. Ramey, *A History of African American Poetry*, 233.

3. Breman, *The Heritage Series of Black Poetry*, n.p.

4. Legêne and Chateau, "Négritude in the Netherlands."

5. Rosey E. Pool to Julia Fields, 9 February 1966, SxMs 19/1/1, Rosey E. Pool Collection, University of Sussex.

6. Dakar folder, SxMs 19/4/36/8, Rosey E. Pool Collection, University of Sussex.

7. Eakin, *The Ethics of Life Writing*, 6–8.

8. Rosey E. Pool to Boele van Hensbroek, 26 February 1969, in Rudi Wesselius's possession. This letter was never sent.

9. Stoler, *Along the Archival Grain*, 96, 155.

10. Hall, "Encoding, Decoding," 128–38.

11. Smethurst, "The Black Arts Movement and Historically Black Colleges and Universities," 90fn13.

12. Meijer, *"M'n hart stond van stocht bijna stil!,"* 13.

13. Legêne, *Spiegelreflex*, 83–118; Sontag, "The Image-World," 80–94.

14. Jan Romein, quoted in Baggerman and Dekker, "'De gevaarlijkste aller bronnen,'" 8.

15. Rosey E. Pool to Mae Mallory, 5 July 1963, SxMs 19/1/2, Rosey E. Pool Collection, University of Sussex.

BIBLIOGRAPHY

Abrams, Lynn. *Oral History Theory*. London: Routledge, 2016.
Abuys, Guido, and Dirk Mulder. *Een gat in het prikkeldraad: Kamp Westerbork, ontsnappingen en verzet*. Hooghalen: Herinneringscentrum Kamp Westerbork, 2003.
Agamben, Giorgio. *Remnants of Auschwitz: The Witness and the Archive*. New York: Zone Books, 1999.
Anstadt, Milo. *Kruis of Munt: Autobiografie, 1920–1945*. Amsterdam: Contact, 2000.
Arbeiders-schrijvers-collectief "Links Richten." *Links richten: Maandblad uitgegeven door Arbeiders-schrijvers-collectief "Links Richten."* Amsterdam: Van Gennep, 1973.
Babb, Valerie M. *Whiteness Visible: The Meaning of Whiteness in American Literature*. New York: New York University Press, 1998.
Baggerman, Arianne, and Rudolf Dekker. "'De gevaarlijkste aller bronnen': Egodocumenten." *TSEG/Low Countries Journal of Social and Economic History* 1, no. 4 (2004): 3–22.
Baldwin, Kate A. *Beyond the Color Line and the Iron Curtain: Reading Encounters between Black and Red, 1922–1963*. Durham, N.C.: Duke University Press, 2002.
Beachy, Robert. *Gay Berlin: Birthplace of a Modern Identity*. New York: Knopf, 2014.
Berenskoetter, Felix. "Friendship, Security, and Power." In *Friendship and International Relations*, edited by Simon Koschut and Andrea Oelsner, 51–71. Basingstoke, UK: Palgrave Macmillan, 2014.
Bindas, Kenneth J. "Re-remembering a Segregated Past: Race in American Memory." *History and Memory* 22, no. 1 (2010): 113–34.
Block, Gay, and Malka Drucker. *Rescuers: Portraits of Moral Courage in the Holocaust*. New York: Holmes and Meier, 1992.
Blom, Hans. "Verzet als norm." *Maatstaf* 34, no. 1 (1986): 20–29.
Blom, Hans, and Joël J. Cahen. "Joodse Nederlanders, Nederlandse joden en joden in Nederland, 1870–1940." In *Geschiedenis van de Joden in Nederland*, edited by Hans Blom, David J. Wertheim, Hetty Berg, and Bart Wallet, 247–310. 1995. Reprint, Amsterdam: Balans, 2017.

Boas, Jacob. *Boulevard des Misères: The Story of Transit Camp Westerbork*. Hamden, Conn.: Archon, 1985.

Boef, August Hans den, and Sjoerd van Faassen. *"Verrek, waar is Berlijn gebleven?" Nederlandse schrijvers en hun kunstbroeders in Berlijn 1918–1945*. Amsterdam: Bas Lubberhuizen, 2002.

Bontemps, Arna. *American Negro Poetry*. New York: Hill and Wang, 1963.

Boom, Bart van der. *"Wij weten niets van hun lot": Gewone Nederlanders en de Holocaust*. Amsterdam: Boom, 2012.

Bordo, Susan. *Unbearable Weight: Feminism, Western Culture, and the Body*. Berkeley: University of California Press, 1993.

Boter, Babs, and Lonneke Geerlings. "Neerkijken en rondzien: Twee reizigers uit Nederland portretteren en presenteren Harlem." *Tijdschrift voor Geschiedenis* 129, no. 3 (2016): 393–414.

Boter, Babs, and Marleen Rensen. Introduction to *Unhinging the National Framework: Perspectives on Transnational Life Writing*, edited by Babs Boter, Giles Scott-Smith, and Marleen Rensen, 7–16. Leiden: Sidestone Press, 2020.

Boyd, Melba Joyce. *Wrestling with the Muse: Dudley Randall and the Broadside Press*. New York: Columbia University Press, 2004.

Braber, Ben. "Passage naar vrijheid: De groep-Van Dien." Master's thesis, University of Amsterdam, 1986.

Braber, Ben. *Passage naar vrijheid: Joods verzet in Nederland 1940–1945*. Amsterdam: Balans, 1987.

Braber, Ben. *This Cannot Happen Here: Integration and Jewish Resistance in the Netherlands, 1940–1945*. Amsterdam: Amsterdam University Press, 2013.

Bregstein, Philo, Johanna Katherina Bloemgarten, and Salvador Bloemgarten-Barends. *Herinnering aan Joods Amsterdam*. 1978. Reprint, Amsterdam: De Bezige Bij, 1999.

Breines, Winifred. *The Trouble between Us: An Uneasy History of White and Black Women in the Feminist Movement*. New York: Oxford University Press, 2006.

Breman, Paul. *The Heritage Series of Black Poetry, 1962 to 1975: A Memoir*. London: private publisher, 2006.

———. *You Better Believe It: Black Verse in English from Africa, the West Indies and the United States*. Harmondsworth, UK: Penguin, 1973.

Brown, Adam. "Beyond 'Good' and 'Evil': Breaking Down Binary Oppositions in Holocaust Representations of 'Privileged' Jews." *History Compass* 8, no. 5 (2010): 407–18.

Brown, Sterling A. *The Collected Poems of Sterling A. Brown*. Edited by Michael S. Harper. Evanston, Ill.: Northwestern University Press, 1996.

———. "Liedje voor kinderen." In *De neger zingt: Amerikaansche negerlyriek*, edited by Jan H. Eekhout, 16. Amsterdam: Uitgeversmaatschappij-Holland, 1936.

Buys, Anneke. "The Marvellous Gift for Friendship: A Biography of Rosey E. Pool, 1905–1971." Unpublished manuscript, 1986, typescript.

Byron, Kristine A. *Women, Revolution, and Autobiographical Writing in the Twentieth Century: Writing History, Writing the Self*. Lampeter, Wales: Edwin Mellen Press, 2007.

Campbell, James. *Middle Passage. African American Journeys to Africa, 1787–2005*. New York: Penguin, 2006.

Carew, Jan. "Paul Robeson and W. E. B. Du Bois in London." *Race and Class* 46, no. 2 (2004): 39–48.

Carew, Joy G. "Translating Whose Vision? Claude McKay, Langston Hughes, Paul Robeson, and the Soviet Experiment." *Intercultural Communication Studies* 23, no. 2 (2014): 1–16.
Caruth, Cathy. *Trauma: Explorations in Memory*. Baltimore, Md.: Johns Hopkins University Press, 1996.
——— . *Unclaimed Experience: Trauma, Narrative, and History*. Baltimore, Md.: Johns Hopkins University Press, 2016.
Cashin, Sheryll D. *The Agitator's Daughter: A Memoir of Four Generations of One Extraordinary African-American Family*. New York: PublicAffairs, 2008.
Cheyette, Bryan. *Diasporas of the Mind: Jewish and Postcolonial Writing and the Nightmare of History*. New Haven, Conn.: Yale University Press, 2014.
Christie, Ian. "Eastern Avatars: Russian Influence on European Avant-Gardes." In *The Emergence of Film Culture: Knowledge Production, Institution Building, and the Fate of the Avant-Garde in Europe, 1919–1945*, edited by Malte Hagener, 143–61. New York: Berghahn, 2017.
Conway, Jill K. *When Memory Speaks: Exploring the Art of Autobiography*. New York: Knopf, 1998.
Cornelissen, Igor. "Tegen het fascisme." In *De taaie rooie rakkers: Een documentaire over het socialisme tussen de wereldoorlogen*, edited by Igor Cornelissen, Ger Harmsen, and Rudolf de Jong, 148–73. Utrecht: Ambo-Boeken, 1965.
Crenshaw, Kimberlé. "Mapping the Margins: Intersectionality, Identity, Politics, and Violence against Women of Color." *Stanford Law Review* 43, no. 6 (1991): 1241–99.
Curnel, Jonathan Brandon. "In the Shadows of Birmingham: The 1962–1963 Huntsville Civil Rights Movement." Master's thesis, American Military University, 2015.
Davis, James, *Eric Walrond: A Life in the Harlem Renaissance and the Transatlantic Caribbean*. New York: Columbia University Press, 2015.
Dawes, Laura. *Childhood Obesity in America: Biography of an Epidemic*. Cambridge, Mass.: Harvard University Press, 2014.
De Grazia, Victoria. *Irresistible Empire: America's Advance through Twentieth-Century Europe*. Cambridge, Mass.: Belknap Press of Harvard University Press, 2005.
Dewey, Anne, and Libbie Rifkin. *Among Friends: Engendering the Social Site of Poetry*. Iowa City: University of Iowa Press, 2013.
Dewulf, Jeroen. *Spirit of Resistance: Dutch Clandestine Literature during the Nazi Occupation*. Rochester, N.Y.: Camden House, 2010.
Dittmer, John. *Local People: The Struggle for Civil Rights in Mississippi*. Urbana: University of Illinois Press, 1994.
Doneson, Judith E. "The American History of Anne Frank's Diary." *Holocaust and Genocide Studies* 2, no. 1 (1987): 149–60.
Düring, Marten. "The Dynamics of Helping Behavior for Jewish Refugees during the Second World War: The Importance of Brokerage." In *Knoten und Kanten*, vol. 3: *Soziale Netzwerkanalyse in Geschichts- und Politikforschung*, edited by Markus Gamper, Linda Reschke, and Marten Düring, 321–37. Bielefeld: Transcript, 2015.
Dyer, Richard. *White: Essays on Race and Culture*. London: Routledge, 1997.
Eakin, Paul John. *The Ethics of Life Writing*. Ithaca, N.Y.: Cornell University Press, 2004.
Edgcomb, Gabrielle Simon. *From Swastika to Jim Crow: Refugee Scholars at Black Colleges*. Malabar, Fla.: Krieger, 1993.

Eekhout, Jan H., ed. *De neger zingt:* Amerikaansche negerlyriek. Amsterdam: Uitgeversmaatschappij-Holland, 1936.

Eekman, Menno, and Herman Pieterson. *Linkssocialisme tussen de wereldoorlogen: Twee studies.* Amsterdam: Stichting Beheer IISG, 1987.

Elteren, Mel van. *Imagining America: Dutch Youth and Its Sense of Place.* Tilburg: Tilburg University Press, 1994.

Enckevort, Maria Gertrudis van. "The Life and Work of Otto Huiswoud: Professional Revolutionary and Internationalist (1893–1961)." PhD diss., University of the West Indies, 2001.

Erll, Astrid. *Memory in Culture.* Basingstoke, UK: Palgrave Macmillan, 2011.

Espinaco-Virseda, Angeles. "'I feel that I belong to you': Subculture, *Die Freundin,* and Lesbian Identities in Weimar Germany." *spacesofidentity* 4, no. 1 (2004): 83–113.

Fehr, Beverley, *Friendship Processes.* Thousand Oaks, Calif.: Sage, 1996.

Figer, Theobald. "Vragen aan een arbeidersvrouw." Translated by Rosey E. Pool. *De proletarische vrouw: Blad voor arbeidsters en arbeidersvrouwen* 25–26, no. 767 (1930): 1.

Flanzbaum, Hilene. *The Americanization of the Holocaust.* Baltimore, Md.: Johns Hopkins University Press, 1999.

Floyd-Thomas, Juan M. "Between Jim Crow and the Swastika: African American Religio-Cultural Interpretations of the Holocaust." *Black Theology* 12, no. 1 (2014): 4–18.

Foster, Gwendolyn Audrey. *Performing Whiteness: Postmodern Re/Constructions in the Cinema.* Albany: State University of New York Press, 2003.

Friedländer, Saul. *Nazi Germany and the Jews, 1933–1945.* New York: Harper Perennial, 2009.

Fuller, Hoyt. *Journey to Africa.* Chicago: Third World Press, 1971.

Gaines, Kevin Kelly. *American Africans in Ghana: Black Expatriates and the Civil Rights Era.* Chapel Hill: University of North Carolina Press, 2006.

Galesloot, Hansje, and Susan Legêne. *Partij in het verzet: De CPN in de Tweede Wereldoorlog.* Amsterdam: Pegasus, 1986.

Galesloot, Hansje, Susan Legêne, and Joop Morriën, eds. *De Waarheid in de oorlog: Een bundeling van illegale nummers uit de jaren '40–'45.* Amsterdam: Pegasus, 1980.

Gans, Evelien. *De kleine verschillen die het leven uitmaken: Een historische studie naar joodse sociaaldemocraten en socialistisch-zionisten in Nederland.* Amsterdam: Vassallucci, 1999.

———. "'Vandaag hebben ze niets—maar morgen bezitten ze weer tien gulden': Antisemitische stereotypen in bevrijd Nederland." In *Polderschouw: Terugkeer en opvang na de Tweede Wereldoorlog: Regionale verschillen,* edited by Conny Kristel, 313–53. Amsterdam: Bakker, 2002.

Garvey, Ellen Gruber. *Writing with Scissors: American Scrapbooks from the Civil War to the Harlem Renaissance.* Oxford: Oxford University Press, 2013.

Gasman, Marybeth. *Envisioning Black Colleges: A History of the United Negro College Fund.* Baltimore, Md.: Johns Hopkins University Press, 2007.

Gasman, Marybeth, and Roger L. Geiger. *Higher Education for African Americans before the Civil Rights Era, 1900–1964.* New Brunswick, N.J.: Transaction, 2012.

Gay, Peter, *Weimar Culture: The Outsider as Insider.* 1968. Reprint, New York: Norton, 2001.

Geerlings, Lonneke, "'23a Paradise,' a Dutch 'Salon' in North London: Rosey E. Pool's promotion of African American Poetry in the 1950s and 1960s." In *International Solidarity Movements in the Low Countries during the Twentieth Century: New Perspectives and Themes*, edited by Kim Christiaens, John Nieuwenhuys, and Charles Roemer, 127–28. Berlin: De Gruyter 2020.

———. "Heynemann, Susanne." *Digitaal Vrouwenlexicon van Nederland*, July 4, 2018. http://resources.huygens.knaw.nl/vrouwenlexicon/lemmata/data/Heynemann.

———. "'Much More Freedom of Thought Than Expected There': Rosey E. Pool, a Dutch Fellow Traveler on Holiday in the Soviet Union (1965)." In *Tourism and Travel during the Cold War: Negotiating Tourist Experiences across the Iron Curtain*, edited by Sune Bechmann Pedersen and Christian Noack, 123–38. London: Routledge, 2019.

———. "Performances in the Theatre of the Cold War: The American Society of African Culture and the 1961 Lagos Festival." *Journal of Transatlantic Studies* 16, no. 1 (2018): 1–19.

———. "A Visual Analysis of Rosey E. Pool's Correspondence Archives: Biographical Data, Intersectionality, and Social Network Analysis." *CEUR Workshop Proceedings* 1339 (2015): 61–67. http://ceur-ws.org/Vol-1399/paper10.pdf.

———. "W. E. B. Du Bois at Ons Suriname, Amsterdam: Transnational Networks and Dutch Anti-Colonial Activism in the Late 1950s." In *Unhinging the National Framework: Perspectives on Transnational Life Writing*, edited by Babs Boter, Marleen Rensen, and Giles Scott-Smith, 81–97. Leiden: Sidestone Press, 2020.

Geerlings, Lonneke, and Ellen de Vries. "'Er is heel wat goed te maken': Rosey Pool en Nola Hatterman, witte culturele bemiddelaars voor 'zwarte' kunst." In *Het andere postkoloniale oog Onbekende kanten van de Nederlandse (post)koloniale cultuur en literatuur*, edited by Michiel van Kempen, 193–202. Hilversum: Verloren, 2020.

Gill, Glenda E. "The Alabama A. and M. Thespians, 1944–1963: Triumph of the Human Spirit." *Drama Review* 38, no. 4 (1994): 48–70.

Gilman, Sander L. *Fat: A Cultural History of Obesity*. Cambridge, UK: Polity, 2008.

Gilroy, Paul. *Against Race: Imagining Political Culture beyond the Color Line*. Cambridge, Mass.: Belknap Press of Harvard University Press, 2001.

———. *The Black Atlantic: Modernity and Double Consciousness*. Cambridge, Mass.: Harvard University Press, 1993.

Ginneken, Jaap van. *Kurt Baschwitz: A Pioneer of Communication Studies and Social Psychology*. Amsterdam: Amsterdam University Press, 2018.

Goldenberg, Jennifer. "'I had no family, but I made family': Immediate Post-War Coping Strategies of Adolescent Survivors of the Holocaust." *Counselling and Psychotherapy Research* 9, no. 1 (2009): 18–26.

Goldstein, Eric L. *The Price of Whiteness: Jews, Race, and American Identity*. Princeton, N.J.: Princeton University Press, 2006.

Graaff, Bob de, and Lidwien Marcus. *Kinderwagens en korsetten: Een onderzoek naar de sociale achtergrond en de rol van vrouwen in het verzet, 1940–1945*. Amsterdam: Bakker, 1980.

Graham, Shane. "Black Atlantic Literature as Transnational Cultural Space." *Literature Compass* 10, no. 6 (2013): 508–18.

Graham, Shane, and John Walters, eds. *Langston Hughes and the South African Drum Generation: The Correspondence*. New York: Palgrave Macmillan, 2010.

Granovetter, Mark S. "The Strength of Weak Ties." *American Journal of Sociology* 78, no. 6 (1973): 1360–80.

Greenberg, Cheryl Lynn. *Troubling the Waters: Black-Jewish Relations in the American Century*. Princeton, N.J.: Princeton University Press, 2006.

Greene, Roberta R., and Sandra A. Graham. "Role of Resilience among Nazi Holocaust Survivors: A Strength-Based Paradigm for Understanding Survivorship." *Family and Community Health* 32, no. 1 (2009): s75–s82.

Griffioen, Amber L. "Regaining the 'Lost Self': A Philosophical Analysis of Survivor's Guilt." In *Altered Self and Altered Self-Experience*, edited by Alexander Gerner and Jorge Gonçalves, 43–57. N.p.: Norderstedt Books on Demand, 2014.

Gross, Michael L. "Jewish Rescue in Holland and France during the Second World War: Moral Cognition and Collective Action." *Social Forces* 73, no. 2 (1994): 463–96.

Grünberg-Klein, Hannelore. *Zolang er nog tranen zijn*. Amsterdam: Nijgh en Van Ditmar, 2015.

Hall, Stuart. "Encoding, Decoding." In *Culture, Media, Language: Working Papers in Cultural Studies, 1972–1979*, edited by the Centre for Contemporary Cultural Studies, 128–38. 1973. Reprint, London: Routledge, 1980.

——. "Political Belonging in a World of Multiple Identities." In *Conceiving Cosmopolitanism: Theory, Context, and Practice*, edited by Steven Vertovec and Robin Cohen, 25–31. Oxford: Oxford University Press, 2002.

Halldórsdóttir, Erla Hulda. "The Narrative of Silence." *Life Writing* 7, no. 1 (2010): 37–50.

Harmsen, Ger. *Blauwe en rode jeugd: Ontstaan, ontwikkeling en teruggang van de Nederlandse jeugdbeweging tussen 1853 en 1940*. 1961. Reprint, Nijmegen: SUN, 1973.

Harney, Elizabeth. *In Senghor's Shadow: Art, Politics, and the Avant-Garde in Senegal, 1960–1995*. Durham, N.C.: Duke University Press, 2004.

Hartveld, Leo, Frits de Jong Edz, and Dries Kuperus. *De Arbeiders Jeugd Centrale AJC: 1918–1940, 1945–1959*. Amsterdam: Van Gennep, 1982.

Hatcher, John. *From the Auroral Darkness: The Life and Poetry of Robert Hayden*. Oxford, UK: Ronald, 1984.

Hausmann, Frank-Rutger. "English and Romance Studies in Germany's Third Reich." In *Nazi Germany and the Humanities: How German Academics Embraced Nazism*, edited by Anson Rabinbach and Wolfgang Bialas, 341–64. London: Oneworld, 2014.

Hayden, Robert. *Collected Poems*. Edited by Frederick Glaysher. New York: Liveright, 1996.

——. *How I Write/1*. New York: Harcourt Brace Jovanovich, 1972.

——. *Kaleidoscope: Poems by American Negro Poets*. New York: Harcourt, Brace and World, 1967.

Heath, Gordon. *Deep Are the Roots: Memoirs of a Black Expatriate*. Amherst: University of Massachusetts Press, 1992.

Heddon, Deirdre. "Performing Lesbians: Constructing the Self, Constructing the Community." In *Auto/Biography and Identity: Women, Theatre, and Performance*, edited by Maggie B. Gale and Vivien Gardner, 217–38. Manchester, UK: Manchester University Press, 2004.

Hereford, Sonnie W., and Jack D. Ellis. *Beside the Troubled Waters: A Black Doctor Remembers Life, Medicine, and Civil Rights in an Alabama Town*. Tuscaloosa: University of Alabama Press, 2011.

Herlemann, Beatrix. "Het Exil als operatiebasis: De Duitse communistische emigratie in Nederland, 1933–1945." In *Nederland en het Duitse exil, 1933–1940*, edited by Kathinka Dittrich and Hans Würzner, 127–43. Amsterdam: Van Gennep, 1982.

Herman, Judith Lewis. *Trauma and Recovery: The Aftermath of Violence, from Domestic Abuse to Political Terror*. London: Pandora, 1997.

Hilberg, Raul. *Perpetrators, Victims, Bystanders: The Jewish Catastrophe, 1933–1945*. New York: Aaron Asher Books, 1992.

Hillesum, Etty. *Etty: The Letters and Diaries of Etty Hillesum, 1941–1943*. Edited by Klaas A. D. Smelik. Ottawa: William B. Eerdmans, 2002.

Hofmeester, Karin. *Jewish Workers and the Labour Movement: A Comparative Study of Amsterdam, London, and Paris, 1870–1914*. Aldershot, UK: Ashgate, 2004.

Hondius, Dienke. *Blackness in Western Europe: Racial Patterns of Paternalism and Exclusion*. New Brunswick, N.J.: Transaction, 2014.

———. *Return: Holocaust Survivors and Dutch Anti-Semitism*. Westport, Conn.: Praeger, 2003.

Hondius, Dienke, and Miep Gompes-Lobatto. *Absent: Herinneringen aan het Joods Lyceum Amsterdam, 1941–1943*. Amsterdam: Vassallucci, 2001.

Horne, Gerald. "Who Lost the Cold War? Africans and African Americans." *Diplomatic History* 20, no. 4 (1996): 613–26.

Hughes, Langston. "Black Writers in a Troubled World." In *Colloquium: Function and Significance of African Negro Art in the Life of the People and for the People (March 30–April 8, 1966)*, 505–10. Paris: Editions Présence Africaine, 1968.

———. *The Collected Works of Langston Hughes: Essays on Art, Race, Politics, and World Affairs*. Columbia: University of Missouri Press, 2001.

———. "Nazi and Dixie Nordics." In *Civil Rights since 1787: A Reader on the Black Struggle*, edited by Jonathan Birnbaum and Clarence Taylor, 318–20. New York: New York University Press, 2000.

Hyman, Paula E. "Keeping Calm and Weathering the Storm: Jewish Women's Responses to Daily Life in Nazi Germany, 1933–1939." In *Women in the Holocaust*, edited by Dalia Ofer and Lenore J. Weitzman, 39–54. New Haven, Conn.: Yale University Press, 1998.

Ibsch, Lrud. "Writing against Silence: Jewish Writers of the Generation-after in the Netherlands, Germany, Austria, and France." In *The Dutch Intersection: The Jews and the Netherlands in Modern History*, edited by Yosef Kaplan, 389–402. Leiden: Brill, 2008.

Jong, Rudolf de. "Kunst en Cultuur." In *De taaie rooie rakkers: Een documentaire over het socialisme tussen de wereldoorlogen*, edited by Igor Cornelissen, Ger Harmsen, and Rudolf de Jong, 223–49. Utrecht: Ambo-Boeken, 1965.

Jouwe, Nancy. "Standing at the Crossroads: The Black, Migrant, and Refugee Women's Movement in the Netherlands." *Historica* 39, no. 3 (2016): 3–8.

Kaplan, Carla. *Miss Anne in Harlem: The White Women of the Black Renaissance*. New York: Harper, 2013.

Kaplan, Cora. *Victoriana: Histories, Fictions, Criticisms*. Edinburgh: Edinburgh University Press, 2007.

Katsinas, Stephen G. "George C. Wallace and the Founding of Alabama's Public Two-Year Colleges." *Journal of Higher Education* 65, no. 4 (1994): 447–72.

Keating, Ann Durkin. "'Keep up the agitation': Rev. Jerry Forshey and a KKK Cross from Jackson, Mississippi." *Journal of the Illinois State Historical Society* 107, no. 1 (2014): 45–76.

Kellner, Bruce. "'Refined Racism': White Patronage in the Harlem Renaissance." In *The Harlem Renaissance*, edited by Harold Bloom, 53–66. Philadelphia: Chelsea House Publishers, 2004.

Kim, Daniel Won-gu. "'We, Too, Rise with You': Recovering Langston Hughes's African (Re)Turn 1954–1960 in *An African Treasury*, the *Chicago Defender*, and *Black Orpheus*." *African American Review* 41, no. 3 (2007): 419–41.

Kinnamon, Keneth. "Anthologies of African-American Literature from 1845 to 1994." *Callaloo* 20, no. 2 (1997): 461–81.

Klandermans, Bert. "Motivation and Types of Motives (Instrumental, Identity, Ideological Motives)." In *The Wiley-Blackwell Encyclopedia of Social and Political Movements*, edited by David A. Snow, Donatella della Porta, Bert Klandermans, and Doug McAdam, 778–80. Malden, Mass.: Wiley-Blackwell, 2013.

Knegtmans, Peter Jan. "Voor wetenschap en maatschappij: Het zelfbeeld van studenten in de Sociaal-Democratische Studentenclubs." In *Keurige wereldbestormers: Over studenten en hun rol in de Nederlandse samenleving sedert 1876*, ed. Leen Dorsman and Peter Jan Knegtmans, 39–51. Hilversum: Verloren, 2008.

Kolk, Bessel A. van der. *The Body Keeps the Score: Mind, Brain and Body in the Transformation of Trauma*. London: Allen Lane, 2014.

———. "The Compulsion to Repeat the Trauma." *Psychiatric Clinics of North America* 12, no. 2 (1989): 389–411.

Kolker, Robert. *Film, Form, and Culture*. London: Routledge, 2016.

Kooten Niekerk, Anja van, and Sacha Wijmer. *Verkeerde vriendschap: Lesbisch leven in de jaren 1920–1960*. Amsterdam: Feministische Uitgeverij Sara, 1985.

Kramer, Gerhard F. *Portugal am Pranger: Der portugiesische Kolonialismus. Feind der Völker Afrikas*. Berlin: Dietz, 1964.

———. *We Shall March Again*. New York: Putnam, 1955. Translation of Gerhard F. Kramer, *Wir Werden Weiter Marschieren*. Berlin: Blanvalet, 1952.

Kramer, Santje. *De keuken van kamp Westerbork: Alle dagen stamppot*. NPO documentary, August 2016.

Kruse, Kevin M., and Stephen G. N. Tuck, eds. *Fog of War: The Second World War and the Civil Rights Movement*. New York: Oxford University Press, 2012.

Krystal, Henry. "Trauma and Aging: A Thirty-Year Follow-Up." In *Trauma: Explorations in Memory*, edited by Cathy Caruth, 76–99. Baltimore, Md.: Johns Hopkins University Press 1996.

Kuipers, Giselinde. "1 oktober 1957, Donald Jones verschijnt in *Pension Hommeles*: De rol van gekleurde acteurs in Nederlandse televisiehumor." In *Cultuur en migratie in Nederland: Kunsten in beweging 1900–1980*, edited by Rosemarie Buikema and Maaike Meijer, 291–306. The Hague: SDU, 2003.

Kuitenbrouwer, Maarten. *De ontdekking van de derde wereld: Beeldvorming en beleid in Nederland, 1950–1990*. The Hague: SDU, 1994.

Kushner, Tony. "Britain, the United States, and the Holocaust: In Search of a Historiography." In *The Historiography of the Holocaust*, edited by Dan Stone, 253–75. London: Palgrave Macmillan, 2004.

Kynaston, David. *Modernity Britain: 1957–62*. London: Bloomsbury, 2015.

Laanes, Eneken. "Unsayable or Merely Unsaid?" In *Haunted Narratives: Life Writing* in an Age of Trauma, edited by Gabriele Rippl, 123–28. Toronto: University of Toronto Press, 2013.

Labun, Alona, Rafael Wittek, and Christian Steglich. "The Co-Evolution of Power and Friendship Networks in an Organization." *Network Science* 4, no. 3 (2016): 364–84.

Laney, Monique. *German Rocketeers in the Heart of Dixie: Making Sense of the Nazi Past during the Civil Rights Era.* New Haven, Conn.: Yale University Press, 2015.

Langer, Lawrence L. "The Americanization of the Holocaust on Stage and Screen." In *Anne Frank: Reflections on Her Life and Legacy*, edited by Hyman Aaron Enzer and Sandra Solotaroff-Enzer, 198–202. Urbana: University of Illinois Press, 2000.

———. *Versions of Survival: The Holocaust and the Human Spirit.* Albany: State University of New York Press, 1982.

Last, Dick van Galen. *De zwarte schande: Afrikaanse soldaten in Europa, 1914–1922.* Edited by Ralf Futselaar. Amsterdam: Atlas Contact, 2012.

Leach, Laurie. *Langston Hughes: A Biography.* Westport, Conn.: Greenwood Press, 2004.

Lee, Carol Ann. *The Hidden Life of Otto Frank.* New York: Perennial, 2003.

Legêne, Susan. *Spiegelreflex: Culturele sporen van de koloniale ervaring.* Amsterdam: Bakker, 2010.

Legêne, Susan, and Eugène Chateau. "Négritude in the Netherlands: Humanism and the Cultural Programme of Rosey E. Pool." Paper presented at NINSEE symposium "Trajectories of Emancipation," Vrije Universiteit Amsterdam, 30 June 2009.

Lester, Julius. *Lovesong: Becoming a Jew.* 1988. Reprint, New York: Skyhorse, 2013.

———. "The Stone That Weeps." In *Testimony: Contemporary Writers Make the Holocaust Personal*, edited by David Rosenberg, 192–210. New York: Times Books, 1989.

Lev-Wiesel, Rachel, and Marianne Amir. "Growing Out of Ashes: Posttraumatic Growth among Holocaust Child Survivors—Is It Possible?" In *Handbook of Posttraumatic Growth: Research and Practice*, edited by Lawrence G. Calhoun and Richard G. Tedeschi, 248–63. New York: Routledge, 2009.

Lewin, Lisette. *Het clandestiene boek, 1940–1945.* Amsterdam: Van Gennep, 1983.

Leydesdorff, Selma. "When All Is Lost: Metanarrative in the Oral History of Hanifa, Survivor of Srebrenica." In *Listening on the Edge: Oral History in the Aftermath of Crisis*, edited by Mark Cave and Stephen Sloan, 17–32. Oxford: Oxford University Press, 2014.

———. *Wij hebben als mens geleefd: Het Joodse proletariaat van Amsterdam 1900–1940.* Amsterdam: Meulenhoff, 1987.

Leys, Ruth. *From Guilt to Shame: Auschwitz and After.* Princeton, N.J.: Princeton University Press, 2009.

Lipschits, Isaac. *De kleine sjoa: Joden in naoorlogs Nederland.* Amsterdam: Mets en Schilt, 2001.

Lipstadt, Deborah E. "America and the Memory of the Holocaust, 1950–1965." *Modern Judaism* 16, no. 3 (1996): 195–214.

———. *Denying the Holocaust: The Growing Assault on Truth and Memory.* New York: Free Press, 1993.

Lowe, Maria R. "An 'Oasis of Freedom' in a 'Closed Society': The Development of Tougaloo College as a Free Space in Mississippi's Civil Rights Movement, 1960 to 1964." *Journal of Historical Sociology* 20, no. 4 (2007): 486–520.

———. "An Unseen Hand: The Role of Sociology Professor Ernst Borinski in Mississippi's Struggle for Racial Integration in the 1950s and 1960s." *Leadership* 4, no. 1 (2008): 27–47.

Lowe, Maria R., J. Clint Morris, and Madeline L. Pizzo. "Academic Agitators in Mississippi: Advancing the Cause of Racial Equality at Millsaps College and Tougaloo College." Paper presented at American Sociological Association Annual Meeting, Washington, D.C., August 2000.

Lubbers, Annette. *Lloydhotel*. Amsterdam: Lubberhuizen, 2004.

Madgett, Naomi Cornelia Long. *Exits and Entrances*. Detroit, Mich.: Lotus Press, 1978.

Matera, Marc. *Black London: The Imperial Metropolis and Decolonization in the Twentieth Century*. Berkeley: University of California Press, 2015.

McAdam, Doug. "Recruitment to High-Risk Activism: The Case of Freedom Summer." *American Journal of Sociology* 92, no. 1 (1986): 64–90.

McQuaid, Kim. "Race, Gender, and Space Exploration: A Chapter in the Social History of the Space Age." *Journal of American Studies* 41, no. 2 (2007): 405–34.

McWilliams, Nancy. "The Psychology of the Altruist." *Psychoanalytic Psychology* 1, no. 3 (1984): 193–213.

Mechanicus, Philip. *In depôt: Dagboek uit Westerbork van Philip Mechanicus*. Amsterdam: Polak en Van Gennep, 1964.

Meijer, Maaike. *"M'n hart stond van stocht bijna stil!" (F. Harmsen van Beek): Dichters en hun biografen*. Maastricht: Maastricht University, 2014.

Meilof, Jan. *Een wereld licht en vrij: Het culturele werk van de AJC*. Amsterdam: Stichting Beheer IISG, 1999.

Melkman, Joseph. "David Cohen." *Studia Rosenthaliana* 4, no. 2 (1970): 219–27.

Melnick, Ralph, *The Stolen Legacy of Anne Frank: Meyer Levin, Lillian Hellman, and the Staging of the Diary*. New Haven, Conn.: Yale University Press, 1997.

Meltzer, Milton. *Langston Hughes: A Biography*. New York: Crowell, 1968.

Meriwether, James. *Proudly We Can Be Africans: Black Americans and Africa, 1935–1961*. Chapel Hill: University of North Carolina Press, 2002.

Michielse, Hendrik Cornelis Marie. *Socialistiese vorming: Het Instituut voor Arbeidersontwikkeling (1924–1940) en het vormings- en scholingswerk van de Nederlandse sociaal-demokratie sinds 1900*. Nijmegen: Socialistiese Uitgeverij Nijmegen, 1980.

Michman, Jozeph, Hartog Beem, and Dan Michman. *Pinkas: Geschiedenis van de joodse gemeenschap in Nederland*. Amsterdam: Contact, 1999.

Mollenhorst, Gerald, Beate Völker, and Henk Flap. "Social Contexts and Personal Relationships: The Effect of Meeting Opportunities on Similarity for Relationships of Different Strength." *Social Networks* 30, no. 1 (2008): 60–68.

Monroe, Kristen Renwick. "Cracking the Code of Genocide: The Moral Psychology of Rescuers, Bystanders, and Nazis during the Holocaust." *Political Psychology* 29, no. 5 (2008): 699–736.

Moore, Bob. *Refugees from Nazi Germany in the Netherlands, 1933–1940*. Dordrecht: Nijhoff, 1986.

Moore, David Chioni. "Local Color, Global 'Color': Langston Hughes, the Black Atlantic, and Soviet Central Asia, 1932." *Research in African Literatures* 27, no. 4 (1996): 49–70.

Moraal, Eva. *Als ik morgen niet op transport ga . . . : Kamp Westerbork in beleving en herinnering*. Amsterdam: De Bezige Bij, 2014.

Morgan, Kathryn Pauly. "Describing the Emperor's New Clothes: Three Myths of Educational (In-)Equity." In *The Gender Question in Education: Theory, Pedagogy, and Politics*, edited by Ann Diller, Barbara Houston, Kathryn Pauly Morgan, and Maryann Ayim, 105–22. Boulder, Colo.: Westview, 1996.

Morrison, Toni. *Playing in the Dark: Whiteness and the Literary Imagination*. New York: Vintage, 1992.

Moss, Steven L. "NASA and Racial Equality in the South, 1961–1968." Master's thesis, Texas Tech University, 1997.

Munro, John. "Imperial Anticommunism and the African American Freedom Movement in the Early Cold War." *History Workshop Journal* 79, no. 1 (2015): 52–75.

Newport, Barry, ed. *A Hand and Flower Anthology: Poems and Fables Commemorating Erica Marx and the Hand and Flower Press*. N.p.: privately printed, 1980.

O'Brien, Mike J. *We Shall Not Be Moved: The Jackson Woolworth's Sit-In and the Movement It Inspired*. Jackson: University Press of Mississippi, 2013.

Olweus, Dan. "Bullying at School: Long-Term Outcomes for the Victims and an Effective School-Based Intervention Program." In *Aggressive Behavior: Current Perspectives*, ed. L. Rowell Huesmann, 97–130. New York: Plenum Press, 1994.

Ott, Katherine, Susan Tucker, and Patricia P. Buckler. *The Scrapbook in American Life*. Philadelphia: Temple University Press, 2006.

Parmar, Inderjeet. *Foundations of the American Century: The Ford, Carnegie, and Rockefeller Foundations and the Rise of American Power*. New York: Columbia University Press, 2012.

Pattynama, Pamela. "Etnocentrisme en waarheid." In *Vrouwenstudies in de jaren negentig: Een kennismaking vanuit verschillende disciplines*, edited by Margo Brouns, Mieke Verloo, and Marianne Grünell, 211–32. Bussum: Coutinho, 1995.

Perlstein, Daniel. "Teaching Freedom: SNCC and the Creation of the Mississippi Freedom Schools." *History of Education Quarterly* 30, no. 3 (1990): 297–324.

Pol, Angelique van der. "Mazirel, Laura Carola." *Digitaal Vrouwenlexicon van Nederland*, 4 July 2016. http://resources.huygens.knaw.nl/vrouwenlexicon/lemmata/data/Mazirel.

Polletta, Francesca. *It Was like a Fever: Storytelling in Protest and Politics*. Chicago: University of Chicago Press, 2006.

Ponse, Barbara. "The Social Construction of Identity and Its Meanings within the Lesbian Subculture." In *Social Perspectives on Lesbian and Gay Studies: A Reader*, edited by Peter M. Nardi and Beth E. Schneider, 246–60. Abingdon, UK: Routledge, 2013.

Pool, Rosey E. "'Advocaat pro deo' pleit voor allen." *Vrije Geluiden: Radio- en Televisieprogrammablad van de VPRO*, 6 September 1958, 6.

———. "African Renaissance." *Phylon* 14, no. 1 (1953): 5–8.

———. "Anne Frank: The Child and the Legend." *World Order* 6, no. 3 (1972): 51–56.

———. "Arbeiderstooneel en film te Berlijn." *De nieuwe weg* 4 (1929): 125–27.

———. *Beperkt zicht*. Amsterdam: Querido, 1945.

———. "Beyond the Blues: Modern Trends in Afro-American Poetry." *American Society of African Culture Newsletter*, supplement, no. 24 (1962): 4–5.

———, ed. *Beyond the Blues: New Poems by American Negroes*. Aldington, UK: Hand and Flower Press, 1962.

———. *Black and Unknown Bards: A Collection of Negro Poetry*. Aldington, UK: Hand and Flower Press, 1958.

———. "Ça Ira," *Kentering* 2, no. 4 (1925): 56–57.

———. "Clubnieuws," *Kentering* 3, no. 5 (1926): 79.
———. "De Diets-Akademiese Leergang te Amsterdam," *Kentering* 3, no. 7 (1926): 110–11.
———. "De kunst van den neger." *Vrij Nederland*, 3 August 1946, 7.
———. "Een reuze-baan!!!" In *Een gat in het prikkeldraad: Kamp Westerbork, ontsnappingen en verzet*, edited by Guido Abuys and Dirk Mulder, 16–17. Hooghalen: Herinneringscentrum Kamp Westerbork, 2003.
———. "Feest," *Kentering* 2, no. 8 (1926): 117.
———. "Geven en Nemen: Afrikaanse Renaissance." *Vrij Nederland*, 11 October 1952, n.p.
———, ed. *Ik ben de Nieuwe Neger: Gedichten, rijmen, liedjes en dokumenten uit 300 jaar verzet van de Amerikaanse neger*. The Hague: Bakker, 1963.
———. "Ik zie, ik zie, wat jij niet ziet . . . namelijk: Toneel in Londen." *Vox Guyanae* 3, no. 6 (1959): 32–36.
———. "Kleurbekentenissen," *Vrij Nederland*, 25 September 1965, n.p.
———. "Kleurbekentenissen," *Vrij Nederland*, 15 December 1965, n.p.
———. *Lachem om niet te huilen*. Rotterdam: Lemniscaat, 1968.
———. "Onbetwistbaar en luisterrijk zwart! Het Eerste Wereld-Festival van Negerkunst te Dakar," *AVRO-Bode*, 29 May 1966, 11–13.
———. *'n Engelse sleutel: Een ABC over het "Perfide Albion."* Amsterdam: De Boer, 1957.
———. "The Negro Actor in Europe." *Phylon* 14, no. 3 (1953): 258–67.
———. "Perspectieven van een artistiek Pan-Afrika: Eerste wereldfestival voor negerkunst in Dakar." *Vrij Nederland*, 23 April 1966, n.p.
———. "Robert Hayden, Poet Laureate: An Assessment." *Negro Digest* 15, no. 8 (1966): 39–47.
———. "Schril licht op zwarte zijde der democratie in Amerika, het land van de zeven vrijheden. Dertien millioen negers vernederd door geschreven en ongeschreven wetten." *Haarlems dagblad*, 22 April 1947, 2.
———. "UNO in Croydon." *Vrij Nederland*, 17 February 1951, 8.
———. "Vijfentwintig minuten 'Damnyankee.'" *Vrij Nederland*, 12 March 1966, n.p.
———. "Wat is 'normal' in Alabama? Dagelijks leven in het zuiden." *Vrij Nederland*, 17 April 1965, 15.
Pool, Rosey E., and Paul Breman, eds. *Ik zag hoe zwart ik was: Verzen van Noord-Amerikaanse Negers*. The Hague: Bakker, 1958.
Portelli, Alessandro, "What Makes Oral History Different?" In *Oral History, Oral Culture, and Italian Americans: Italian and Italian American Studies*, edited by Luisa Del Giudice 21–30. New York: Palgrave Macmillan, 2009.
Presser, Jacques, *Ondergang: De vervolging en verdelging van het Nederlandse jodendom, 1940–1945*. Vol. 1. The Hague: Staatsuitgeverij, 1985.
Procter, James, editor. *Writing Black Britain, 1948–1998: An Interdisciplinary Anthology*. Manchester, UK: Manchester University Press, 2000.
Putnam, Robert. *Bowling Alone: The Collapse and Revival of American Community*. New York: Simon and Schuster, 2000.
Radde, Gerd. "Fritz Karsens Reformwerk in Berlin-Neukölln." In *Schulreform, Kontinuitäten und Brüche: Das Versuchsfeld Berlin-Neukölln, 1912 bis 1945*, edited by Gerd Radde, 175–87. Opladen: Leske und Budrich, 1993.
Ramazani, Jahan. *A Transnational Poetics*. Chicago: University of Chicago Press, 2009.

Ramey, Lauri, and Paul Breman, editors. *The Heritage Series of Black Poetry, 1962–1975: A Research Compendium*. Aldershot, UK: Ashgate, 2008.

Rampersad, Arnold. *I Dream a World*. Vol. 2 of *The Life of Langston Hughes*. 1988. Reprint, New York: Oxford University Press, 2002.

———. *I, Too, Sing America*. Vol. 1 of *The Life of Langston Hughes*. 1986. Reprint, Oxford: Oxford University Press, 2002.

Ratcliff, Anthony J. "When Négritude Was in Vogue: Critical Reflections of the First World Festival of Negro Arts and Culture in 1966." *Journal of Pan African Studies* 6, no. 7 (2014): 167–86.

Rawlins, William K., and Laura D. Russell. "Friendship, Positive Being-with-Others, and the Edifying Practices of Storytelling and Dialogue." In *Positive Psychology of Love*, edited by Mahzad Hojjat and Duncan Cramer, 30–43. Oxford: Oxford University Press, 2013.

Renders, Hans. *Gevaarlijk drukwerk: Een vrije uitgeverij in oorlogstijd*. Amsterdam: De Bezige Bij, 2004.

Rich, Adrienne. "Compulsory Heterosexuality and Lesbian Existence." *Signs: Journal of Women in Culture and Society* 5, no. 4 (1980): 631–60.

———. "When We Dead Awaken: Writing as Re-Vision." *College English* 34, no. 1 (1972): 18–30.

Riet, Frank van. *De bewakers van Westerbork*. Amsterdam: Boom, 2016.

Righart, Hans, and Piet de Rooij. "In Holland staat een huis: Weerzin en vertedering over 'de jaren vijftig.'" In *Een stille revolutie? Cultuur en mentaliteit in de lange jaren vijftig*, edited by Paul Luykx and Pim Slot, 11–18. Hilversum: Verloren, 1997.

Rijsdijk, Mink van. *Reünie op papier: Joodse oorlogskinderen kijken terug op hun jaren aan die "wonderlijke school."* Weert: Van Buuren, 2000.

Rive, Richard. *Writing Black*. Cape Town: David Philip, 1981.

Roebuck, Julian B., and Komanduri S. Murty. *Historically Black Colleges and Universities: Their Place in American Higher Education*. Westport, Conn.: Praeger, 1993.

Roo, Jos de. "Praatjes voor de West: De Wereldomroep en de Antilliaanse en Surinaamse literatuur, 1947–1958." PhD thesis, University of Amsterdam, 2014.

Rosen, Jules, et al. "Sleep Disturbances in Survivors of the Nazi Holocaust." *American Journal of Psychiatry* 148, no. 1 (1991): 62–66.

Rossouw, P. J. "Die bevrydingstryd: Biblioterapie as kognitiewe herstrukturering by slagoffers van gewapende konflik in Suidelike Afrika." In *De helende kracht van literatuur: Over Nederlands en Suid-Afrikaans oorlogsproza*, edited by Chris van der Merwe and Rolf Wolfswinkel, 33–59. Haarlem: In de Knipscheer, 2002.

Rothberg, Michael. *Multidirectional Memory: Remembering the Holocaust in the Age of Decolonization*. Stanford, Calif.: Stanford University Press, 2009.

Rozett, Robert. "Jewish Resistance." In *The Historiography of the Holocaust*, edited by Dan Stone, 341–63. London: Palgrave Macmillan, 2004.

Santen, Salomon. *Dapper zijn omdat het goed is: Brieven uit de cel*. 1993. Reprint, Amsterdam: De Bezige Bij, 2012.

Saunders, Max. *Self Impression: Life-Writing, Autobiografiction, and the Forms of Modern Literature*. Oxford: Oxford University Press, 2010.

Schoppmann, Claudia. *Days of Masquerade: Life Stories of Lesbians during the Third Reich*. New York: Columbia University Press, 1996.

Schuyf, Judith. *Een stilzwijgende samenzwering: Lesbische vrouwen in Nederland, 1920–1970*. Amsterdam: Stichting Beheer IISG, 1994.

Schwegman, Marjan, and Jolande Withuis. "Moederschap, van springplank tot obstakel: Vrouwen, natie en burgerschap in twintigste-eeuws Nederland." In *Geschiedenis van de vrouw*, vol. 5, *De twintigste eeuw*, ed. Georges Duby and Michelle Perrot, 557–83. Amsterdam: Agon, 1993.

Seidman, Michael. *Transatlantic Antifascisms: From the Spanish Civil War to the End of World War II*. Cambridge: Cambridge University Press, 2018.

Siertsema, Bettine. *Uit de diepten: Nederlandse egodocumenten over de nazi concentratiekampen*. Vught: Skandalon, 2007.

Singh, Minati. "Mood, Food, and Obesity." *Frontiers in Psychology* 5, no. 925 (2014): 1–20.

Smaldone, William. *Confronting Hitler: German Social Democrats in Defense of the Weimar Republic, 1929–1933*. Lanham, Md.: Lexington, 2009.

Smethurst, James. "The Black Arts Movement and Historically Black Colleges and Universities." In *New Thoughts on the Black Arts Movement*, edited by Lisa Gail Collins and Margo Natalie Crawford, 75–91. New Brunswick, N.J.: Rutgers University Press, 2006.

———. "'Don't Say Goodbye to the Porkpie Hat': Langston Hughes, the Left, and the Black Arts Movement." *Callaloo* 25, no. 4 (2002): 1225–36.

Smith, Sidonie, and Julia Watson, eds. *Reading Autobiography: A Guide for Interpreting Life Narratives*. 2001. Reprint, Minneapolis: University of Minnesota Press, 2010.

Sontag, Susan. "The Image-World." In *Visual Culture: The Reader*, edited by Jessica Evans and Stuart Hall, 80–94. London: Sage, 1999.

Spurlin, William J. *Lost Intimacies: Rethinking Homosexuality under National Socialism*. New York: Peter Lang, 2009.

Staub, Ervin. "The Psychology of Bystanders, Perpetrators, and Heroic Helpers." *International Journal of Intercultural Relations* 17, no. 3 (1993): 315–41.

Staub, Ervin, and Johanna Vollhardt. "Altruism Born of Suffering: The Roots of Caring and Helping after Victimization and Other Trauma." *American Journal of Orthopsychiatry* 78, no. 3 (2008): 267–80.

Stearns, Peter N. *Fat History: Bodies and Beauty in the Modern West*. New York: New York University Press, 1997.

Steen, Bart van der. "'Kiest Sneevliet uit de cel!' Henk Sneevliet, de RSP en de verkiezingen van 1933." *Leidschrift* 22, no. 3 (2007): 79–88.

Steen, Bart van der. "Met de Roode Auto op reis: Een fragment uit de memoires van Jef Last." *Onvoltooid verleden* 23 (2007): 7–27.

Steen, Bart van der, and Ron Blom, eds. *Wij gingen onze eigen weg: Herinneringen van revolutionaire socialisten in Nederland van 1930 tot 1950*. Delft: Eburon, 2011.

Steen, Margit van der. *Drift en koers: De levens van Hilda Verwey-Jonker (1908-2004)*. Amsterdam: Bakker, 2011.

Stoler, Ann Laura. *Along the Archival Grain: Epistemic Anxieties and Colonial Common Sense*. Princeton, N.J.: Princeton University Press, 2009.

Stroom, Gerrold van der. "The Diaries, *Het Achterhuis*, and the Translations." In *The Diary of Anne Frank: The Revised Critical Edition*, edited by Harry Paape, Gerrold van der Stroom, and David Barnouw, 59–77. New York: Doubleday, 2003.

Stutje, Jan Willem. "Antisemitisme onder Nederlandse socialisten in het 'fin de siècle.'" *BMGN: Low Countries Historical Review* 129, no. 3 (2014): 4–26.
Sugrue, Thomas. "Hillburn, Hattiesburg, and Hitler: Wartime Activists Think Globally and Act Locally." In *Fog of War: The Second World War and the Civil Rights Movement*, edited by Kevin M. Kruse and Stephen Tuck, 87–102. Oxford: Oxford University Press, 2012.
Sundquist, Eric J., *Strangers in the Land: Blacks, Jews, Post-Holocaust America*. 2005. Reprint, Cambridge, Mass.: Harvard University Press, 2009.
Talwar, Victoria, Heidi M. Gordon, and Kang Lee. "Lying in the Elementary School Years: Verbal Deception and Its Relation to Second-Order Belief Understanding." *Developmental Psychology* 43, no. 3 (2007): 804–10.
Tarrow, Sidney G., *Power in Movement: Social Movements, Collective Action, and Politics*. Cambridge: Cambridge University Press, 1994.
Taylor, Verta, and Nancy E. Whittier. "Collective Identity in Social Movement Communities: Lesbian Feminist Mobilization." In *Frontiers in Social Movement Theory*, edited by Aldon D. Morris and Carol McClurg Mueller, 104–29. New Haven, Conn.: Yale University Press, 1992.
Tedeschi, Richard G., and Lawrence G. Calhoun. "The Posttraumatic Growth Inventory: Measuring the Positive Legacy of Trauma." *Journal of Traumatic Stress* 9, no. 3 (1996): 455–71.
Thompson, Julius Eric. *Dudley Randall, Broadside Press, and the Black Arts Movement in Detroit, 1960–1995*. Jefferson, N.C.: McFarland, 1999.
Tichelman, Fritjof. "Hendricus Josephus Franciscus Marie (Henk) Sneevliet." *Biografisch Woordenboek van het Socialisme en de Arbeidersbeweging in Nederland)* 1 (1986): 111–19.
Turner, Jeffrey A. *Sitting in and Speaking Out: Student Movements in the American South, 1960–1970*. Athens: University of Georgia Press, 2010.
Turner, Joyce Moore. *Caribbean Crusaders and the Harlem Renaissance*. Urbana: University of Illinois Press, 2005.
Veldmeijer, Susan. "Considering Art: The Role of De Brug, the ASB, and the Socialistische Kunstenaarskring in the Production, Distribution, and Reception of Notions on Art and the Position of the Artist." Master's thesis, Utrecht University, 2014.
Verwey-Jonker, Hilda. "De ideologie van de SDAP (1930–1940)." In *Van brede visie tot smalle marge: Acht prominente socialisten over de SDAP en de PVDA*, edited by Jan Bank and Stef Temming, 11–30. Alphen aan den Rijn: Sijthoff, 1981.
Vogel, Shane. "Closing Time: Langston Hughes, and the Queer Poetics of Harlem Nightlife." *Criticism* 48, no. 3 (2006): 397–425.
Von Eschen, Penny M. *Race against Empire: Black Americans and Anticolonialism, 1937–1957*. Ithaca, N.Y.: Cornell University Press, 1997.
Vree, Frank van. *In de schaduw van Auschwitz: Herinneringen, beelden, geschiedenis*. Groningen: Historische, 1995.
Vries, Ellen de. *Nola: Portret van een eigenzinnig kunstenares*. Schoonhoven: Klapwijk en Keijsers, 2009.
Vries, Manfred Kets de. "Leadership Coaching and the Rescuer Syndrome: How to Manage Both Sides of the Couch." Working paper, 2010.
Walker, Alice. "In Search of Our Mothers' Gardens." In *Worlds of Difference: Inequality*

in the Aging Experience, edited by Eleanor Palo Stoller and Rose Campbell Gibson, 48–53. 1994. Reprint, Thousand Oaks, Calif.: Pine Forge Press, 2000.

Webb, Clive. *Fight against Fear: Southern Jews and Black Civil Rights.* Athens: University of Georgia Press, 2001.

Wekker, Gloria. *White Innocence: Paradoxes of Colonialism and Race.* Durham, N.C.: Duke University Press, 2016.

Wijfjes, Huub. *VARA: Biografie van een omroep.* Amsterdam: Boom, 2009.

Wilford, Hugh. *The Mighty Wurlitzer: How the CIA Played America.* Cambridge, Mass.: Harvard University Press, 2008.

Williamson, Joy Ann. "Black Colleges and Civil Rights: Organizing and Mobilizing in Jackson, Mississippi." In *Higher Education and the Civil Rights Movement: White Supremacy, Black Southerners, and College Campuses,* edited by Peter Wallenstein, 116–37. Gainesville: University Press of Florida, 2008.

Withuis, Jolande. "Mothers of the Nation: Post-war Gendered Interpretations of the Experiences of Dutch Resistance Women." In *When the War Was Over: Women, War and Peace in Europe, 1940–1956,* edited by Claire Duchen and Irene Bandhauer-Schöffmann, 29–43. London: Leicester University Press, 2000.

Wright, William D. *Black History and Black Identity: A Call for a New Historiography.* Westport, Conn.: Praeger, 2002.

Young, Christopher M. "Alabama's *Rocket City*: Cotton, Missiles, and Change in Huntsville and Madison County." *Huntsville Historical Review* 41, no. 1 (2016): 1–24.

Zichem, Frank, *Beeldspraak: Nola Hatterman (en de konsekwente keuze)* TV documentary 1982.

Zijderveld, A. C. "Vrij zinnig eigenzinnig: De cultuur en traditie van de VPRO." In *Een vrij zinnige verhouding: De VPRO en Nederland, 1926–1986,* edited by J. H. J. van den Heuvel, Hans Daalder, and Johan Cornelius Hendrik Blom, 147–80. Baarn: Ambo, 1987.

Zohar, Ada H., Lotem Giladi, and Timor Givati. "Holocaust Exposure and Disordered Eating: A Study of Multi-Generational Transmission." *European Eating Disorders Review* 15, no. 1 (2007): 50–57.

Zoonen, Liesbet van. "Pia, Maartje, Hennie en Joop: De opkomst van de vrouwelijke nieuwslezer." *Tijdschrift voor Vrouwenstudies* 121, no. 4 (1991): 470–83.

INDEX

Acre, Israel, 169
Ailey, Alvin, 163
Alabama, 143–54; A&M College, 143–54 passim; Birmingham, 139, 145, 205n76; Black writer's conference, 151, 152; Huntsville, 143–54; Normal, 143, 151; racial segregation, 145; Talladega College, 122; Tuskegee College, 146; University of Alabama, Huntsville, 152, 207n13; University of Alabama, Tuscaloosa, 146, 206n13
Albarda, Willem, 21
Albion College, 200n11
Allen, Samuel, 3, 151, 167
Alma, Peter, 24
altruism, 115, 121–22
American Society of African Culture (AMSAC), 159, 160, 174
anticolonialism, 104, 167
antifascism, 46, 47, 53, 57, 67; Van Dien group, 51, 61, 189n97
antinationalism, 22, 105
antisemitism, 13, 18, 46, 65, 76, 100, 123, 137–38; anti-Jewish measures in Nazi Germany, 39–40; anti-Jewish measures in Netherlands, 47–48
Ast, Bruno, 54, 188n59
Atlanta, Ga., 3, 4, 115, 124, 125
Atlanta Daily World, 125
Atlanta University, 120, 161

Baarn, Netherlands, 60–64, 67
Baez, Joan, 130

Bahá'í faith, 6, 26
Baldwin, James, 82, 130, 159, 165
Baraka, Amiri, 85, 165
Baschwitz, Kurt, 54, 188n59
BBC, 63, 97, 99–100, 201n43; BBC Dutch Service, 97; BBC Radio, 97, 100
Beittel, Adam Daniel, 129, 138, 139, 205n73
Belafonte, Harry, 159, 165
Belgium, 19
Benin treasures, 163
Berlin, 27–42; burning of Reichstag building, 39, 40; help to German Jews, 40; lesbian subculture, 27, 35, 36, 37, 38; 1933 book burning, 40; University of Berlin, 42, 132, 186n89
Beugeling, Mies, 15, 180n28
Bier, Jakob Hermann, 59–60
Birmingham, Ala., 139, 145, 205n76
Black Arts Movement, 85
Black Atlantic, 71, 79, 89, 93, 94, 164, 166, 167
Black Power, 153
Blok, Hetty, 102
Bond, Horace Mann, 161
Bond, Julian, 86, 157, 195n27
Boone House group, 89
Borinski, Ernst, 127, 129–32, 137, 139, 140
Bramall, Eric, 197n9
Braun, Wernher von, 143, 152–53, 206n4
Brecht, Bertolt, 29
Breman, Paul, 89, 103–4, 119, 166, 173, 174
Britten, Benjamin, 155
Bronkers, Aaf, 60
Bronkers, An, 60

Brooks, Gwendolyn, 82, 157
Brown, Sterling, 3, 4
Bunche, Ralph, 130
Burroughs, Margaret, 151, 152, 174
Bussum, Netherlands, 106

Campbell, Ambrose, 99
Cardozo, Ben Lopez, 40
Carew, Jan, 158
Carmiggelt, Simon, 99
Carroll, Vinnette, 81, 89, 100, 196n46
Catholicism, 62
Césaire, Aimé, 94, 126, 138, 163, 203n75
Chaffee, Lois, 140, 205n77
Chattman, Johnny Earl, 128
Clark, Rubastine M., 128
Collins, Jessie, 167
Collins, Leslie M., 85
communism, 41, 46, 74, 157; Communist Party of the United States of America (CPUSA), 69, 158; Dutch Communist Party (CPH/CPN), 31, 51; German Communist Party (KPD), 40, 50, 51, 68
concentration camps: Auschwitz, 1, 53, 54, 55, 58, 59, 63, 75, 187n35, 188n59; Bergen-Belsen, 124, 202n66; Sobibór, 55, 56, 136
Congress of Racial Equality (CORE), 138, 140
Conley, Binford, 146
Connor, Edric, 81
Connor, Pearl, 100
Cook, Mercer, 163, 164
Cullen, Countee, 3, 16, 68, 70, 73, 76, 77, 90, 149, 191n19, 193nn61–62, 194n72
Cunard, Nancy, 84, 192n21
Cuney, Waring, 73, 90, 167

Danner, Margaret, 85, 88, 90, 151, 152, 167, 196n49
Davis, Ossie, 165
Delaware, 120
Detroit, Mich., 89–90, 115–17, 119
Dickinson, Emily, 37, 63
Dietrich, Marlene, 35, 36
Dixon, Jack, 97–99, 101, 103, 108
Dodson, Owen, 83, 151, 155, 174
Dordrecht, Netherlands, 74
Dorsey, Charles, 145
Du Bois, Shirley Graham, 79, 94, 104, 163, 174

Du Bois, W. E. B., 79, 126, 138, 155, 163, 193n61, 198n45, 208n4; in Netherlands, 103–5
Dunham, Katherine, 156

Edman, Marion, 115, 116
Ehrlich, Max, 60
Einstein, Albert, 29
Ellington, Duke, 163, 164
Ellison, Ralph, 157, 165
Enwonwu, Ben, 64
Epstein, Sally, 34
Evans, Mari, 151, 152
Evers, Medgar, 205n73

Fabio, Sarah Webster, 87
Fauset, Jessie, 3, 157
feminism, 94
Fields, Julia, 90, 91, 167
Fischer, Lena, 35, 36, 40, 49
Fisk University, 6, 124, 166, 196n61
Five Pound Press, 63, 190n106
Fowlkes, William, 125, 202n71
Frank, Anna (sister-in-law), 54
Frank, Anne, 48–50, 97, 113–26, 131; Pool's translation of diary, 67, 113, 115
Frank, Edith, 50
Frank, Leonhard, 16, 34
Frank, Margot, 118, 119
Frank, Otto, 67, 120, 123, 126, 191n13, 202n58, 202n63
Fulbright Program, 113, 115, 199n1
Fuller, Hoyt, 151

Gaffel, Wim, 18
Garner, Lela, 128
Gatlin, Joyce, 128
Gbeho, Philip, 164
Germany: Munich, 40; Nazi Germany, 39–42
Gershwin, Ira, 94, 155
Ghana, 162–63; Ghanaians in London, 92
Girl Scouts, 14–15
Goes, Frank van der, 11
Golf, Naomi, 128
Greensboro, N.C., 124, 131
Gruber, Max, 46, 57

Haldane, J. B. S., 46
Hall, Mary Ann, 128
Hampton, Lionel, 160

Hand and Flower Press, 84
Hansmann-Knopp, Cilly, 191n17
Haringman, Max, 24
Harris, Ruth Bates, 206n4
Hatterman, Nola, 66, 68–69, 73, 174, 191n17, 191n19
Hayden, Robert, 93, 124, 151, 166, 174, 196n61, 202n66
Heath, Gordon, 81–83, 95, 99–110, 115, 174
Hepburn, Audrey, 103
Heppner, Albert, 188n59
Hernton, Calvin, 86
Heymann-David, Alice, 50, 60
Heynemann, Susanne, 40, 60–63, 67
Highland Park, Mich., 116
Hill, Mozell, 120, 201n43
Hillesum, Etty, 63, 190n11
Himes, Chester, 157, 167
Hirschfeld, Kurt, 187n35
Hirschfeld, Magnus, 29, 37
Hitler, Adolf, 3, 32, 33, 39, 41–43, 45, 47, 50, 56, 58, 72, 104, 105, 125
Holborn College of Languages (London), 83, 199n1
Hollander, Arie den, 180n21
Hollander, Ine den, 14
Holst, Henriette Roland, 16, 24, 34
homosexuality, 100, 162
Howard University, 3, 173
Hughes, Langston, 3, 17, 70–73, 77, 79, 82, 83, 85, 90, 92, 94, 149, 150, 193n61; in Amsterdam, 162; homosexuality, 162; in London, 91; Pool's friendship with, 155–68
Huiswoud, Otto, 69, 102, 104, 158
Huiswoud-Dumont, Hermie, 69, 102, 104, 158
Huntsville, Ala., 143–54
Hutson, Jean Blackwell, 166
Hyman, Earle, 83, 100, 174

Ibo, Wim, 101, 174
Indonesia, anticolonial activism in, 31, 104, 105
Inness-Brown, Virginia, 210n59
International Lenin School, Moscow, 191
International Red Aid, 40
Isenburg, Ursel ("Isa"), 75, 79, 81–83, 100, 134, 162, 177
Israel, 120, 123; Acre, 169
Italy: Perugia, 40; Spoleto, 163

Jackson, Etta M., 128
Jacobs, Cilia, 54, 188n59
Jacobs-Gast, Martha, 54, 188n59
Jahn, Jan-Heinz, 164
Jansma, Arie, 191n17
Jessurun, Joost (cousin), 60–61
Jessurun, Marie, 60
Jewish Council, Netherlands, 49, 52, 53, 58, 64, 154
Jewish Lyceum, Amsterdam, 48, 49, 52, 59, 60, 188n53
John, Erroll, 198n27
Johnson, Gloria, 201n45
Johnson, James Weldon, 68, 73, 149, 191n19, 193n61
Johnson, William Spaarndam, 102
Johnson Publishing Company, 165, 210n64
Jones, Alando X., 207n40
Jones, Claudia, 81
Jones, Donald, 101, 102, 109
Jong, Année Rinzes de, 32

Kalamazoo, Mich., 117, 188
Karl Marx Schule (Berlin), 29, 35, 39, 134
Killens, John O., 151
Kincaid, Oteria, 128
King, Ed, 135
Kinsbergen, Nora ("Noor"), 24
Knöchel, Wilhelm, 191n17
Knoxville College (Tenn.), 90
Koestner-Swiat, Priscilla, 118
Kramer, Gerhard F., 27, 29, 33, 34, 37–39, 182n2, 182n7, 183n39, 184n59, 184n65
Ku Klux Klan (KKK), 127, 143

LaGrone, Oliver, 90
Laine, Cleo, 81, 100, 101
Lasekan, Akinola, 164
Last, Jef, 24, 25, 32, 71, 83, 134, 157
Lebeer, Paul, 164
Leiden, Netherlands, 21–22
Lenin, Vladimir, 30, 31, 158
lesbianism, 35–39, 82, 100, 162
Lester, Julius, 125
Levi, Ernst, 50
Levin, Meyer, 67, 123, 191n13
Liège, Belgium, 19
Lincoln University, 161
Little Rock, Ark., school desegregation, 84, 105, 109
Livingstone College (N.C.), 148, 207n28

Lloyd Hotel (Amsterdam), 45, 57
Loggem, Manuel van, 157
Lopes Cardozo, Benjamin, 40
Lorde, Audre, 85, 157
Löwenberg, Martin, 51–53
Lubbe, Marinus van der, 40

Madgett, Naomi Long, 86, 89, 90, 196n47
Malcolm X, 166
Manley, Edna, 192n21
Mann, Stanley, 99
Marx, Erica, 84
Marxism, 20, 21, 46
McCarthyism, 103, 158, 163
McKay, Claude, 3, 73, 82, 149, 193n61
Mengele, Josef, 59
Meyer, Hajo, 49, 50, 187n35
Michel, Mijrtiel, 188n59
Michigan: Albion College, 200n11; Detroit, 89–90, 115–17, 119; Highland Park, 116; Kalamazoo, 117, 188; Wyandotte, 117; Ypsilanti High School, 117
Mississippi, 6, 121, 123, 145, 148; Freedom Schools, 140, 205n77; Mississippi State Sovereignty Commission, 127, 135; Tougaloo College, 127–41, 148, 169, 205n76
Modisane, Bloke, 92, 93, 201n45
Mol, Albert, 78, 83, 174
Mols-de Leeuwe, Enny, 70
Mongo, Frank, 193n46
Monkau, Marius, 102
Morehouse College (Atlanta), 195n27
Morrison, Richard D., 147, 148, 152, 153
Mug-de Gooijer, Jeanne, 17, 18
Mulisch, Harry, 99
Munich, Germany, 40

Nashville, Tenn., 93, 124, 196n61
National Aeronautics and Space Administration (NASA), 143, 145, 152, 206n4
National Association for the Advancement of Colored People (NAACP), 69, 92, 104, 138, 139, 205n73, 205n76
Nazi Party (NSDAP), 33, 34
negritude, 138, 159, 164–66
Netherlands: Baarn, 60–64, 67; Bussum, 106; Dordrecht, 74; Leiden, 21–22
Nicol, Davidson, 156
Nigeria: Festival of Negro Art and Culture in Africa and America (Lagos), 159–62; Nigerians in Dakar, 163–64; Nigerians in London, 80; Nigerians in Netherlands, 99
Nkosi, Lewis, 201n45
Normal, Ala., 143, 151
Norman, Memphis, 128, 139
North Carolina, 124, 131
Notowicz, Nathan, 50, 58

obesity, 14, 20, 66, 76–77
Odetta, 160
Odufré, Joes, 98, 197n9
Okigbo, Christopher, 156, 166
Olatunji, Michael, 160
Olf, Bill, 193n46
Oosie, Majo, 193n46
orientalism, 73, 88, 164
Oudegeest, Jan, Jr., 20
Overst, Hyman, 17

Pach, Stella, 57
Padmore, George, 81
Palestine, 49, 57
Palfi, Marion, 29
pan-Africanism, 159
Pankey, Aubrey, 100
Paris, 16, 40, 79, 95, 99–101, 157, 191n13
Parkes, Frank, 92
Payant, Lee, 100, 101
Perugia, Italy, 40
Peters, Brock, 100
Petry, Ann, 71
philanthropy, 121
Pinkston, Jutha, 128
Polak, Henri, 23
Pool, Jozef ("Jopie"; brother), 12, 19, 54, 155
Pool, Louis (father), 9, 11–15, 19, 52, 54–56, 63, 67, 75, 136, 154
Pool-Jessurun, Jacoba ("Cobie"; mother), 9, 10, 11–14, 19, 78, 191n8
Pool-van Blankenstein, Roosje (grandmother), 28
Porter, Dorothy, 3
Pothuis-Smit, Carry, 24
Prabhu, Pandarinath Hari, 201n45
Premsela, Benno, 162
Prentiss, Audrey, 128, 137–38
primitivism, 73, 85, 88
Pudovkin, Vsevolod, 30, 31

Querido publishers, 73, 83

Randall, Dudley, 85, 87, 151, 152, 196n49
resistance: within Camp Westerwork, 53–54, 56–60; in Nazi Germany, 40; Van Dien group, 50–51, 53–54, 57–58, 60–61, 67, 187n35, 188n59, 189n97; Westerweel group, 187n35; during World War II, 50–52
Rive, Richard, 91
Robeson, Essie, 81
Robeson, Paul, 81, 155
Route, William, 128, 133

Sadberry, Evelyn, 128
Sannes, Goswijn, 24
Schmidt, Annie M. G., 101, 198n30
Schönemann, Friedrich, 42, 185n88
Scottsboro Boys, 42, 143
Scouts, Girl, 14–15
Senegal, 156, 163–66, 210n59
Senghor, Leopold, 94, 138, 159, 164, 165
Shakespeare, William, 63
Simmons, Clifford, 156
Simone, Nina, 155, 160, 161
sit-ins: Greensboro, N.C., 124; Jackson, Miss., 139–40; Tougaloo, Miss., 129
Sluis, Meijer van der, 69, 70
Smith, Muriel, 81, 100
Sneevliet, Henk, 31, 32, 183n24
Snodgrass, William, 90, 196n49
social democracy, 33, 104, 131; Amsterdam Social Democratic Student Club (SDSC), 21, 22; Berlin Association of Social Democratic Students, 182n2; Dutch Social Democratic Workers' Party (SDAP), 11, 12, 15, 16, 20, 23, 24; Dutch Workers Youth Center (AJC), 15, 17, 22, 24, 32, 90, 174; German Social Democratic Party (SDP), 31, 33, 129
socialism: Independent Socialist Party (OSP), 32; Revolutionary Socialist Party (RSP), 31, 32; Socialist Artists Circle (SKK), 24; Socialist Youth Union (SJV), 32
Société Africaine de Culture (SAC), 159
South Africa, 91; and England, 91, 92; and Netherlands, 22, 99
Soviet Union, 74, 104, 157, 158; American-Soviet space race, 145; Sovkino, 30–31, 38–39

Soyinka, Wole, 159, 163
Spain, 12, 157, 161, 167; Spanish Civil War, 157, 161
Spingarn, Arthur, 92, 94, 138
Spoleto, Italy, 163
Stein, Gertrude, 82
Sterman, Django, 102
Sterman, Otto, 102, 104, 174, 198n29
Stertzenbach, Werner, 56–60, 63, 190n111
Stowe, Harriet Beecher, 68
Student Nonviolent Coordinating Committee (SNCC), 86, 130
Suriname: *Ons Suriname*, 104; Surinamese people living in Amsterdam, 16, 68, 69, 73, 99, 158

Talladega College, 122
teetotalism, 11
Tehuis Oosteinde, 45, 50, 52, 58–60, 188n59
television: in England, 99; in Netherlands, 95, 97, 98, 99, 101, 105, 106, 108–11, 197n9; in United States, 114, 196n47
theater, 15, 29, 30, 101
theosophy, 15, 23, 26, 181n58; Theosophical Association, 15
therapy, 133, 136, 138, 140
Thivy, John A., 103
Tingen, Frits, 16, 122
Toklas, Alice B., 82
Tolson, Melvin, 71, 73, 82, 157
Tougaloo College, 127–41, 148, 169, 205n76; Tougaloo Nine, 129
trauma, 65, 70, 75–78, 133–34, 136, 138, 154; posttraumatic growth, 138
Truth, Sojourner, 82
Tubman, Harriet, 47, 149
Ture, Kwame, 130
Tuskegee College, 146

United Negro College Fund (UNCF), 92, 120–21, 135, 148, 201n45
University of Alabama: Huntsville, 152, 207n13; Tuscaloosa, 146, 206n13
University of Amsterdam, 24, 75
University of Berlin, 42, 132, 186n89

vegetarianism, 19
Verwey-Jonker, Hilda, 20, 21
Vinson, Audrey L., 147, 148, 150, 154
Visdrager, Shelly, 202n66

Vleeschouwer, Jopie, 190n111
Vorst, Meyer, 188n59
Vos, Margot, 16
Voth, Rhoda M., 135

Walcott, Derek, 157, 166
Wallace, George, 145, 146, 151, 153, 206n13
Walrond, Eric, 84
Washington, Booker T., 82
Wayne State University (Detroit), 89, 90, 196n49
Wees, Gijsbertus Martinus van, 60–63
Welch, Elisabeth, 81
Welk, Ehm, 30
Wessel, Horst, 34
Wesselius, Eva, 62
Wesselius, Rudi, 62, 174
West African Arts Club, London, 81
Westerbork, 53–60
Weston, Randy, 160
White Citizens' Council, 127, 130

Wijk, Paula van, 102
Williams, Annie Belle, 128
Williams, Dianella, 128, 134
Willis, Melinda Lois, 128
Wilmington, Del., 120
Wilson, Jimmy, 105, 109
Wiseman, Victor H., 201n45
Wolkers, Jan, 99
Wright, Richard, 71, 73, 158
Wyandotte, Mich., 117

X, Malcolm, 166
Xavier University (New Orleans), 123

Yevtushenko, Yevgeny, 164
Ypsilanti High School (Mich.), 117
Yu, Chin, 99

Zionism, 123, 57; Hadassah women's organization, 120

Politics and Culture in the Twentieth-Century South

*A Common Thread: Labor, Politics, and
  Capital Mobility in the Textile Industry*
BY BETH ENGLISH

*"Everybody Was Black Down There":
  Race and Industrial Change in the Alabama Coalfields*
BY ROBERT H. WOODRUM

*Race, Reason, and Massive Resistance:
  The Diary of David J. Mays, 1954-1959*
EDITED BY JAMES R. SWEENEY

*The Unemployed People's Movement:
  Leftists, Liberals, and Labor in Georgia, 1929-1941*
BY JAMES J. LORENCE

*Liberalism, Black Power, and the
  Making of American Politics, 1965-1980*
BY DEVIN FERGUS

*Guten Tag, Y'all: Globalization and the
  South Carolina Piedmont, 1950-2000*
BY MARKO MAUNULA

*The Culture of Property: Race, Class,
  and Housing Landscapes in Atlanta, 1880-1950*
BY LEEANN LANDS

*Marching in Step: Masculinity, Citizenship,
  and The Citadel in Post-World War II America*
BY ALEXANDER MACAULAY

*Rabble Rousers: The American Far Right in the
  Civil Rights Era*
BY CLIVE WEBB

Who Gets a Childhood?: Race and Juvenile Justice in Twentieth-Century Texas
BY WILLIAM S. BUSH

*Alabama Getaway: The Political Imaginary and the
  Heart of Dixie*
BY ALLEN TULLOS

*The Problem South: Region, Empire, and the
  New Liberal State, 1880-1930*
BY NATALIE J. RING

*The Nashville Way: Racial Etiquette and the
  Struggle for Social Justice in a Southern City*
BY BENJAMIN HOUSTON

*Cold War Dixie: Militarization and Modernization
   in the American South*
BY KARI FREDERICKSON

*Faith in Bikinis: Politics and Leisure in the
   Coastal South since the Civil War*
BY ANTHONY J. STANONIS

*Womanpower Unlimited and the Black Freedom
   Struggle in Mississippi*
BY TIYI M. MORRIS

New Negro Politics in the Jim Crow South
BY CLAUDRENA N. HAROLD

Jim Crow Terminals: The Desegregation of American Airports
BY ANKE ORTLEPP

*Remaking the Rural South: Interracialism, Christian Socialism,
   and Cooperative Farming in Jim Crow Mississippi*
BY ROBERT HUNT FERGUSON

*The South of the Mind: American Imaginings of
   White Southernness, 1960–1980*
BY ZACHARY J. LECHNER

*The Politics of White Rights: Race, Justice,
   and Integrating Alabama's Schools*
BY JOSEPH BAGLEY

*The Struggle and the Urban South:
   Confronting Jim Crow in Baltimore before the Movement*
BY DAVID TAFT TERRY

*Massive Resistance and Southern Womanhood:
   White Women, Class, and Segregationist Resistance*
BY REBECCA BRUCKMANN

I Lay This Body Down: The Transatlantic Life of Rosey E. Pool
BY LONNEKE GEERLINGS

www.ingramcontent.com/pod-product-compliance
Lightning Source LLC
Chambersburg PA
CBHW020804230426
43666CB00007B/854